Praise for *Neighbor Lo*

"Many of us have wished for a book that would provide an account of our pandemic days that is honest, accessible, critically informed, and deeply faith based. Jason Mahn has written exactly such a book. His book consists of daily notes as he lived through a year of pandemic. We get to watch his mind work and his words form as his children, his reading, his memory, and a host of other forces impact his thinking. In the end, his writing is a passionate call to vocation in this 'moment of summoning.' The book is such a compelling read because two things happen. We find our own vexed thinking echoed; at the same time, we find ourselves led in generative ways beyond our own thinking. This book is a deep gift for any reader who wants to engage our present circumstance as a chance for fresh faithful, generous, emancipated obedience."

—Walter Brueggemann, Columbia Theological Seminary

"Part memoir, part diary, part commission, and yet wholly authentic, *Neighbor Love through Fearful Days* offers readers a window into one person's pursuit of purpose amid the early months of the COVID-19 pandemic. In Jason Mahn's words, I found insight and challenge, wisdom and confession, all as he invited us to see our own stories alongside his as we together make sense of our callings in this unprecedented time. This book will stir you to reflection and to action in a profoundly good way."

—Drew Tucker, university pastor and director of the
Center for Faith and Learning at Capital University

"The year 2020 is one many would rather forget than remember. But Jason Mahn's *Neighbor Love through Fearful Days* helps us see that remembering rightly is pivotal to navigating any crisis purposefully. This smart and beautifully written reflection merits thoughtful reading and wide discussion by campuses and congregations alike."

—Tim Clydesdale, vice provost, dean of graduate studies, and professor
of sociology at the College of New Jersey

"A relevant and meaningful book written not only *for* our moment—but from *within* that very moment. Read it and heed its clarion call to love, lament, and listen . . . and to remember, reflect, and resist the triple pandemics of our time: racism, COVID-19, and environmental disasters."

—Jacqueline Bussie, award-winning author of
Outlaw Christian and *Love without Limits*

"In *Neighbor Love through Fearful Days*, Jason Mahn offers himself as a thoughtful and honest reflection partner in the complicated, difficult, and ultimately life-affirming task of discerning vocation and the call to love in this moment. By sharing experiences, relationships, provocative readings, musings on current events, conversations, and memories, Mahn shows us how paying attention is the starting place for addressing the questions that matter: Who are we to be, and what are we to do in the here and now?"

—Sergia Hay, associate professor of philosophy
at Pacific Lutheran University

"Jason Mahn combines a sharp intellect with a pastoral heart. His deeply spiritual reflections on our common life in the midst of a pandemic are part memoir, part confession, and part theological primer. Mahn writes with an honesty and a vulnerability about our vocation as Christians to love our neighbors well even and especially in a time of social distancing. Through his honest, poignant prose, Mahn allows himself to be seen in a way that makes me, likewise, feel seen and heard."

—Mindy Makant, associate professor of religious studies and director
of youth and family ministry at Lenoir-Rhyne University

"Jason Mahn has done something both rare and relevant. He has written about our callings in medias res, where all of us always find ourselves. The fresh, retrospectively sculpted journal entries that chart his own halting and continuing efforts to live the 'summoned' life of a Christian, loving responsibility in 'fearful days' of multiple pandemics, include many other stories as well. This book captures the vocabulary of vocation as well as any book we know."

—Mark R. Schwehn and Dorothy C. Bass, editors of *Leading Lives That Matter: What We Should Do and Who We Should Be* (2nd ed., 2020)

"Coming in the heart of this book, the chapter 'Dear Amy—June 15, 2020' crystallizes what is best about *Neighbor Love through Fearful Days*: Jason Mahn's willingness to interrogate his own failures and hold others like him accountable, his ability to speak with authenticity and vulnerability, and his commitment to mine a theological tradition alongside the responsibilities of his own profession as an educator. Through fragments and stories captured as the world turned itself outside in, we feel the texture of a time and are called into an as-yet-undetermined future."

—Caryn Riswold, McCoy Family Distinguished Chair in Lutheran Heritage and Mission at Wartburg College

"While reading *Neighbor Love through Fearful Days*, I found myself reliving my own pandemic-driven fears and wonderment about the common good versus my personal well-being. Anyone interested to profoundly consider the scriptural injunction to 'love your neighbor as yourself' will find a treasure in Jason Mahn's reflections written in real time during the 2020 pandemic."

—Rev. Mark Wilhelm, executive director of Network of Colleges and Universities, Evangelical Lutheran Church in America

"The global COVID-19 pandemic upended so much of life, including most of the ways we make meaning in life together. What does vocation—that process of being shaped by the needs and callings of others—look like in COVID times? Lutheran university professor Jason Mahn offers real-time reflections on the daily choices of life, work, and neighbor love at a time when masking, social distancing, and renewed reckoning with the long legacy of white supremacy mark our days. Drawing on the wisdom of Søren Kierkegaard, Marge Piercy, Ta-Nehisi Coates, Toni Morrison, Jesus, and the students who've become his teachers, Mahn weaves a rich tapestry of reflections on what it means to embody neighbor love in days where pandemic fears threaten fundamental commitments of faith, hope, and love. A tender, convicting, provocative, soul-nourishing read."

—Deanna Thompson, director of the Lutheran Center for Faith, Values, and Community and Martin E. Marty Regents Chair in Religion and the Academy at St. Olaf College

"If the language of 'finding your calling' or 'discerning your vocation' sometimes seems hollow or abstract, Jason Mahn's book will provide the remedy. These diary-like reflections offer practical wisdom and a sense of direction, drawn from the experience of living through pandemic and quarantine: hardship, frustration, and fear, yes, but also moments of revelation and even of joy. This book reminds us all—teachers and students, parents and children, activists and contemplatives—to make plans for what we will do with this 'one wild and precious life.'"

—David S. Cunningham, director of Network for Vocation in Undergraduate Education (NetVUE), Council of Independent Colleges

"Jason Mahn has written a book for all of us, for everyone searching for meaning and justice in a time of suffering, uncertainty, and intersecting existential threats. Amid the global Covid-19 pandemic, long overdue racial reckoning, and unrelenting climate change, Mahn offers powerful and prescient 'real-time' reflections that name both our fears and our hopes. With engaging and accessible prose, he weaves together personal stories with the wisdom of philosophers, theologians, and poets. I highly recommend this book."

—Lori Brandt Hale, professor of religion, Augsburg University

NEIGHBOR LOVE THROUGH FEARFUL DAYS

NEIGHBOR LOVE THROUGH FEARFUL DAYS

FINDING PURPOSE AND MEANING IN A TIME OF CRISIS

JASON A. MAHN

Fortress Press
Minneapolis

NEIGHBOR LOVE THROUGH FEARFUL DAYS
Finding Purpose and Meaning in a Time of Crisis

Cover design: Love Arts Design

Print ISBN: 978-1-5064-7947-7
eBook ISBN: 978-1-5064-7948-4

To students at Augustana College—
beside whom I am grateful to be called to learn;

and to Asa, Gabe, and Laura—
no one with whom I'd rather be quarantined

You have called your servants to ventures of which we cannot see the ending, by paths as yet untrodden, through perils unknown.

—Eric Milner-White and G. W. Briggs,
"Prayer of Good Courage"

CONTENTS

PREFACE

I saw a T-shirt this last summer that simply read, "2020 SUCKS." It would be hard to disagree. Still, I tried to make the best of it, like so many others.

As an author and college teacher, I've spent twenty years grappling with the ideas of others and trying to think about and express my own ideas clearly while leading students in doing the same. For me, then, making the best of 2020 involved careful attention to the crises we are living through, as well as to works of love to which we are called, even and especially in fearful days. The present book both talks about and enacts such reflective practice.

As I explain more fully in the introduction, I wrote the first draft of these reflections in real time—as I was encountering the shared hardship, my own fear and anxiety, and an emerging sense of meaning and purpose that I here describe. While I have revised all the chapters and cut others entirely, I haven't smoothed over the fragmentary, journal-entry form of each. The book as a whole is focused on neighbor love in fearful days, but that primary theme emerged from these pages rather than being the plan from the start. Indeed, although I felt called to start writing in March of 2020, I didn't really know what I was writing until midsummer, when I wrote the introduction. Perhaps the final form does not entirely "flow" to the degree that college students schooled in transition statements expect. The upshot, though, is a book now filled with short chapters that are each self-contained, attending to unique insights while together addressing age-old questions that take on particular urgency in times of pain and fear: Who is my neighbor? To what am I called? How shall I live?

Jesus answered the first of those questions by telling the parable of the Good Samaritan. It's a parable that I wrestle with throughout this book as I try to courageously care for others and (no less difficult) to graciously receive their care for me. Parables are short, pithy stories that carry tremendous meaning about the depth of human brokenness and the mysteries of hope and healing. They carry so much meaning, in fact, that they cannot easily be translated into takeaway "morals" or "points." It might sound heretical, but I hope the stories about my own life and the lives of family members, neighbors, and students that fill this book feel a bit like parables—short, reflective stories that try to get to the heart of holy lessons that would be hard to learn in other ways.

Writing them has been both gift and task. I hope the same for your reading.

INTRODUCTION

Storying Our Lives in Times of Pain and Crisis

Let me tell you what I wish I'd known
When I was young and dreamed of glory.
You have no control:
Who lives,
who dies,
who tells your story?
  —Lin-Manuel Miranda, *"Who Lives, Who Dies, Who Tells Your Story"*

If posts on Facebook are any indication, my family spent the Fourth of July weekend during the summer of 2020 doing what countless other families did: we subscribed to Disney+ so that we could stream the filmed version of Lin-Manuel Miranda's sensational Broadway musical, *Hamilton*. The musical is a work of historical revisionism, as it reframes and retells the stories of America's Founding Fathers from an otherwise marginal point of view. Alexander Hamilton was previously known for little more than being that wig-wearing white dude on the ten-dollar bill. In the musical, he goes from unsung hero to underdog victor (although a tragic one), champion of immigrants (they "get the job done"), and rags-to-riches trailblazer who decidedly will *not* throw away his shot.

Since its debut in 2015, *Hamilton* has been widely celebrated by most but scrutinized and criticized by some. For critics, the historical revisionism passes over into revisionist history—a retelling that cleans up and distorts the actual historical record. The protagonist throws shade at Thomas

Jefferson for relying on slaves to produce Virginia's wealth. But the musical fails to note that Alexander Hamilton, too, acquired slaves when he married into the wealthy Schuyler family; supported the "three-fifths clause" of the Constitution; and made many other compromises whenever they gave him the best shot at developing a strong central government or at profiting personally. Some see the hip-hop score and multicultural cast as obscuring "darker" truths about who the Founding Fathers really were and what the country they founded really is. The genocide of Native Americans, on whose land all these events unfold, receives not a single shout-out.[1]

Of course, every story simplifies the facts of history—and necessarily so. Stories are always told from a particular point of view. They raise certain characters into heroes or villains, relegating others to the ensemble or to silence. Stories, unlike history per se, have clear plots that thicken through rising action and finally reach a climax before the resolution or denouement.

What I like about *Hamilton*—besides it giving my kids something to do in the car—is that it invites rather than obscures careful, critical attention to what stories get told, which perspectives get reconsidered, and who benefits. The color-conscious casting of the musical ensures that we notice the irony of people of color playing the part of slave owners and hopefully talk about it. The celebration of immigrants "getting the job done" prompts us to reconsider the stories we tell about contemporary immigrants, some of which are rather disparaging. When King George so whimsically serenades the colonies, assuring them that "when push comes to shove, I will kill your friends and family, to remind you of my love," we who live in the United States should reflect on how often we, too, have killed in the name of peace or democracy or law and order or economic growth or other forms of paternalistic, colonizing "love." After (spoiler alert) Hamilton is killed by Aaron Burr in a duel, George Washington begins the final number, "Who Lives, Who Dies, Who Tells Your Story," which reevaluates the very story of the self-made, autonomous man that he had believed when he was young and that *Hamilton* otherwise tells.

None of us is in control. The very stories of our lives depend on being told and retold by others.

I am writing this book during the spring and summer of 2020, a time when none of us is in control. I tell a story *about* that same time; in this sense, these are "real-time" reflections. It is a story about living through a period when the world as we know it is being shattered by COVID-19 and one or two additional pandemics, depending on how you count.

The story begins in March, after a novel coronavirus (SARS-CoV-2) reached American shores and it became clear that this was serious—really, really serious. Restaurants and shops closed down. Colleges, universities, and K–12 schools told their students not to return to classes after spring break; instead, schools would move online. States mandated their residents to stay at home unless their work was deemed essential. Cable news channels counted cases and deaths. A shortage of toilet paper in early March gave way to a shortage of morgues by the end of April. People taped construction-paper hearts to their windows and left thank-you notes and hand sanitizer for postal carriers. Sports disappeared. *Flattening the curve, social distancing, six feet apart,* and *sheltering in place* became household terms.

Interwoven with this crisis in personal and public health was the hemorrhaging of the economy. By the end of July, the gross domestic product (GDP) plummeted to almost two-thirds of its previous annual rate. The US unemployment rate, which has averaged at about 5.75 percent since World War II, skyrocketed to almost 15 percent in April. This pandemic-driven recession, like the coronavirus itself, immediately targeted the most vulnerable. Grocery store and fast-food workers who were deemed "essential" wondered whether that really meant "disposable." The debate over how and whether to reopen the economy started to fall along partisan lines, with maskless libertarians protesting shelter-in-place orders and demanding their right to work, while liberals shamed the maskless and boycotted businesses that neglected safety precautions. The pandemic-driven recession is certainly a symptom of COVID-19, but treating it can worsen the disease. States in the Sun Belt that reopened aggressively around Memorial

Day soon saw a spike in cases and shut back down by the Fourth of July. Some wonder whether a global, capitalistic economy, with safety nets for the few and instability for the many, primarily experiences the effect of the health crisis or is closer to being its cause.

While the COVID-19 outbreak and economic meltdown happened in lockstep, a third pandemic broke out later in the summer, surprising many with its force and speed. Many of us who, in the words of Ta-Nehisi Coates, "believe ourselves white"[2] responded to the belated news reports of Ahmaud Arbery's murder on February 23 by a father-son team of vigilantes much like we had responded to early reports of the coronavirus outbreak in Wuhan, China—with interest in and mild concern for something affecting *other* people. The same was true for Breonna Taylor's death on March 13 by the Louisville Police Department. But then George Floyd died under the knee of Minneapolis police officer Derek Chauvin on May 25, and our nation's longtime pandemic of police brutality and systemic racism fully presented itself to all of America, not just to those it impacted firsthand. Like the virus, this pandemic was no longer something happening to others, something we—I myself, as a white person, included—could forget about simply by turning off the news. An accompanying outbreak of uprisings, vigils, and protests hit Minneapolis and spread throughout the world. *Eight minutes 46 seconds*, *die-in protests*, and *defund the police* also became household terms. It turns out that in, with, and under the COVID-19 pandemic was the equally deadly pandemic of police brutality, widespread white supremacy, and the mass incarcerations and executions of Black America—a pandemic that some who believe themselves white had been privileged enough to previously ignore while people of color lived with its chronic pain.

Taking institutionalized racism alongside an extractive economy, partisan politics, and global contagion, it becomes difficult to sort out the primary disease from its symptoms and underlying conditions. Is this one pandemic or many? If the latter, they certainly feed off one another. A person of color is more likely to be hospitalized or die from COVID-19 than a white person, and that likelihood correlates with the risk of obesity, type 2 diabetes, and a number of other conditions, each with disparities along racial lines. The physical health of Black and brown Americans correlates, in turn, with insufficient health care, the working conditions of essential/disposable workers (including undocumented workers in dangerous meat-packing plants), and a lack of access to fresh food within food deserts. Poor neighborhoods with ubiquitous access to Little Debbies and liquor but not healthy produce did not pop up by chance or because of the "lifestyle choices" of their residents. They are the product of redlining, or racially biased mortgage lending that made homeownership and generational wealth available to white Americans through the sequestering of Black folks to monthly rentals in substandard neighborhoods that are policed to this day by white officers who live on the other side of town.[3]

You can see how in telling just this slice of the story, I have already had to make interpretive decisions about protagonists, antagonists, plots, and subplots. (In fact, I have only alluded to a fourth, underlying pandemic manifesting itself through the others—modern, Western humanity's alienation from the nonhuman world, which has led us to the "long emergency" of climate change and up to the edge of Earth's seventh mass extinction, which may just do humanity in.) No telling of a story comes from history ready at hand. The same events can thus be storied in wildly different ways. Indeed, one weekend in July, my wife and I debated with another baseball parent about whether COVID-19 was even real. We said we were glad to be back at baseball after the team took fourteen days off when a player's older sibling tested positive. He said it was an overreaction and that the team wasn't playing well because of the hiatus. We said that there were parents of players who were very high risk and that winning tournaments didn't really matter. He said you had to take some calculated risks and that the dangers had been inflated by liberal media. One hundred fifty thousand dead in the United States, we said. He said those numbers were definitely inflated.

That every story is perspectival does not mean that there is nothing but perspective and no such thing as truth. People can and will disagree, but there's a big difference between doing so with facts, argument, evidence, and an openness to learning, on the one hand, and by flippantly reposting the latest conspiracy theory on social media and unfriending those who disagree, on the other.

I teach religion at a Lutheran liberal arts college. One primary goal of being liberally educated (meaning *widely* educated) is the ability to critically and constructively participate in public debates of real importance. (Some of them, like debates about COVID-19 or racialized violence, may literally affect who lives, who dies, and who tells the story.) We hope that our graduates get not only well-paying jobs but also the skills needed to read a graph and know what it is and is not saying; to come away from a long novel with deeper empathy for different life experiences; to be suspicious of theories that are so all explanatory that no evidence seems to count against them; and to cast an informed vote, to join the PTA, to participate in a protest, to buy local foods, and to otherwise serve the common good. Liberal arts education helps young people hear stories with critical and self-critical ears. Who are the heroes, and what are their flaws? Who is villainized? Is transformation or redemption still open to them? What kind of story is this? Whose interests does it serve? Who gets to tell it?

Actually, the ability to critically investigate the stories we tell is only half of what it means to be liberally educated. The other half involves the ability to tell stories and thus to make meaning in the first place. Liberal arts colleges, especially those that are church related, want our students to form character as well as acquire skills. To form and know your character is to come to know yourself as *a* character in a larger story. It is to find yourself in a story that you did not create but can fully own and narrate. It is to understand yourself and your world as having a plot, meaning, and purpose—above and beyond the random incidences and coincidences that too often decide how we live. This is another way of saying that church-related liberal arts schools educate for *vocation*. They want students to form the kinds of selves and live the kinds of lives that are attuned to—and can capably respond to—the needs and callings of others.

Questions about one's sense of calling or vocation direct attention not only toward *doing* but also toward *being*. To consider one's callings quickly pushes past the immediate and pragmatic (What should I do with my time and skills?) to questions of personhood, agency, purpose, and meaning: Who am I? Why am I here? How shall I live? Those rather deep questions can only be adequately answered by thinking of one's life in terms of a story. To ask about one's story is to ask about one's sense of self—about one's gifts and passions and how they might be cultivated to respond to the needs of the world.

I have said that this is a book about the spring and summer of 2020, when pandemics ravaged the world. Really, it is about my sense of being called to act in particular ways and to become a particular kind of person; it is about my sense of responsibility for my family, my students, my neighbors, and myself throughout these challenging days. (I say "these" rather than "those" because I am writing this in the midst of them.) Because one's personal vocation can only be fleshed out by reflecting on the story of one's life, this is a book that tries to tell the story of callings new and old. I sometimes clearly hear and fully heed those callings. Just as often, I strain to listen for them, confuse them with my own loud longings, and occasionally ignore them altogether. Finally, because the very stories of our lives depend on the telling and retelling of others, this book includes some stories about past and present students, family members, neighbors near and far, and the God whom (I believe) is coauthor, at least, of our collective story. Reflecting on these stories helps me to come to terms with my own—just as telling this slice of my story might help others live theirs.

So this is a story about a sense of responsibility, a summer of suffering, and my and others' storied selves. In each case, however, telling the story as I do so here remains a tension-filled, complex process. This is for three reasons. First, while I and so many others feel called to do good and needed work during this time of crisis, it is hard to know how to answer that summoning while also being told to shelter in place. How do we think about our lives as called toward courageous and meaningful work during this time—from protesting to volunteering to getting an education—when we must shelter in place and continue to wait? Second, we know that we are living through a momentous juncture, one that matches 9/11 or the Great Depression in shaping our national identity (one might say history has its eyes on us), and yet this summer seems so absurd, meaningless, and senseless. Our cries of "Why?" echo about, sounding hollow, as intense and enduring suffering interrupts the normal ways of making meaning of things. Finally, there is the tension between coming to know and own our vocations by reflecting on our lives in terms of story and the fact that, on the one hand, stories can't be fully told until they are done, while on the other hand, we must live our lives before they are finished. The challenge of living a reflective life of purposeful work gets even more complicated when one is trying to reflect and act in the middle of crises whose end is unknown—a challenge I have felt even more acutely after I decided to tell this story, the end of which I don't yet know.

These three tensions cut through the book you are holding from beginning to end. Indeed, they are the stuff of the book—that which I explore as I come to terms with our lives and responsibilities in times of crisis. I want to say more about each.

Summoning While Sheltering

My colleague M., who teaches in our music department, reached out to me after our college had begun distance learning with an email that named the acute sense of responsibility—to students, colleagues, friends, and family members—that she and so many others were feeling in the face of a frightening pandemic. "If this is not a moment of summoning," she said, "I don't know what is."

That language of summoning comes from the political and cultural commentator David Brooks, whom M. and I read in an "Education for

Vocation" seminar that I coordinated for faculty.[4] Brooks contrasts the "well-planned life" with a "summoned life." The former considers itself as a project that should be defined early on and then lived out strategically and purposely. The well-planned life is driven by goals; the one living it articulates ambition, makes plans, crosses items off bucket lists.

Brooks doesn't denigrate the vision of the well-planned life. Yet he clearly favors the kind of responsible, well-considered life that often doesn't make headlines—at least not in the United States, with its preference for stories of lone heroes who carve their own paths (including, I would add, stories that the United States often tells of itself). This second kind of life, the summoned life, exercises its agency by being attentive and responsive to others. The summoned life doesn't, first of all, ask what the individual wants to do and then plan for how to accomplish it. Rather, it looks to the situation and web of relationships in which it finds itself, asking how to respond. Such lives can be incredibly meaningful, but the meaning and purpose come through a different kind of effort.

The summoned life is open to the pleas, gifts, needs, interruptions, and summons of others. It is not aimless, endlessly drifting, or thrown about by circumstance. It, too, is a life of reflection, intention, and responsibility. Indeed, one might argue (Brooks is only suggestive here) that a life open to being summoned is more meaningful and responsible than the well-planned life. Because the meaningfulness isn't intended in advance, it comes to include meaningful work (and play) that couldn't be planned for and yet still comes as gift and task. The summoned person is supremely "response-able" in a primary sense—*able* to *respond* to new circumstances, open and responsive to others.

To be "educated for vocation" is to embark on a summoned life. *Vocation* comes from *vocare*, or "calling" or "summons," which in turn comes from *vox*, or "voice." To discern a vocation is to hear and respond to the voices of others—whether one identifies it as the voice of God or hears it as the summoning (sometimes a desperate cry) for help and healing by particular communities of human and nonhuman creatures. At best, college students not only strive for fulfilling and successful careers but also form lives of careful discernment and creative, responsible work with and for a world that so desperately needs them.

Some find the language of vocation a bit wonky or too easily confused with vocational-technical (vo-tech) training or the callings of Catholic priests. (Before the sixteenth century, and still today in some Catholic quarters, only monks, nuns, and priests were said to have vocations. Martin Luther democratized the meaning of vocation to include any and all work—both paid and unpaid—that serves the common good. Brewing beer, changing diapers, and serving as a soldier were Luther's frequent examples.) Critics of the term often propose "meaningful work" or a "life of purpose" as good alternatives. I've got no real problem with that, except that *making* meaning and *pursuing* purpose, unlike *finding* these or being called or summoned, maximize the individual's self-authorship and are therefore more easily confused with a fully planned life of one's choosing. By contrast, understanding one's life as called forth by others puts the emphasis on its embeddedness within relationships (with God, with other humans, with particular communities and the whole created order). This is why so many church-related colleges talk about work that serves the common good.

It is also why Lutheran schools like my own lean so heavily on Martin Luther's fondness for the biblical language of "the neighbor" when they consider human work in the world. In a passage I cite in an early entry, Luther claims, "No one needs even one of these works to attain righteousness and salvation. For this reason, in all of one's works a person should in this context be shaped by and contemplate this thought alone: to serve and benefit others in everything that may be done, having nothing else in view except the need and advantage of the neighbor."[5] Luther thought that many of us are stuck desperately trying to create our own lives in order to impress other people and, ultimately, appease God. Whether with delusions of grandeur or with desperation and despair, we assume that we must earn our worth, make our own meaning, and otherwise "justify" ourselves. But when such a self-creating, self-justifying person is interrupted by a gracious God who, in Luther's favored language, extends justification by grace through faith, they can finally cease to focus on themselves and fully attend to what someone else is going through. Grace, which redoubles as calling, has freed them to do good work. They can and will do whatever they can so that their neighbors can flourish.

While *vocation* and *neighbor love* come primarily out of Jewish and Christian traditions, people from different religious and secular backgrounds translate the idioms into their own terms. While Christians come to humble service because their Lord humbly serves, they shouldn't be surprised to find Jews engaged in the same service, who come in the spirit of *tikkun olam*—from the hope that by doing small acts that contribute to God's ongoing creation, humans can "heal the world." And they shouldn't be surprised to find Muslims responding to the Qur'an's exhortation to "strive in the way of God with a service worthy of Him" (22:78). When Buddhists live out their callings with the Heart Sutra on their lips or when lovers of the Bhagavad Gita come with intentions to act for good simply and purely—"intent on action / not on the fruits of action"[6]—Christians should see them as partners. Finally, when secular students at church-related colleges return from service-learning trips to Guatemala or Appalachia with an "epiphany of recruitment,"[7] a powerful sense of direction and purpose, they will probably interpret the summons as issuing from particular places and people, rather than from God. Still, they should be able to understand religious students who interpret the experience differently, and the two groups should be able to learn from one another.

The onset of COVID-19 challenged everyone's sense of purposeful work. Office professionals with clear divisions between work life and home life found themselves summoned (or simply compelled) to homeschool children during their own endless Zoom meetings. Some workers in the service industry (grocery store clerks, for example) were honored and thanked; others (fast-food workers) were scrutinized and scolded even more than usual by the customers they were serving. While some were given increased protections and provisions, many workers—maybe especially those honored—did not find their "necessary," "sacrificial," and "heroic" work to be compensated fairly. Accolades may have simply masked their exploitation.

Students of all ages who previously could fulfill one of their primary callings simply by showing up for class and doing their homework had to take wholesale responsibility for their learning while negotiating clumsy online learning platforms. College students who felt drawn to selective schools and immersive learning found themselves back at home fighting for broadband space with siblings; many mused over whether community college online courses would feel any different. International students who could not make it back to their home countries spent the summer worrying about their student visa statuses from designated dorms on largely deserted campuses. Those who did make it home now wonder whether they will be able to reenter the United States or whether it is worth returning.

Maybe this is what my colleague M. meant when she said that this was a moment of summoning. Many of our well-planned lives are on hold. Some are gone for good. That's the moment—a very long and painful moment—when we might hear the call to become a different sort of persons, ones more attuned to what is needed here and now, regardless of prior ambitions.

Making Sense of Meaningless Suffering

People go to great lengths to explain why tragedies happen. When Hurricane Katrina struck New Orleans fifteen summers ago, it left in its wake not only massive destruction of human life and property but also a number of religious and secular explanations for why God (or Mother Earth) was angry with us. Conservative Christians saw the storm as God's way of punishing evildoers, driving unbelievers to conversion, and preparing the elect for the Rapture. God was angry with the United States for abortion, or homosexuality, or its lack of unqualified support for the State of Israel. Liberal environmentalists had their explanations as well. Mother Earth was fighting back against our conspicuous consumption and idolatrous worship of fossil fuels. Violent storms are consequences or comeuppances for the violence humans have inflicted on Her.[8]

Whether coming from the right or left, explanatory accounts make sense of a storm that its victims only experience as utterly absurd. *It makes sense* that the hurricane struck New Orleans (or so the explainers explain) given that the Gulf Coast is home to over a quarter of the nation's oil refineries or that the Big Easy is known for its sexual license and immorality. Connecting dots and perceiving patterns allow people to double down on meaningful worldviews, even and especially in the face of meaningless tragedies.

Explanations for why suffering makes sense are known in philosophical and theological quarters as "theodicies"—literally, the justification or defense (*diké*) of God (*theos*) and of God's ways. To offer a theodicy is to "justify the ways of God to men" or, more philosophically, to offer a defense of the rational or moral coherence of the universe as "the best of all possible worlds."[9]

Theodicies (those defenses) and theodicists (the defenders) are as old as time remembered. The Hebrew Bible's most maddening book is Job, a story of God accepting Satan's bet concerning whether a man named Job, who was entirely innocent and righteous, would continue to praise God if God were to take away all his livestock, his children, and his health. God takes the bet and allows Satan to wreak destruction. The rest of the book of Job consists of Job sitting on a pile of dung, lamenting his plight and imploring God to explain Godself. Job's so-called friends sit shiva with him silently at first and then desperately try to explain his senseless suffering.

Sunday school teachers might say that the book of Job has a take-away lesson. ("If you're patient like Job, God will reward you with even more livestock and a brand-new family!") For anyone who actually reads it, though, it is a confounding story, one that troubles neat and easy understandings of God, suffering, justice, morality, and meaning. It is only Job's friends (and not Job or the book itself) who patiently present explanations for why he suffers. They begin with the most prevalent reason—suffering is punishment for sin. Later, they change tactics, insisting that if Job's plight is not the consequence of sin, it must be God teaching him a lesson. Whether as punishment for some hidden disobedience or a cosmic ruler slap by a habit-wearing teacher, suffering—they insist—is all part of the master plan.

Except that it's not, which Job and the reader know. In my reading, the book of Job primarily indicates all the problems with our desperate attempts to situate suffering within an airtight explanation. The problem with explaining why suffering makes sense (whether in light of past wrongdoing, future vindication, or something else) is that such explanations and theodicies often rationalize, justify, or defend the pain as reasonable and right. The friends treat Job like a conceptual puzzle to be solved rather than as a friend calling them toward compassion. In their attempts at comprehension, they sidestep his actual affliction, explaining it away.

So why do we do it? Why do we so regularly and so desperately seek to explain tragedy in ways that make sense of it as part of an overarching plan or metaphysical worldview? Explanations and other meaning-making *work*. They sometimes work for good and often work for bad, but they work. That, I think, is why we seek them.

There are studies that show that people who get lung cancer after a life of chain-smoking more easily accept their sickness and death and are more content through the end of their lives compared with those who get lung cancer for no apparent reason. When lung cancer makes sense within understood frameworks of cause and effect (as spelled out on cigarette packs), its victim feels less victimized, or at least not senselessly so. With explanation at hand, those suffering come to terms more easily with their plight.[10]

In *Man's Search for Meaning*, Holocaust survivor Viktor Frankl claims that the primary force driving humanity is its search for meaning. The greatest torment of the camps, he writes, was not the hunger, cold, abuse, or looming death but the "unreasonableness of it all." But Frankl also writes of an ultimate sense of meaning and purpose that can be experienced and affirmed, even in moments of doom and despair. He recalls a time he was forced to work in a trench under a gray sky, grieving for what had become of his life: "I was struggling to find the *reason* for my sufferings, my slow dying. In a last violent protest against the hopelessness of immanent death, I sensed my spirit piercing through the enveloping gloom. I felt it transcend that hopeless, meaningless world, and from somewhere I heard a victorious 'Yes' in answer to my question of the existence of an ultimate purpose."[11] Life itself carries tremendous meaning when, even amid the experience of utter abandonment, a person affirms it.

While the search for meaning can lead people to accept lung cancer or survive genocide with their souls intact, we know that it can sometimes do more harm than good. Consider the spouse who stays in an abusive marriage, having come to believe that they deserve it or that God has sent the suffering as their "cross to bear." That hunger, abject poverty, exploitation, or abuse is ordained by God or that those suffering will be compensated with heavenly bliss if only they endure their suffering patiently (like Job!)—such explanations anesthetize the suffering of some while justifying the apathy of others. At the same time, there are ways to find meaning that don't amount to giving explanations. Much depends on *how* we think about suffering. Is it only a problem to be solved? What then do we do with problems that have no solutions—like the "problem" of our mortality? Suffering cannot be solved with greater technological precision or a more refined philosophical theory. We are called to know it in other ways.

The Impossible Necessity of "Real-Time" Reflections

Most authors write introductions to their books at the very beginning or the end of the writing process. I'm writing this one halfway through the time of overlapping pandemics that I trace in what follows. Actually, we're not "halfway" through, nor do we even know what that would mean. We only know that we're anxious and fearful and want it all to end.

All acute suffering has an anachronistic character, Dorothee Soelle claims in her book *Suffering*.[12] Those not suffering rush toward the future; the afflicted remain stuck in another time, which passes with agonizing slowness. Cheap consolations try to pull them toward closure, assuring the sufferers that everything happens for a reason and will work itself out in the end. Those explanations won't help and will probably feel like the patronizing rationalizations of Job's so-called friends. We can only help, says Soelle, by stepping into the time frame of those who are suffering.

This is what I have tried to do in the present book—to step into a time of painful catastrophes and equally painful transformations, of quick despair and slow hope, while they are happening. The book reflects on our interconnected lives as they slouch forward.

Church-related liberal arts colleges ask students to do real-time reflections all the time. We ask them to take stock of their education, to consider what they thought they knew and how that is giving way to new learning and growth. What is more, we ask them to take stock of their lives, to consider who they thought they were and how that is giving way to an unfolding sense of vocation, meaning, and purpose. I'm not sure educators realize just how difficult this is. Reflecting on one's life while living it is a bit like holding a mirror while biking in order to see and improve one's peddling. It's difficult, although necessary and humanizing work. (I mean the work of reflection, not tricky bike maneuvers.)

Socrates said that the unexamined life is not worth living. Philosophy (the "love of wisdom") was for Socrates the way one lived an examined life—overturning false assumptions, thinking about thinking, taking reason wherever it leads one, even to the acceptance of death. All deep learning includes careful logic and persistent self-evaluation. Without reflecting on what makes for a just society and a well-lived life, we act haphazardly and reactively rather than responsibly and purposefully.

Kierkegaard said that life can be understood backward, but it must be lived forward. For Socrates, human understanding brings us right to the brink—if not over the edge—of acting reasonably and justly, while for

Kierkegaard, a wide ditch always remains. No matter how carefully we think, we can never think ourselves into decision. Every important decision must break with deliberation and take a leap of faith.

When Kierkegaard was young, he—like so many young people—was searching for who he was. He writes the following in his journal: "What I really need is to get clear about *what I must do*, not what I must know, except insofar as knowledge must precede every act. What matters is to find a purpose, to see what it really is that God wills that *I* shall do; the crucial thing is to find a truth which is truth *for me*, to find *the idea for which I am willing to live and die*."[13] Socrates most fears the unreflective life, one that acts without thinking; Kierkegaard fears a life of idle speculation or endless rumination, one that tells itself it needs to read some more books before beginning a paper or that has worked through Anselm's ontological proof for God's existence but can't bring itself to pray.

They are, of course, both right. Neither thoughtless living nor lifeless thought will do. Self-knowledge is crucial, but only insofar as it enables us to inhabit our daily decisions and everyday work with an increased sense of their and our own value. Reflection at its best enables one to connect the life of the mind with the rest of one's life. Reflective, purposeful students know all kinds of things about, say, organic chemistry or third-wave feminism. But they also know why those things matter, for whom they matter, and how they matter in their own lives.

It is not always that way, of course. In much of our everyday lives, there remain conspicuous gaps between what we know, how we live, and how we talk about each. This brings to my mind a story about a friend I knew as a young adult.

I met P. at Luther Seminary in St. Paul, Minnesota, where we were two academic MA students, surrounded by a sea of "MDivs"—master of divinity students—who felt called to ordained ministry. P. was wicked smart—not only encyclopedic in what he knew but also patient and perceptive in finding connections between seemingly unrelated facts. P. also had a stutter. Eating lunch together in the campus dining hall, he would be eloquent for minutes on end while he spoke about Lyotard on meta-narratives or Julian of Norwich's *Revelations of Divine Love*. The stutter would return only when there was a break in his train of thought, as though he were keeping his foot on the gas while in park to keep a low-idling car from dying. One day, in a rare moment of open vulnerability between us, P. told me the reason he was in the master's program and why he read so extensively. He believed that if he became immersed deeply enough in ideas and books, his mind would never idle and so his tongue would never stammer.

That conversation has stayed with me over the past twenty years, probably because it hits close to home. I don't have a speech impediment, but I do easily confuse words (sometimes comically so, to my kids' amusement). I sometimes lose my ability to express even the easiest of ideas, especially when I am tired and sometimes when standing in front of a classroom of college students. This was most noticeable—both to me and to my students, who rated me low on "clarity" in their course evaluations—when I started teaching at my Lutheran liberal arts college over a decade ago. What was it about that time? Certainly I was exhausted, with two toddler sons having night terrors and getting ear infections while my wife was spending her nights on call as a hospital chaplain and I was trying to publish my first book (on Søren Kierkegaard) and otherwise earn my keep as a young college professor. More to the point, though, it was a time when there was a big gulf between the life of my mind and the everyday life I was living. Looking back now, it seems that all my verbal halts and hesitancies were stumbling about in that ditch.

Some years later, the problem subsided, or at least I ceased to be anxious about it. I found myself finishing sentences that would have ensnared me earlier. Or I would notice my mixed-up words and even laugh at them while continuing to peddle forward. What was it about *this* time? I was sleeping more, certainly. But I think I was also getting out of my own head long enough to attend to the needs of my family and students. Reflection provided the bridge between the life of my mind and my everyday callings.

I could speak more meaningfully and coherently about things that mattered. I stopped stammering when I reflected on the story of my life.

I have said that this is a book of stories about responding to the central calling to love and serve our neighbors in times of crisis. It is the culmination of decades of reflective practice, even if I am writing it over the course of less than a year.

Why write the chapters of this story in real time, before I know how all of it will end? In short, because I see no ending to the stories of our summonings that would allow us to hear them more clearly amid these fearful days. In fact, thinking about the struggle only in light of its resolution will probably simplify the story and so distort it. If, for example, we wait to come to terms with 2020 only once a vaccine has been tested, approved, and administered widely, the story we tell about the time before becomes the story of questing after a cure, neatly contained and easily understood in light of the end. Our lives are not so easily understood and contained. What we are living through right now is not just a long chapter before the end of COVID-19 or the end of injustice, or poverty, or the climate crisis. We should be able to tell stories about our lives before they are over. Otherwise, as Aristotle suggests, we would not be able to assess the character of our lives until we're dead.

To reflect on meaning, purpose, and callings while living through fearful days is no easy task, especially when many are eager to skip to the end. "We are a species," writes Kelly Corrigan, "of unreliable narrators desperate for closure."[14] Our desperation is particularly fraught these days. Anxiously wanting this long chapter to end, we conjecture about the future—whether churches will really reopen by Easter, whether the economy will rebound by September, whether a vaccine will be ready by the end of 2020.

Here, then, are some real-time reflections on our unfinished stories during a prolonged time with no end in sight. I don't presume that the book will affect who lives, who dies, and who (Who?) ultimately will tell our stories. I've only tried to be honest about the vulnerability and beauty of our precious, mysterious lives.

PART 1

WHO IS MY NEIGHBOR?

(March and April)

BANISHING SNAKES—MARCH 17, 2020

It's St. Patrick's Day. I'm up a few hours before my sons Asa, age fourteen, and Gabe, twelve, who are on the second week of a now three-week spring break. The odds of them returning to public school before Easter decline with each COVID-19 news report.

Are there any news reports other than those about the coronavirus? I scroll down the *New York Times* Morning Briefing sent to my inbox this morning—past President Trump's advice to limit social gatherings to fewer than ten people at a time, past reports of testing delays, past the order for residents in France to stay in their homes for fifteen days, past updates on the death toll in Italy (today at 2,100), past the postponement of the Kentucky Derby, past the release of actors Tom Hanks and Rita Wilson from the hospital, and past an opinion piece about how social distancing doesn't have to be lonely—until I get to an article about Syrian refugees and another about Russian shell companies accused of meddling in the 2016 election.

Like my sons, I wonder when and in what form education will resume. On Friday, the Lutheran college where I teach religion announced that our own spring break would begin one week early, effective at four o'clock that very afternoon. We told students to take with them their computers, books, class notes, and other school supplies on the chance that we would have to move to distance learning two weeks from now. That "chance" is now nothing short of a likelihood, and "likelihood" seems to be our administration's calming way of saying that, in fact, our residential liberal arts college will almost certainly look a lot like the University of Phoenix for the rest of the academic year.

I passed two senior female students, J. and S., Friday afternoon, as campus was already eerily quiet. Both were in my honors seminar three years ago. S. had been ready to present her religion senior thesis at the Midwest American Academy of Religion conference before it was canceled last week. "We are in great classes that we really enjoy," they said. "And it's our senior year and our friends are now scattering in every direction. We are supposed to go home but this *is* our home." Students such as these deeply know both grief and gratitude, their callings as students, and the value of true friends, even if it sometimes takes a worldwide pandemic to put those sentiments into words. I told them to be *well*—in the deepest sense of that word. I admit that I don't know what that means.

The 330 million people living in the United States are no doubt figuring out what being well means in this chaotic situation and anxious time. I imagine that they—like me—are primarily concerned with their own physical safety and that of their immediate family members and close friends. But will we also check in on our neighbors? Or will social distancing amount to spiritual and moral distancing out of fearful concern for me and mine?

I remember hearing a presentation from Lutheran pastor Jonathan Strandjord about the Jewish philosopher Emmanuel Levinas when I was in seminary long ago. Strandjord unpacked Levinas's radical idea that being interrupted by "the face of the other" would compel a person to turn inside out in pursuit of justice. In Levinas's words, the other's very otherness should make one take the bread out of one's own mouth, so to speak, relinquishing it to the other.[1] Strandjord was asked during a Q and A how such self-sacrifice could ever happen, given that people are so self-concerned, so "curved in upon themselves"—as the Augustinian-Lutheran understanding of sin would have it. He responded by saying that neither he nor Levinas nor Jesus thought that the real barrier to

4

neighbor love was an individual's *self*-concern, strictly speaking. The problem is exactly what sometimes passes as neighbor love—love for my family or my friends or nation or race or others whom I deem as my neighbors. We must pry open love that seems so naturally selective, so fiercely focused on the communities to which we belong. Love needs to be summoned and stretched through unbidden encounters with the alien, the stranger, the one deemed enemy. At the same time, this stretched love cannot get too drawn out, becoming thin and immaterial like a fog in which all cats appear gray.

The challenge of broadening without weakening love was difficult enough when I first met Strandjord in person and Levinas through his writings twenty-five years ago. Since then, the self-selecting virtual communities of the like-minded on social media and the echo chambers they produce, along with the now dramatic rise in nativism and racism and the unprecedented quarantine-like divide between liberals and conservatives, mean that one is less and less likely to be summoned by a neighbor who does not already belong to one's social group or political party. Online communities have been thoroughly gerrymandered through a gazillion friend requests and like buttons. Ironically enough, it is now just as likely that the neighbor who does in fact need the bread from your mouth is literally your neighbor—the one who lives down the street, whom you recognize through the window of your car but haven't yet (be)friended, virtually or otherwise.

I'm trying here to describe the log in my own eye, not the speck in others more liberal or conservative. It was just two days ago that my wife Laura (an ordained pastor) and I were watching NBC's *Meet the Press* together on Sunday morning, a rare occurrence made possible by the cancellation of her church service. We watched the political and cultural commentator David Brooks describe his fear that the same vicious self-protection and lack of compassion that accompanied the 1918 ("Spanish") flu pandemic would follow the spread of COVID-19. He noted that while some tragedies generate feelings of solidarity and acts of kindness (consider the days immediately following 9/11, before any declaration of war), pandemics typically do the opposite. Conserving moral energy and cultivating moral righteousness to protect themselves and family, people cease to come to the aid of others. Mutual suspicion and competition increase, as does class warfare. Laura and I were taken aback when Brooks articulated his fears. Is this really where we are headed? Narrow concerns driving cutthroat competition and disregard for others? Class warfare?

And yet by Sunday afternoon, there I was, standing before the half-empty shelves of our local Aldi supermarket, buying provisions to add to our mostly full refrigerator. With the meat section particularly picked over, I briefly wondered whether I should leave the corned beef brisket, two turkey tenderloins, and a package of wild-caught flounder for someone with less access to affordable protein. But the shelves had already been thinned, and there were reports of people stockpiling food and amassing cleaning products, and my family was behind on all of it. Would I be morally culpable for not dwelling on the needs of a faceless other who may or may not be needier than we are? Later, as I rearranged the freezer so that everything would fit, I assured myself that Aldi would get restocked overnight.

I am writing these daily entries because I am scared—scared not only for my family's health and safety (although that too, as my anxious grocery buying shows), but also for how I will respond to this pandemic, what will become of me, morally and spiritually, and what will become of my Christian calling to love and serve the neighbor. Brooks's Sunday morning opinion piece was entitled "Pandemics Kill Compassion, Too: You May Not Like Who You're about to Become." I want to like who I'll become, although I know not who that will be.[2]

I'm here committing to taking stock of this pandemic and more so of my own and others' responses to it in thought, word, and deed. I'll wake up early, make coffee, and type out my queries and musings related to regard for neighbors in a time of fear.

Laura and I told our boys that we would need to be intentional with one another and our neighbors during this time. We haven't done much yet, but I hope some seeds will grow. We're praying for those we know who are older, are alone, or have compromised immune systems: Grandpa-Great, Grandma S., members of Laura's church, the homeless in our town who no longer have access to computers and daily shelter at the library, the mother of two young friends, my colleague's spouse who has cancer. Laura is going grocery shopping tonight to buy food for homebound members of her church. We've committed to writing regular letters to people we'd otherwise visit. Will this field of concern open outward? Can it do so without thereby getting overly abstract and self-conspicuously pious, as prayers for "the whole world" sometimes do? How can we structure the weeks or months ahead along the lines of the old Benedictine discipline of *ora et labora*, of prayer and work, repeated throughout each day? Will either be effective in welcoming and sheltering the neighbor?

* * *

I'm finishing this entry in the afternoon, after the first death from COVID-19 in our state of Illinois was announced and the state of Kansas declared that all public schools would go online through the end of year. Our St. Patrick's Day cabbage and corned beef brisket simmers in the slow cooker. Among the legends attributed to Saint Patrick is the miracle of banishing all venomous snakes from Ireland by chasing them into the sea after they attacked him during a forty-day fast. In these forty days of Lent, the nation is beginning to ready itself for a widespread virus that will not so easily be washed away. Besides the virus itself, we will need to resist a legion of crafty serpents that would have us rationalize disregard for others out of protection for our own. Banishing those snakes—loving the neighbor in anxious and fearful times—could turn out to be the miracle of our age.

SITTING SHIVA—MARCH 19, 2020

Today is the first day of spring. Yesterday, the last day of winter, was a bustle of activity. Laura was up and off to her church early, where she announced suspension of Sunday worship through mid-April, planned the videos she will post to Facebook in lieu of live sermons, looked in on congregation members, and led her last Wednesday Lenten prayer service. I spent the morning online with a hundred of my colleagues going over the tools and best practices of teaching and learning online—how to use Moodle and Google, Zoom and Loom, forums and chat rooms and blogs (oh my!). In the afternoon, I reached out to the students in my classes—including S., the student prematurely nostalgic for the college she'll graduate from in May. I've become more and more personal with students over my sixteen years of teaching, but my emails yesterday were full-blown parental and pastoral. I told them that I missed them dearly (which is true for almost all of them), that this was an emotionally exhausting time, and that they should try to establish rhythms of sleeping at night and being awake in the day, do some simple breathing meditation, go for walks, hug their family members, and wash their hands. I told them that I would check in by video chat soon.

It was also yesterday that President Trump declared that the coronavirus pandemic is the war of our time. Former Vice President Joe Biden and Senator Bernie Sanders had already compared confrontation with the virus to the waging of a war. French President Emmanuel Macron was more direct still. "We *are* at war," he repeatedly declared when addressing his citizens two days ago, ordering them to stay in their homes for all but essential activities. In the United States, the administration considered invoking a wartime production act that would allow the government to mobilize industries for national service, requiring them to produce medical supplies and surgical masks. Headlines currently show a number of predictions that COVID-19 casualties may exceed those of World War II.

War language is powerful language, the language of power. Many thus interpret the administration's talk of war positively; after early forays into glib optimism and empty assurances, politicians invoke war to exhibit clear resolve, to gird their loins, and to prepare for battle. Yet I think that much of our work ahead will be the far less unilateral work of patiently waiting out this infectious storm, of learning to care for the infected and affected, of grieving the loss of loved ones. There is much more that we will need to bear and survive rather than conquer and control. War language may be not only irrelevant but also counterproductive to these efforts.

I think of the week immediately following the attacks of 9/11. There was widespread fear and confusion, of course, but also countless makeshift memorials, solidarity vigils, and spontaneous help among strangers. There was an affectionate, palpable patriotism of the most profound kind. It was as if the nation was sitting shiva, purposely persisting in our grief while we waited on one another. That week was incredibly meaningful, whether we were watching images on television or roaming New York like it was a giant prayer labyrinth. It even had something of an overabundance of meaning, as though the importance of every story of firefighters working twelve-hour shifts, every photo of a missing person or hot-dog vendor passing out water, was heightened against the background of the meaningless tragedy itself. Paradoxically, though oversaturated with meaning, none of it meant any one thing. Or rather, because we couldn't situate 9/11 within a well-defined framework of understanding, we didn't know *what* it meant, which became part of the very enigma that we were so devotedly circumambulating. We had no national myth or collective story into which we could insert the event of 9/11 as climactic action before moving straightaway toward resolution.

And then we declared war. According to longtime war correspondent Chris Hedges, war gives meaning like nothing else. Americans know war; we know how to make sense of things when we are at war. We honor the fallen, pray for soldiers, hang flags, supplement the national anthem with "America the Beautiful" and color guards and flyovers. Bush's declaration of war had the almost magical effect of transforming victims into heroes, terrorists into enemy soldiers, our passive mourning into active resolution, and our collective dread before God-knows-what into a clear mission to rid the world of evil.[3] There were some small casualties; for example, most of the international community sitting shiva with us collected their things and quietly departed. But by and large, to be at war was much more understandable and reassuring than the meaning-soaked meaning-less grief from which we were emerging.

For the record, I hope that we beat COVID-19—kick the shit out of each small set of genes enclosed in fatty lipid molecules and armored with protein spikes. My concern is for the collateral damage to our collective character and individual dispositions that waging war can yield. Will we be patient and kind? Will we be able to truthfully accept and faithfully bear this tragedy, even as we try to conquer it? How will we care for those who cannot be cured—a question made painfully difficult by the six or more feet of space that could separate the dying from their families? How well will we grieve—privately in our homes, locally in shifts of ten, and collectively as a human race?

Trump continues to call the coronavirus "the Chinese virus." Am I right to hear echoes of "gooks" fought overseas or the "thugs" demonized in a war on drugs? If killing people requires their prior dehumanization, perhaps attacking a virus depends on its racialization. Already, too, speeches about containing COVID-19 include commands for a more militarized border security, lest a storm of sick immigrants infect us and strains our health care system.

These are some cracks in the armor, but the language of war mostly carries out its mission in garnering collective resolve, eradicating critique, and justifying the moral righteousness of those engaged. This goes for wars on diseases as well as on terrorists or criminals. In her profound work, *Glimpsing Resurrection*, Deanna Thompson, who was diagnosed with stage IV cancer in 2008, writes about how "those of us who live with cancer [often] are cast in the role of warriors called on to battle the cancer with all the ammunition we've got." Swapping out a story of battle for the lens of trauma, Thompson asks what it would mean to live well with loss. She writes about, and with, "a different, non-military focused vocabulary to talk about what it means to negotiate life with a serious illness."[4]

For two thousand years, Christians have found such countercultural scripts and practices in the raw lamentations of Job and the Psalms, in Jesus's difficult acceptance of death (complete with a cry from the cross), and in the acceptance of mortality during Ash Wednesday and the self-examination that follows during Lent. For just as long, Chinese culture has sought to "cultivate valley spirit," balancing an aggressive, masculine yang with a supple, feminine yin. Indeed, according to Daoism, the most powerful action is spontaneous nonaction—wu wei, the way of water, which cuts through rock by yielding so masterfully to it. Hindus and Jains practice *ahimsa* (literally, "noninjury"), and Buddhists attend to their breath, letting go of acquisitive desire, hatred, and ignorance. Islam literally means submission, and a Muslim is one who submits. There are plenty of stories and practices that would provide alternatives to war and war making, if we would just draw on their riches.[5]

I gave blood at our regional blood bank today, as I've done fairly regularly over the last several years. I was quick to make the appointment when they called asking for help; it didn't hurt that my kids were in the car listening to my response over Bluetooth. I keep my mind off the red tube attached to my left arm by tallying small acts of kindness alongside acts done out of fear and ignorance. I am giving blood—plus one point. It is, in part, to set an example for my kids rather than to do what is good for goodness's sake—minus one point. The place is packed; beyond the regular row of older men giving platelets, a small line has formed of people wanting to donate blood, having heard that the need was especially high with the recent cancellation of blood drives in local schools—plus two points. While sipping apple juice and eating my granola bar, I overhear two workers discuss whether it was the cleaning crew who stole all the toilet paper from the supply closet—minus one point. Too early for a final score, but kindness seems to be leading at halftime.

* * *

Tonight is beautiful. The sun came out late in the day, its light dispersing throughout the early spring sky at twilight. It's that time when everything becomes more pronounced against the setting sun—almost surreal, as if we were cast in a colorized movie. There is more meaning against the horizon of this meaningless pandemic than I may be able to take in.

SHELTER IN PLACE—MARCH 22, 2020

This is getting real.

I'm up well before dawn after a handful of hours of restless sleep. Last night, Facebook Messenger lit up with rumors of the first case of COVID-19 in our small city. One cryptic message from our neighbor D., who often knows things before they are public, specified that the boys and I should not, under any circumstances, play pickup basketball this afternoon, which we had done a week ago, the last day that my college's rec center was open. No sooner had Laura read me the message than I began to create and connect the dots: I think the wife of the player who likes to drive the lane works in the emergency room. Did he contract it through her? Did Asa or Gabe guard him? Did they use enough hand sanitizer between games? Could they die?

A subsequent text from our neighbor clarified that she just didn't want us having any contact with anyone; basketball was only an example. No need to dwell on the questions above—minus the last one, which kindled my anxiety long after we said goodnight to the boys.

Today is the fourth Sunday of Lent. The gospel lesson is the story of the man born blind, whom an unbeckoned Jesus hastens to heal as the disciples debate over who is to blame for his condition. My family will have "family church" at ten thirty this morning over a chorizo egg bake, which I promised to the boys last night. Sitting under a warm blanket on the couch, watching the sky spit sleety snow, my contemplations and writing this morning feel especially like prayer—or at least like the difficult (non) action of paying attention, which Simone Weil identifies as the essence of prayer.[6]

We will abide by the Illinois governor's executive order to "stay at home," one of five statewide decrees at present. "Shelter in place" is no longer being used for these orders, given that the phrase conjures frightening images of active shooters and classroom lockdowns in many people's minds—especially those of Gen X, who have trained for school shootings since they were in kindergarten. For me, though, to shelter seems much more accurate to the purposeful action asked of us. Deriving from the word *shield*, to shelter is to take guard—and more so, to protect those who need guarding, as in providing lodging for the homeless poor or taking in stray animals. My putting an egg bake in the oven, Laura's designing of word games for the kids, and our planning of hikes with our dog Gracie at Sylvan Island—each action makes shelter for our family. The difficulty is how to shield those who are not already under our roof. Whom else will I be called on to shelter? What can hospitality look like across property lines?

Two days ago, I received an email from E., a recent graduate from my college and former student in my upper-level seminar, Suffering, Death, and Endurance, who moved to Boston to look for jobs and attend to his mental health. Students like E. make me proud to teach at a Lutheran liberal arts school. He identifies as nonreligious but would visit during my office hours to discuss faith and hope and spiritual wellness. He wrote his final paper in the "Suffering" class on the theodicy of hip-hop music, which first turned me on to the prophetic and profane musical artist Brother Ali. I dare not tally the teaching versus the learning that I give/receive from students like E.

He reported last week that the streets and squares of Boston have been disconcertingly quiet, like the calm before a storm. "Still, it's not all bad," he writes. "People are settling into their new norm. I'm starting to get involved with the mutual-aid networks popping up across the country. It's wonderful to see how much people are willing to share, both in knowledge and resources. I'm grateful for social media allowing us to stay connected while remaining distant." He says he's been organizing people in his Somerville neighborhood, ensuring that channels of communication remain open. And then, with characteristic humility, E. asks me for advice about how to talk with people about the pandemic itself. He confesses, "I'm not sure how to talk about this moment in time we're living through. I want to be a source of stability, but I don't want to be more than what I am."

There's so much here to comment on, including all the ways that E. is enacting neighbor love much more creatively than I am. I am particularly struck by the wisdom of not wanting to be more than he is. He could have said that he didn't want to overextend himself or that he didn't want to do more than he could effectively do. But his language is about personhood and character, not activities and tasks.

He's writing about his sense of calling, that understanding of oneself and one's necessary limits that must be carefully discerned and then courageously lived out in service to others. While many idealistic young adults bravely want to change the world in whatever ways they dream up, E. has intuited the more discerning insight of American author and activist Parker Palmer—namely, that pretending you are something you're not is a recipe for resentment, then fatigue, and then cynicism. We must rather, in Palmer's words, "accept that our lives are dependent on an inexorable cycle of seasons, on a play of powers that we can conspire with but never control." Accepting those God-given limits alongside our God-given gifts can be painful. We inevitably "run headlong into a culture that insists, against all evidence, that we can make whatever kind of life we want, whenever we want it. Deeper still, we run headlong into our own egos, which want desperately to believe that we are always in charge."[7]

E. is discerning his deepest self and its responsive and purposeful work in the world, even as he keeps one eye open for an ambush of his ego. I am proud of him and wrote back saying as much.

The networks of church-related higher education of which I am a part have, over the last couple of decades, doubled down on their central missions to educate for vocation. From *vocare* (calling) and *vox* (voice), *vocation* is something one hears (usually metaphorically) and then responds to—or not. Many identify the ultimate Caller as God, who uses the voices of human and nonhuman creatures to beckon a person toward work for the flourishing of all creation. Others hear the call as originating from particular people and places who call out for help and compassion. Either way, undergoing education for a life of vocation provides a very different understanding of higher education than the leading consumerist model. Students don't only pay for college to get a degree that gets them opportunities to advance their chosen careers. They also—and more importantly—accept the invitation to carefully listen for and critically understand what the world most needs and then develop skills by which they can capably and confidently respond. While many, if not most, students come to college primarily to get a good paying job (and there's nothing wrong with that), among them are students such as E., many of them first-generation college students and others with a strong sense of appreciation for this opportunity, who have a handle on their gifts and passions and are ready to leverage them for the flourishing of the common good.

My questions about neighbor love are easily translated into the idiom of purposeful callings. Lutheran higher education follows its namesake, Martin Luther, in equating vocation with love and service to the neighbor. Whereas before the sixteenth century "godly work" had been the work of the professionally religious or explicitly religious work (such as taking a pilgrimage), Luther redirected such work away from the desperate attempt to please God and toward the free, creative, and even joyful effort to work on behalf of the neighbor. As Luther put it five hundred years ago in "The Freedom of a Christian," "No one needs even one of these works to attain righteousness and salvation. *For this reason*, in all of one's works a person should in this context be shaped by and contemplate this thought alone: to serve and benefit others in everything that may be done, having nothing else in view except the need and advantage of the neighbor."[8] When the old self, the ego, is upended by the unearned gift of divine love, it then—and "for this reason"—can finally see what the neighbor actually needs and will do what it can to respond. Luther assumed that the transformative turnaround happens in baptism, whose waters drown a person's pious perfectionism, together with their doubt and despair. For most today, death of ego and the rebirth of a summoned life probably only come from brushes with actual death. Being made to face our mortality—for example, by sheltering in place, glimpsing the vulnerability of our families, or getting sick ourselves—can kill the implicit "theology of self-reliance" to which we otherwise so fanatically cling. Self-reliance is replaced by the gift of grace, which then redoubles as gracious attention to others.[9]

My colleague from our music department, M., also reached out by email last week. She is a wise leader within this year's "Education for Vocation" faculty seminar. She wrote to me of that key vocational discernment question we had discussed a few weeks before: "To what am I being summoned?"[10] Then, referencing the worldwide pandemic, she wrote, "If this is not a moment of summoning, I don't know what is."

COMMONPLACES—MARCH 29, 2020

The penitential season of Lent lasts forty days in the Christian calendar—not including Sundays, which are joyful anticipatory glimpses of Easter. Traditionally, today is called Passion Sunday, the beginning of two weeks of Passiontide, which continues into Holy Week and culminates in Holy Saturday, when Jesus lies in the tomb, his fellow Jews rest on the Sabbath, and nothing much else happens. Liturgical time is stitched together like a multimedia collage—so much more impasto, folds, and texture than our secular, monochromatic clock time. Today—Passion Sunday—is simultaneously a twenty-four-hour reprieve between the twenty-eighth and twenty-ninth day of Lent, the beginning of the observance of Jesus's final days, and a day of preemptively remembering a resurrection that will be celebrated two weeks from now.

I wish I could say that I waited a week since last writing out of conscious fidelity to Lenten rhythms. The truth is that my planned-for patterns of work and prayer, of caretaking and contemplation, have felt rather haphazard this past week. Asa and Gabe are essentially being homeschooled and self-taught until their public schools design online curricula. We wake them at seven-thirty; until lunch, they read books and write chapter summaries or work through math problems on the computer, with a snack break and quick game of ping-pong midmorning. After lunch and "recess" (whiffle ball or driveway basketball), the boys return to their morning studies or work on longer projects. So far, they have researched the specs of various computers and delivered case-making presentations on the one they want us to buy. This coming week, science will consist of researching the soil and light conditions of each of our eight raised beds to decide where to plant different vegetables. Fine arts entails Skyped-in piano lessons, as well as writing, directing, and performing an original scene inspired by *The Office*.

We have begun calling our midmorning break from work "coffee break," following Holden Village, a remote intentional community in the North Cascade Mountains, where we have lived with college students for six weeks in midwinter. Holden has been a joyful place for us, a place of rhythm and rest and of being real. Naming our midmorning pause "coffee break" invokes a little sacramental charm into these banal days. (The irony that "coffee break" in both substance and name is surpassingly mundane is not lost on me.) Later today, we will use Holden Evening Prayer as our Sunday worship, where bread crust and fruit-punch Gatorade will become the everyday things of God.

Laura is moving ahead with plans to open "NEST Café" (Nourish Everyone Sustainably Together). Part of a pay-what-you-can nonprofit movement, the restaurant will serve locally sourced meals for a suggested donation. Those who can afford to do so can pay in full or pay more to support others. Those with fewer means can pay less or volunteer in exchange for a meal. She got news of the official nonprofit status this week and continues to consult with her board; the website is finally up and running. Serving basic needs in a communal space where rich and poor become *companions* (literally, those who share bread) is deeply needed in our diverse community, which is segregated between a largely Black west end, white folks up the bluff, and the *Floreciente* (Spanish for "blooming") neigh-borhood to the east. Laura still hopes to open the café a year from now, but she's getting nervous that the need for companionship will be seen as a luxury when so many in our community are merely trying to survive.

I converted my Encountering Religion class to an online format, swap-ping out our planned visits to local synagogues, churches, and mosques for chatroom conversations with local faith leaders. In the past week, I've also taken out two unwieldy bushes along our property line and planted fruit trees in their place, prepared the raised beds for planting, built a small retaining wall around the main garden, began to clean and repair a chicken coop that was given to us by a couple who recently had twins (two more kids and so no more chickens), mended a fence that I broke while moving said coop, and otherwise looked after our quarter-acre lot.

We've picked up Zicam, aspirin, and sugar-free spearmint gum for the elderly couple across the street. We've bought bread, lunch meat, and plastic baggies for the homeless shelter downtown, whose indoor soup kitchen has become a sidewalk sack-lunch service. We got takeout last night from El Patron in order to support a local business—and, in truth, because they make a damn good #11 combo.

I realize that all of this sounds incredibly commonplace and parochial—especially from someone who wrote a dozen days ago of being summoned by the needy face of the neighbor and taking bread from my mouth in response. I may be settling for more comfortable callings. Some, however, will argue that I am only now getting it right, that faithful love of and service to the neighbor usually has little to do with extraordinary responses.

A pastor and professor at another Midwestern Lutheran college notes that *vocation* is often associated with heroically challenging the injustices of the world, whereas most days, our callings are lived out "in the nitty-gritty of life, far out of the spotlight."[11] Luther, too, asks the person who is ready to make a religious pilgrimage or do some other so-called saintly work to consider whether they have not already been called. Haven't you, he rhetorically asks spiritual-seekers, always been "a husband or a wife or a son or a daughter or a servant?"[12] Questing after one's purpose in life or heroically working for justice might in fact distract from all the commonplace ways that neighbor love is normally, meaningfully enacted. Luther and my colleague suggest that the very stuff of God is particularly present in the everyday—sealed into plastic baggies and takeout containers, rooted in fruit trees, and woven together like chicken coops.

I'm only half convinced. I want to believe, and many days do, that the reality that Christians call God can be found in very ordinary stuff, for those with eyes to see. But I also know all too well how easy it is for me to whittle down the commandment to love my neighbor as myself into something more manageable. It *felt good* to stand six feet behind the woman in front of me at the cash register of El Patron before asking the server how business was holding up, to tip well and tell her we'd be back, before hauling four #11s home in my Prius. That feeling is about me, not her. It would seem that commonplaces can also be subtly infused with pious self-importance, for those with eyes to see.

* * *

Luke's gospel tells the story of a lawyer who asks Jesus, "Who is my neighbor?" The lawyer really wanted "to justify himself" (10:29)—hoping the answer would fall within a manageable sphere of concern. Jesus responds with the parable of the Good Samaritan. Like other parables, it has an overabundance of meaning that both responds to and deconstructs the question posed. Any lesson learned is not easily grasped apart from the story itself:

> Jesus replied, "A man was going down from Jerusalem to Jericho, and fell into the hands of robbers, who stripped him, beat him, and went away, leaving him half dead. Now by chance a priest was going down that road; and when he saw him, he passed by on the other side. So likewise a Levite, when he came to the place and saw him, passed by on the other side. But a Samaritan while traveling came near him; and when he saw him, he was moved with pity. He went to him and bandaged his wounds, having poured oil and wine on them. Then he put him on his own animal, brought him to an inn, and took care of him. The next day he took out two denarii, gave them to the innkeeper, and said, 'Take care of him; and when I

come back, I will repay you whatever more you spend.'" (Luke
10:30–35)

Jesus ends with a question for the lawyer:

"Which of these three, do you think, was a neighbor to the man
who fell into the hands of the robbers?"
[The lawyer] said, "The one who showed him mercy."
Jesus said to him, "Go and do likewise." (Luke 10:36–37)

It's not only that the Samaritan, the one disregarded and demonized by
Judeans in Jesus's day, should be counted as the neighbor. The Samaritan
is not only a *candidate* for receiving the lawyer's love; he also becomes the
central *exemplar* of neighborly love—of human, warm-blooded care. You
should love like the neighbor you don't yet love, the one loving and neighboring you. The story doubly humbles.

I do feel called to exhibit neighbor love by fulfilling my commonplace
roles as husband, father, teacher, and homeowner. But I also feel convicted
by that call, summoned to give an account of my many shortcomings.
The very command to love my neighbor as myself exposes how readily I
otherwise shave down commandments into conveniences and conventions,
sanctifying self in the name of the neighbor.

I trust that my everyday cares and concerns can move outward,
but only under conditions that are sometimes hard to come by. For
starters, good, commonplace work would seem to depend on the
commonplace—that is, literally, a place of the commons. We need public
sidewalks and bike paths and pedestrian malls lined with locally owned
businesses, as well as vibrant public schools, accessible public parks,
farmer's markets, and other shared places where neighbors can, like the
Good Samaritan, come near enough to strangers to know their need and
thus be moved to neighborliness. Had the road from Jerusalem to Jeri-
cho been an express lane for commuters who pay a toll, the Samaritan

(stuck in traffic on the public highway) would never have noticed the man left half-dead.[13]

On the one hand, the quarantine has led to a further abandonment of shared, public spaces where strangers can neighbor one another. With schools moving to online learning, the actual buildings and schoolyards where students come to know one another remain empty. Learning online may become another step toward the privatization of education for those who can afford it and the abandonment of our country's commitment to education for those who cannot. Other places where strangers could become neighbors are off-limits. Playgrounds have yellow caution tape wrapped around them. Hiking trails have been closed. Outdoor basketball hoops are being disassembled to prevent pickup games. The 6.6 million Americans who applied for unemployment benefits this past week are at home; beyond a lost income, they've lost places of work—places that, ideally, bring together people of different backgrounds and political persuasions so that they can repair roads, do people's taxes, or wait tables alongside one another.

On the other hand, restraint breeds creativity, and many people are finding innovative ways to connect—some even neighboring former strangers. People are leaving hand sanitizer and toilet paper for mail carriers and USPS workers. Last night, in Atlanta, a whole Midtown neighborhood emerged outside and applauded the health care workers leaving their long and dangerous shifts. Free little libraries that used to be stocked with books now sometimes stock a roll or two of toilet paper, with kind notes to neighbors attached. We see more people out running or walking their dogs. Neighbors who formerly drove to Lincoln Park, leaving their cars idling as they followed after protruding cell phones in pursuit of Pokémon, now seem to be walking there and readier to glance up and greet even those foreign to their virtual realities.

To me, the colorful paper hearts that people have been pasting on their front windows symbolize both the loss of commonplaces and their regeneration. Attached to the outside of houses, they mark borders. People are inside here, they announce. You cannot see us because we are quarantining, but we are here and have hearts that go on pumping. The paper hearts also signal attention to others. We see you, they say, out there on the sidewalks and roads, and our hearts are with you in your fear and loneliness. As small signs of connection and compassion, paper hearts try to do what people in public parks and passing bicyclists nodding at one another have tried to do for ages. They say, "I'm here, and I see that you're here too."

WOUNDED HEALER—APRIL 1, 2020

The best April Fools' joke ever played on me was by my father, who reset the alarm clock in the bedroom that I shared with my older brother so that we would wake up for school two hours too early. He then made us breakfast, packed our lunches, and sent us off to the bus stop, where we waited in the dark Minnesota morning for thirty minutes before lumbering back inside to tell him that the bus didn't come. "It's 6 a.m.," he said, stone-faced. "Go back to bed." Only after we stood bewildered for a good five seconds did he add nonchalantly, "April Fools."

It takes me much longer than a good five seconds, after reading the headline this morning announcing that April Fools' Day is canceled, to decide that it is in earnest. I initially determined that the headline itself was a pretty clever case of self-erasing ironic jest (much like the statement "I'm lying right now"). Actually, the headline unironically announces that many are urging the public not to play pranks this year. According to one utterly serious CNN writer, "April Fools' Day pranks are not funny right now. Don't do them." That seems a bit didactic to me, until I realize that the threat of healthy people declaring that they have COVID-19 on social media or intentionally coughing on grocery store produce is all too real.

Still, to throw out all humor would take away a means of coping. Humor, too, is practice in the art of transcendence. Holocaust survivor Viktor Frankl puts humor beside the beauty of nature and music as that which was capable of building resilience and deepening the spiritual lives of those in the camps.[14] Humor can also bring us together as a human community; in his song "Good Lord," Brother Ali asks, "Can you tell me, what language do you laugh in?" Jimmy Fallon surely isn't aiming for transcendence per se, but funny is funny. Commenting on how this week the Empire State Building was illuminated by flashing red and white lights to honor medical workers, he said, "At first, New Yorkers thought it meant Target finally got a shipment of toilet paper."

No fooling: More than 215,000 people have been diagnosed with COVID-19 in the United States—more than any other country on Earth. The death toll just surpassed that of 9/11. The federally mandated social distancing guidelines have been extended through April, which is a self-overturning of the president's earlier hope that things would be up and running by Easter, when Christians could "pack the churches."

After two inmates died, the Bureau of Prisons announced yesterday that federal prisoners will be confined to their cells for fourteen days to stop the spread of the disease. Attorney General William Barr obfuscated about the "particular concerns in this institutional setting"—as if mass incarceration posed something of a workflow challenge. Governor Cuomo appears repeatedly on the nightly news, as New York is again the epicenter of tragedy. He was asked last night whether police would enforce the law about social distancing. The thought of having to do so visibly irritated him; referring to teenagers obliviously hanging out on playgrounds, he snapped, "I mean, how selfish can you get?" Finally, while people like me (employed homeowners with retirement plans and savings accounts) wake up and think "It's April Fools' Day," one hundred million Americans woke up this morning and thought "Rent is due today." They are anxiously wondering whether and when they will receive their portion of the $2 trillion stimulus bill (or the CARES Act) that was signed into law last week.[15]

* * *

My family and I have been in touch with C., a graduate from several years back who is now an intern at a major university hospital in a state hit hard by COVID-19. C. lived in Micah House her senior year, a living-and-learning community dedicated to the ideals of hospitality, service, spirituality, and vocational discernment. She wrote an honors thesis on identity formation through personal narratives among adolescents with chronic diseases. She graduated with a premed major *summa cum laude* (that's Latin for *she's the shit*). She did all this while living with her own chronic, immunosuppressant disease, sometimes taking final exams from a hospital bed. She is now trying to discern her appropriate place in the hospital rotation, having gone into medicine knowing all too well the life-and-death balance of self-care and other care that every nurse and doctor is now negotiating as well.

Reading her texts, I thought of Henri Nouwen's description of "wounded healers"—those who know their own vulnerabilities and limits (like the ultimate limit of mortality) well enough to help others compassionately. Compassionate healers avoid "the distance of pity" but also the "exclusiveness of sympathy" that results from overly identifying with a select group. Like the Good Samaritan, they come near (Luke 10:33) and are moved to help those who summon them. But they know, too, that nobody is helped for long by rash self-sacrifice.

I see something of this balancing act between self-sacrifice and self-care among the health care workers showcased on the evening news. Actually, the balance feels more like wild oscillations and tipping points. Some accept the honorifics of self-sacrificing heroes working on the frontlines. "This is what we do," said one Chicago doctor, after telling the story of having to intubate one of her colleagues.

Last night's news, though, also included a Skype interview with a nurse who quit her job because health workers in her hospital did not have access to adequate personal protective gear. She tearfully pleaded her case before the news-watching audience: "I have a family. I can't get sick. I've got to stay alive to be there for my children." It seems as though all the ubiquitous talk of heroic health care workers willing to sacrifice themselves compels her to explain why she isn't a war-zone deserter. I wish that someone who has to make difficult decisions about what can or should be sacrificed were not regarded as such, even if they didn't have kids.[16]

In *Wounded Healer*, Nouwen resists language of balance, seeing self-knowledge and self-care as the very instruments by which hospitality to others can be offered. He begins his final chapter with a Talmudic (Jewish) story about a rabbi who questions the prophet Elijah about the coming of the Messiah. Elijah tells him that he will find the Messiah at the gates of the city. When the rabbi asks how he will be able to recognize him among all the poor and injured, Elijah identifies the Messiah as the one who distinctively tends to his own wounds: "He is sitting among the poor covered with wounds. The others unbind all their wounds at the same time and bind them up again. But he unbinds one at a time and binds it up again, saying to himself, 'Perhaps I shall be needed: if so I must be ready so as not to delay for a moment.'"[17] Self-care and the care of others isn't so much a balancing act—but rather a rhythm, a pulse, an art. At its most practiced and graceful, it's an art that uses one's own woundedness as a place of connection. Ministers and medics, like the exemplar Messiah, know and look after their own wounds because from them comes their healing power.[18]

I know this to be true of C. She feels called to care for the sick, not despite her sickness, but because of it. She attends to others not on top of, or in place of, her own self-care, but in and through it. The language of self-sacrifice doesn't quite capture how selves are connected through their wounds, or how healing happens together.

The last we heard, C. had been working to help assign incoming COVID-19 patients to medical teams or recommend transfers to affiliate sites. This is important, meaningful work, which also prevents her from having direct contact with patients, minimizing the risk that she will need a hospital bed and ventilator of her own.

* * *

My first name means "healer," which I learned as a kid and liked—although by then I knew that I, like many suburban white kids in the 1970s, was given my name only because it "sounded good." Had I become a nurse or doctor or even a pastor, the name may have meant something more to me. I haven't been a healer, literally or otherwise. I can think of only a handful of times when I've given direct care to someone for more than an hour at a time.

There were those long, late nights when Asa was an infant, and I was up with him as Laura tried to sleep between breastfeedings. I held the back of his head in my hand, my forearm cradling the length of his body, and bounced up and down on the yoga ball, singing quietly, persistently offering the rhythm of our bodies and my voice in exchange for his crying.

A decade later, when my own father went on hospice care, my older brother Aaron ("exulted") and I alternated weekly shifts as his caregiver: emptying his catheter bag, putting fresh Ensure nutrition drinks next to his bed in the living room, playing cribbage, and otherwise caring for a jaundiced, wounded body that was past the point of cure. My father wasn't healed—hospice care is for those who won't be. But there was healing in and through the woundedness, for both of us.

COME CLOSE—APRIL 5, 2020

Along with eyeing paper hearts on the windows of homes and businesses, I've been reading some creative slogans recently. "Let's all step up by stepping back" reads one sign outside a closed store downtown. The big window of my college's library displays encouraging words, now primarily read by international students left on campus: "We will get through this together . . . by staying six feet apart!" An old friend who teaches yoga put "Namaste—From Six Feet Away" on her studio's Facebook page.

Each message, and countless variations, plays with the central irony of building close communities of support and care by keeping our distance from one another. We seem to be circulating them not only for the pleasure of rhyming *away*, *apart*, *distance*, and *get back* with corresponding assurances, but also because that central irony—lending a hand by not touching—is just so counterintuitive. I cannot think of a logo for a community-building nonprofit that does not feature the joining of arms and hands: arms reaching toward each other (Big Brothers Big Sisters of America); outstretched, overlapping arms (Habitat for Humanity); interlocked hands (Boys & Girls Club of America); hands holding up individuals (United Way); multicolored hands meeting in the center (World Relief). What would a logo for mutual support through social distancing look like? Irony is easier to rhyme than to illustrate.

In some ways, new lessons about *not* coming close and *not* lending a (literal) hand will be hard to learn, given our deeply seated assumptions about how to help one another. On this side of the civil rights era, keeping people apart implies segregation, and segregation means scapegoating and sin. It is difficult to imagine building what Martin Luther King Jr. called the beloved community at safe distances. Even more significant, I think, is how quickly we tend to intervene when it comes to bodily health and how difficult it is for us *not* to insert ourselves. "First, do no harm" remains a cornerstone of the Hippocratic Oath, recited by ancient Greek physicians and today's med school graduates. That pledge notwithstanding, contemporary specialized medicine uses whatever interventions it can (however invasive) whenever there's a chance of cure (however improbable). It may be that lives would be of better quality and just as long if we learned to step back and provide sufficient palliative care—such as with hospice care—instead of wielding invasive procedures that have many dying during surgery. (I say this and think that it is true, but I also just asked my mom to revise her living will so that we would be able to intubate her if she contracted COVID-19 and it came to that. There are too many stories of COVID victims spending weeks on ventilators only to recover to not take advantage of lifesaving interventions.)

In other ways, these "new" lessons about keeping distance are old. We've learned them already and sometimes too well. Our nation's leading political philosophy is predicated on the rights of individuals rather than on the collective needs and care of communities. US citizens have been thoroughly schooled in protecting individual rights and not interfering with those of others. No one should violate my rights. No one should get to tell me what to do. No one should cross my individual boundaries or question my autonomy. The feminist theorist Judith Butler sees the worldview here as hinging on "discrete identity."[19]

Butler challenges this individualistic worldview because it advantages people like me (white, straight, cisgender males) at the expense of those whose identities are more fluid than straight, more communal and historically contingent than we who are privileged would like to assume. The very presumption that people are who they are regardless of historical circumstances and the influence of others' identities has been invented for and by the lucky. White privilege hinges on the myth of individuality. It is assumed that inheritors of wealth amassed through the forced labor of others need not be responsible for the sins of their forbearers. They are just individuals, after all. Those born at the bottom of racial hierarchies and into generational trauma are alone responsible for climbing out. As individuals, they have everything they need.

When visceral fear of others is added to the mix, the myth of personal fortitude gets deadly. Womanist theologian Kelly Brown Douglas traces how America's individualistic worldview stems from white property ownership and culminates in a stand-your-ground culture that enables whites to guard their personal space, killing those (like Trayvon Martin) whom they perceive as threats.[20]

* * *

When I came of age in the 1980s and 1990s, fear of AIDS fueled the story of personal protection from others' invasions. Here was a largely lethal chronic condition (AIDS) caused by a human immunodeficiency virus (HIV) that would invade the body's autonomy and turn it against itself. We assumed that the "gay plague" spread when men let themselves be penetrated by other men or when druggies let themselves be contaminated by sharing needles. Those not vulnerable ratcheted up their precautions to a vicious level. We stopped using public toilets and began spinning elaborate explanations for how AIDS was evolution's way of killing off weaker specimens or God's way of punishing evildoers.

Scripts about the virtues of self-protection and the plight of the weak abounded when I was young. It wasn't until college that I began to unlearn what I knew about being a white, straight male. I remember reading an interview with the Black novelist Toni Morrison, who said that white readers often cannot hear what she and other Black authors were saying, but they can and should try to *overhear* them. I began straining to overhear viewpoints that did not put me at the center. I began to push past my learned aversion or indifference to those who were different from me. Looking back now, I can see how this quest to overhear and overcome was still something that I was *doing*; I didn't know how to let myself be *undone*. But the resolve did allow me to come close enough to people I would have otherwise passed by, like a priest or Levite moving to the other side of the road in the story Jesus tells about the Good Samaritan.

The journey continued throughout college and into my second semester of seminary, when I did an internship in Washington, DC, with Episcopal Caring Response to AIDS. There I was befriended by former sex workers and recovering addicts, gay men, the formerly incarcerated, the homeless, and the mentally ill—all of whom were HIV positive or living with AIDS. Even without the epitaph of AIDS, these were folks commonly shamed and shunned, like reincarnations of the lepers of old.[21]

The internship was a lesson in unlearning white space, rugged individualism, and fortified masculinity by learning to touch and be touched. Sometimes, I was the one pushing through boundaries; those moments were still fraught with well-worn scripts of individual resolve and courage. For example, when I would go to the NAMES Memorial Quilt Project to visit D., a gay Filipino man with such a low white blood cell count that he sometimes had 1 percent of a healthy immune system, he and I would greet one another with a kiss, as many in the AIDS community often greeted one another. I wish the kiss were a natural sign of our growing love and respect. It felt more like a forced transgression, one that was no less contrived than the taboo it sought to break. Was I simply playing the part of a different script—say, the scene from *Philadelphia*, when the formerly homophobic lawyer (Denzel Washington) finally touches the lesion-pocked face of Andrew Beckett (Tom Hanks)?

Fortunately, other moments were less orchestrated and thus more transformational. The best came as a disorienting gift, when I found myself unmade and remade within a web of relationships.

Toward the end of my internship, we took thirty HIV-positive/AIDS folks on a weekend retreat to the Maryland coast. Most had never been outside DC's beltway. Many wept when they stepped off the bus and were handed a teddy bear. The retreat ended with a final laying-on of hands and prayers for healing. In predominantly straight, white churches, healing services are an orderly affair. Willing participants approach the pastor one at a time, nodding to receive ointment on their forehead over the sound of muted prayers. Not so in the retreat center chapel. The clay ampulla holding the consecrated oil was passed around like a Sharpie; people eagerly smudged cross-shaped oil on those around them, then turned to be so smothered. Over full-throated petitions for mercy and healing, the throng laid hands on one another's shoulders, backs, heads, and faces, forming an intricate, unwieldy web. You couldn't tell where the taxpayer ended and the welfare recipient began. Where gay ended and straight began. Where felon ended and free began. Where wounded ended and healer and healing began.

The coronavirus pandemic shares a cast of characters with the AIDS crisis. Dr. Anthony Fauci has been a voice of reason in each. Tom Hanks won an Academy Award for playing the victim of one disease; he and his spouse weren't acting when they contracted the other one. Magic Johnson showed the world that hard-bodied straight men could get AIDS; recently, he has been vocal in debunking the myth that Black people can't get or die from COVID-19.

Notwithstanding some shared players, the central scripts diverge, as do the lessons we need to learn. Coming close has been recast from the antidote to AIDS's social death to the primary vehicle of the coronavirus's transmission. Three decades ago, people like me felt called to touch those deemed untouchable; to do so was to debunk the superstitions and deconstruct the stigmatizations of AIDS as a shameful, repulsive, and well-deserved disease. Now we are called to care for neighbors by staying away. Science explains much—but not all—of the difference: whereas AIDS is transmitted through bodily fluids (blood, semen, breast milk) and can be passed to another adult primarily through sex or needle/syringe use, the new coronavirus spreads through invisible respiratory droplets that surround an individual like a murky aura.

It was good that AIDS was demythologized. Stereotyping caricatures needed to be unlearned and stigmatizing metaphors needed to be debunked. But while science may have cleared the space to touch the untouchable, people like me also needed alternative scripts—stories that would recast us as supporting characters within a beloved community.[22]

True stories are buried deep below fictions about individual rights and gender norms—deeper even than the ostensibly storyless discourse of science. Jesus healed lepers by reaching out and touching them, disregarding purity laws. The Good Samaritan "came near" (Luke 10:33) the man on the side of the road, overcoming the visceral xenophobia between Samaritans and Galilean Jews on top of his natural aversion to a half-dead body. When the woman anointed the still-alive body of Jesus for burial, mixing costly oil with her own tears, caressing and kissing his body, she did so knowing exactly "what sort of woman" she was (Luke 7:39 ESV). It takes truthful, powerful stories to counter society's scripts—scripts that include *both* superstitious scapegoating *and* the indifferent "tolerance" and "respect" of secular society.

The Samaritan, after pouring oil and wine on the man's wounds, bandaging them, taking him to an inn, and caring for him there, somehow knew to go away, commissioning the innkeeper to look after the patient. Jesus, too, said he must go away—to ascend to God the Father in heaven—in order for the Comforter to be sent forth (John 16:7 KJV). Some spaces can be so fully charged with emptiness that they move us toward a kindness difficult to measure. We'll need to learn good stories about the lonely voids we feel and the compassion that spans those distances. That story may just become *our* story, if we tell it often and well.

HOLY SATURDAY—APRIL 11, 2020

A month ago, President Trump said that he would open up the economy and Christians would "pack the churches" on Easter. Easter, he admitted, is "such an important day for other reasons," but he would make it even better: "I'll make it an important day for this [reason], too. I would love to have the country opened up, and just raring to go by Easter."[23] A few days later, as coronavirus numbers continued to climb and most of the states remained in lockdown, Trump clarified that his earlier pronouncements were only hopes. He set May 1 as the new goal for getting back to normal.

It's Holy Saturday, the last day of Lent, and the middle day of the Paschal Triduum, the three days central to the Easter story, beginning Thursday night and culminating on Easter morning. Holy Saturday seems fitting for these weeks of waiting, watching, and mourning throughout a pandemic. While the creeds mention the spirit of Jesus descending into hell, the Bible only says that today his body sits in the tomb while his friends observe the Sabbath, grieve, and try to pass an indeterminate time before something else happens or life gets back to normal.

The day tends to get skipped over in contemporary religious observances; it feels mainly like a day in-between and especially the time before—that which we must get through before getting to Easter. Which is also why the day feels symbolic of this perpetual pandemic, something to try to bookend with target dates for getting back to normal. If and when Christians observe Holy Saturday—typically by fasting or by participating in the Easter Vigil—they consecrate the day as meaningful but ambiguously so. Holy Saturday holds the other days together, saving time itself from pure passage and lending gravity to the moment. No resurrection without death. No hope without facing despair. That's a different way of sitting with suffering, and thus forging compassion, than what often passes for hope.[24]

* * *

Yesterday was Good Friday, a terribly ironic name for Jesus's abandonment, trial, torture, and execution. The name seems overly eager to interpret the events in light of the story's ending, to find atoning purpose in the unjust death of this itinerant rabbi lest the hopelessness and meaninglessness of the day overwhelm.

Good Friday has been important to me since childhood. I can remember back forty or so years, seated for the evening Tenebrae service in the wooden pew beside my still-together family at Messiah Lutheran Church. I'd concentrate extra hard on the long biblical accounts of the day Jesus died, punctuated by the extinguishing of candles, trying to feel the suffering of my savior and deriding myself when premature thoughts of dressing up for Easter and getting candy crept in.

Lutheranism, in fact, is a tradition centered on Good Friday. We confess that God can be fully found in a crucified Christ, although we rarely know what that means. The ultimate power of the universe—that which "moves the sun and other stars" (Dante)—is fully revealed in a dead Palestinian Jew, having been tortured by an empire and executed by slow asphyxiation. That puts the point on what Paul means by power made perfect in weakness. The mover of stars is not an abstract Ultimate, not Aristotle's Unmoved Mover, but the one most moved, most capable of passionately, painfully undergoing all that falls on him.

Dante himself identifies true power as the power of love, but most of us have trouble hearing in that anything other than bad pop music. (Right now, I'm desperately trying to get Huey Lewis and the News's "The Power of Love" out of my head.) Truly *passionate* love is love one doesn't fully control, love filled with *pathos*, which sometimes looks as *pathetic* as a dead Palestinian Jew. When Christians confess that vulnerable love is the mover of stars, they should pause to wonder why the universe doesn't collapse in on itself. For his part, Martin Luther tended to revel in such paradoxes or what Lutherans sometimes call the "coincidence of opposites" between power and powerlessness, infinite and finite, freedom and servitude, and saint and sinner.

I think and write a lot about a "theology of the cross"—one name for this understanding of God as fully revealed in, with, and under human suffering and death, in Jesus's cross and in other crosses.[25] Any God that is more than ideology or idol must be found in the experience of Godforsakenness. If God is not also in the heart of darkness, then darkness can overtake light. But if God is there, hanging from the tree, then we can also find God scattered throughout what would otherwise be a Godforsaken world. I write and think this way but rarely move throughout the day as though it were true. Most days I have a vaguer faith in some abstraction called God. That is, my driving, shopping, streaming, 401(k) investing, eating, and other daily habits show implicit faith in an abstract, invulnerable (and nonrenewable) power, in Aristotle's Unmoved Mover, a God whose power is made perfect in more power.

My family ended Good Friday by reading the account of Jesus's death around a wooden dough bowl filled with candles, trying to stay in key while singing slow, repetitive prayers from the Taizé community of monks in France. As you might guess, my favorite Taizé song is "Jesus, Remember Me," which is a line from the thief who is crucified next to Jesus. Somehow, I didn't think to suggest it.

The day before was Maundy Thursday, which commemorates the day that a Jewish Jesus gathered with his friends to celebrate Passover while the forces of death loomed all around. Christians call it Maundy Thursday after the mandate (from the Latin *mandatum*) to remember Jesus in the wine and bread and to wash one another's feet. Whereas I am a Friday kind of guy, my wife Laura is a Maundy Thursday person. She most experiences God and best remembers Jesus within a community called to serve one another.

Laura and I, in being Thursday and Friday people, come together in not really being Easter people, or at least not what passes for Easter people. Which is to say that both of us are suspicious of the self-assurance of other American Christians, which can be a faith in progress and optimism and other abstractions, a faith in faith, the fanatically buoyant belief that everything will work out for the best. Still, our realisms and reservations in the name of a more service-inflected, cruciform hope sometimes simply pass into pessimism, which is no closer to the expectancy of Christian faith than is optimism.

Here as elsewhere, the students I am called to teach are sometime ahead of me in rooting their hopeful, vigilant work in the realities of a wounded world.[26] I've taken note of C., the medical intern making triage decisions, this wounded healer who draws strength from her own chronic illness so she can capably attend to the wounds of others. I've written of E., who, while attending to Boston's mutual-aid networks, also pays attention to his own limits, lest the ambitions of his ego drown out the discernment of his callings. There's also G., who lost two brothers to cancer over the course of a year—the first during the fall of her senior year, followed later that spring by a second diagnosis of cancer in the second brother. Before graduating, G. shared with me the collection of poems that she had written during that grief-stricken senior year. An early poem in the collection, called "It's Not God I Have a Problem With," begins by tracing the way hopeful words such as *intact* and *awaits* crumble under the weight of tragedy:

> *burnt brain*
> *breaking brother*
> heaven awaits—

grace intact—
grace in tact, heaven waits.
Away. intact: holes in brain, holes in tact,

holes in virtue, holes in heaven,
holes in all.
Despair.

As words of hope and normalcy disintegrate, G.'s full-throated lamentations get loud and raw. The poem ends with an unwieldy chain of meanings that overtake any one meaning or moral:

red means anger means
holes in every belief means
mean—this is mean—

means fuck fame fuck "strong" fuck grace and tact
I am weak we were all weak means
twenties means too young and

as he said "I won't believe in god
until there's a cure"

Some will hear only despair and meaninglessness here. I hear those also and fully, and yet something else. Maybe it's the willingness to face feelings of inconsolable loss with the hope, if that's the right word, the hope that if one can move not from, but with that experience of loss, then hope, if that's the right word, will be seasoned, real, cruciform.

Simone Weil suggests in her penetrating essay "The Love of God and Affliction" that God is fully present when we experience the absence of God, and this is because Godforsakenness is shared by an incarnate, crucified God—one who calls out, "My God, My God, why have you forsaken me?"[27] G.'s is a Holy Saturday poem. It refuses to be consoled prematurely or to keep belief systems or positive thinking intact. It instead attends to loss in its full darkness and *therefore* moves forward—not moves on, but forward—closer to a God, if that is the right word, who abides with the abandoned and does not forsake those who feel Godforsaken and *therefore* is a God of redemption.

G. wrote the final poems in her collection in the spring, a half year after her first brother died and just after her second brother was also diagnosed with cancer. The final poem in the collection is entitled "White Elephants, Hope." It begins with an epigraph from T. S. Eliot, "April is the cruelest month, breeding / lilacs out of the dead land," and ends with these sparse lines:

> *I choose lilacs,*
> *but now I am writing elegies*
> *for the living, too.*

Before her senior year ended, G. applied to be part of the Lutheran Volunteer Corps, where she would spend a gap year weaving her life into the fabric of an intentional community that would let her be angry and unsteady without becoming cynical or hopeless. Her second brother also died. She is alive, still living in Minneapolis, still abiding in a time of unhopelessness.

* * *

Meanwhile, on this Holy Saturday, the day between days, Gabe is on the love seat and I'm on the couch, where I've been looking at the blooming pink flowers on our peach tree and watching the black squirrels unique to this region dig in the garden where we just planted radishes, kale, lettuces, and spinach. He's moving from fetal position, tucking bare feet between cushions, to arching over the edge, dangling there, letting the weight of his chest stretch the small of his back. He's wearing the blue sweatshirt that he's worn too many days in a row, along with red-checkered Christmas pajamas that are already too short.

He goes to snuggle with Gracie and Laura in bed before hammering out a particularly jazzy version of "Ubi Caritas" (another Taizé tune) on the bells in the study. When Asa emerges from the tent they pitched in their room, they eat frozen waffles and work out the first-round picks of an imaginary NBA draft.

Laura and I decide to fast until sundown and so go about a day of hiking at Maquoketa Caves with a bodily hunger meant to cultivate a quiet, inner longing for Easter but that mostly just feels like hunger.

Later this evening, I FaceTime with my mother, an Easter person. She asks how Asa and Gabe are doing without seeing friends at school or teammates during their suspended track-and-field and baseball seasons. "Pretty good," I say. "But they're starting to ask whether they will be back to school for sure in the fall and back to cross country and life as normal. And we just couldn't promise any of that." My mom is flummoxed. She suggested that I should be able to assure my kids of at least that much and that it is my role as a parent to give them hope. She may be right, but I didn't admit it. Hope, I hope, will come in other ways.

SIN-SICK—APRIL 17, 2020

We are all in this together. The motto is quickly becoming a mantra of the pandemic. Slogans notwithstanding, much of the back-and-forth on social media oscillates between bestowing broad compassion for everyone in this together and pointing fingers at those to blame for the spread of the virus. "Corona shaming" was coined in recent days to mark what is quickly becoming quite common. Knowing so little about how to protect ourselves and others, coupled with the confusing mixed messages of political leaders, individuals vent their pent-up fears by calling out everyone from celebrities to people they pass in grocery stores for not wearing a mask, or standing too close, or posting a photo of their kids at a backyard birthday party. If, ideally, shared vulnerability brings us together, it also creates anxieties that lead us to lash out, desperate to divide victimizers from victims. If only we could properly blame the source of our fear and pain, both could be minimized. The tragedy would have culprits; at least that would give some sense to this unbounded terror and confusion.

I'm not beyond any of this. Yesterday I walked past teachers and other community volunteers handing out groceries from the parking lot of our local elementary school—two without masks and one with it ineptly strapped around her chin. I cast a quizzical look for a good three seconds, just long enough that they were sure to see it, but not so long that I couldn't have backtracked if they called me out for calling them out.

I'm not sure if solidarity can be predicated on a shared sense of vulnerability. My religious tradition thinks that it can. Asa, my eighth-grader, shared a testimonial about exactly this.

It was four days ago, on Easter Monday. Asa was quoting Bryan Stevenson, who was quoting the physician and anthropologist Paul Farmer, who was quoting the Trappist monk and spiritual writer, Thomas Merton: "We are bodies of broken bones."

This was in my Working with Faith class, which met online Monday to discuss Stevenson's book, *Just Mercy*. The book chronicles the author's legal advocacy for people on death row, poor folk, minors, mothers, the wrongly accused, the mentally ill, and others trapped in our country's rather unjust criminal justice system. I asked the students in the class whether it would be OK if I invited Asa to join us for our conversation about *Just Mercy*. They said yes, so Asa read my copy of the book before sitting in front of his own computer in a different room, his thin face populating one of the nine squares of Zoom's grid view.

Near the end of the session, when I asked if there were meaningful parts of the book that we hadn't yet discussed, Asa raised his hand, lowered his early-teen voice, and quoted the lesson that Stevenson learns from Farmer, Merton, and the incarcerated persons he serves: "We are bodies of broken bones. I guess I'd always known but never fully considered that being broken is what makes us human. We all have our reasons. Sometimes we're fractured by the choices we make; sometimes we're shattered by things we would never have chosen. But our brokenness is also the source of our common humanity, the basis for our shared search for comfort, meaning, and healing. Our shared vulnerability and imperfection nurtures and sustains our capacity for compassion."[28] Stevenson includes these powerful words toward the end of his book, in a moment following the execution of a man he could not "save"; he feels overwhelmed, nearly ready to abandon his calling to serve the imprisoned and work toward reforming the system. The passage articulates his realization that, if anything can sustain his work, it is not reliance on his own commitments, intelligence, and dedication (although those are clear and inspiring). Rather, Stevenson recognizes his own brokenness in the broken lives of those he is serving. Each reflects the other, and the recognition emanates compassion and elicits the call to keep working toward healing and justice.

Michelle Alexander calls mass incarceration America's "new Jim Crow," meaning that prison is the way that our nation continues to legally segregate Blacks from whites, robbing one group of its human rights and securing power for the other. One group is pure and in need of protection; the other is without conscience and thus rightfully stripped of its humanity.[29] Resisting such divisions, Stevenson describes two crisscrossing paths toward a single place we all meet—"Sometimes we're fractured by the choices we make; sometimes we're shattered by things we would never have chosen." We are sometimes broken by what we have done; other times we're broken by things done to us. These are dual paths each of us walks at different times and in different ways, not a distinction between two kinds of people. Each of us is hurt by and hurts others. Each is broken.

Despite the subtitle, *A Story of Justice and Redemption*, *Just Mercy* isn't an explicitly religious book. Yet I find this language of brokenness and the intersecting paths by which we come to it to be deeply Christian stuff. People typically use the word *sin* as a synonym for wrongdoing and *sinful* to describe a wrongdoer. They are rather unpopular words—and rightfully so, given how they have been wielded to castigate and segregate the guilty from the innocent. At its deepest and widest, however, *sin* (or better, *Sin*) points to the state of being sin-sick, of hurting and being hurt, our shared condition of being broken.

When teaching my Gen Z students about Sin (many of whom are even more suspicious of theological language than the general population), I ask them to try to forget what they think they know about the story of "the fall" in order to read Genesis 3 with something of a "second naivete." What is this archetypal myth saying about the human condition?

Certainly, it's a story about moral failure; God commands Adam not to eat of the tree of knowledge of good and evil, but he breaks the rule and eats. Certainly, too, there are punishments for his and Eve's decisions: their childbearing and work in the field become painful; there will be enmity between them and nonhuman creatures. But the story just can't be reduced to a morality lesson about obeying God or suffering the consequences. The two representatives of humankind are, like the rest of us, stumbling, flailing, and then toiling toward healing just as much as they are willfully disobeying and then being justly punished.

The meaning of the story seems to depend on it not making perfect sense. Why shouldn't Eve trust the crafty serpent, who is but a creature created by God? What do we make of the fact that she is made to repeat the commandment given to Adam before she was created—and that she misquotes it, adding that they should not *even touch* the forbidden fruit? What could Adam even make of God's warning of "or you shall surely die" before anything was known about dying and death? It is a story of moral failure, certainly, but it is simultaneously, strangely, also a story of moral learning, of the pain of growing up. Barbara Brown Taylor compares the first sin to a toddler who is told not to touch the hot stove—an instruction that means very little until she is nursing the burn on her hand.[30]

Throughout her book, *Speaking of Sin*, Taylor positions the language of sin and salvation between our criminal justice's language of crime and punishment and our medical language of sickness and cure. Each extreme understands hurting others and being hurt in mutually exclusive ways. Courts maximize personal responsibility and answer crime with punishment. Doctors maximize the no-fault tragedy of getting ill and respond by trying to cure and heal. The religious vision has "more room for paradox" than either extreme.[31] We do sin, but Sin also does us. We are responsible for a condition that also befalls us and that we cannot get out from under. Sin-sick, we hope for a salvation (from *salva*, meaning "health") whose healing and forgiveness cannot finally be separated. As the African American spiritual has it, "There is a balm in Gilead, to heal the sin-sick soul."

If, after rereading Genesis 3 and working through Taylor's short book, my students still don't find sin and salvation helpful in analyzing the human condition, I sometimes resort to personal testimony. "My father was a life-long alcoholic," I say. "He was more than that, of course, but he was that. What kind of language can properly name the power that his addiction had over him? What might both maximize his personal responsibility for choosing to drink *and* name his powerlessness in the face of disease? What could he have hoped for other than salvation—a healing that comes through forgiveness and forgiveness that issues in radical healing?"

Beyond any of our personal experiences with things like addiction, Sin ought to name the powers and principalities that capture us long before we choose them, and salvation the balm for our sin-sick souls. Racism, sexism, consumerism, xenophobia, Islamophobia, and a criminal (in)justice system that issues in mass incarceration—these are other names for Sin. We are born into them, and they get us before we choose them, and yet we must still repent and open ourselves to healing.

At best, the awareness of our shared brokenness, our overlapping susceptibilities to being hurt and to hurting others, enables us to see that we are, in fact, all in this together. Certainly, COVID-19 is a sickness, not a crime. Yet it also exposes our sin. We are learning that those most susceptible to it are the very people who "the system" (i.e., we who benefit from it) have wrongly, guiltily, *sinfully* confined to substandard living conditions, generational poverty, and inadequate health care, not to mention prisons themselves.

In my home state of Illinois, Black people make up 14 percent of the population, while they make up 46 percent of those who have died from COVID-19. Thirty percent of Chicago residents are Black; 70 percent of those who have died to date there from COVID are Black. Statistics are similar for Latinx and Native American populations. Fauci and other doctors link the unequal death rates to other disparities in underlying conditions, including diabetes, hypertension, obesity, and asthma. These factors, along with exposure to the virus itself, follow additional disparities by directly affecting those who work service-industry jobs (including low-wage health care support and/or service and direct-care jobs); those who do not have access to health care; and those who live in crowded urban areas and rely on public transportation, which enables the virus to spread. Like Hurricane Katrina, the virus is amoral, afflicting whom it will, regardless of moral desert. But who is exposed and how bad it will get for them is—again, like Katrina—very much a matter of sinful structures that have been created to protect some through the disproportionate vulnerability of others.[32]

* * *

I taught *Just Mercy* just once before—a year ago in East Moline Correctional Center (EMCC), a low-security prison eight miles east of campus. It was the third course that I taught to incarcerated students at EMCC, and the one I was most nervous to teach. I didn't know what I would do with the anger that would inevitably arise when incarcerated students read about systemic racism and other injustices that are built into our country's policing and legal systems. The sessions in our cinder-block classroom turned out to be transformative, at least for me. The stories of the students put bones on what it means to be broken and worthy of salvation.

Just one example is B., a Hispanic man from Chicago who served twenty-two years after being tried as an adult and convicted for attempted murder at the age of fifteen. "I did it," he said, "no doubt about that." One year before his crime, a fourteen-year-old B. found himself caught in gang-related cross fire in front of his house. He was shot eight times. After crawling to take cover under his porch, a police officer stood over his bleeding body and said sardonically, "See what you gangbangers get?" At that point in his life, B. had not been involved in a gang or gang violence. A year later, he was belatedly committing the crime for which his own trauma was, according to the officer, a fitting (if also preemptive) consequence.

But if B.'s brokenness was composed both of things he did and what was done to him, the paths to redemption are also many. He was a lead mentor in the "men-mentoring-men" prison program. During our last session discussing *Just Mercy*, he spoke of taking younger incarcerated "kids" aside, telling them "they ain't got to be tough." The words didn't always get through, he said, although he sometimes saw a spark in them. He also finds storytelling life-giving. He tries to write something every day, and recently finished the story of his own life. Also a talented artist, he spent much of his time in prison drawing portraits of his friends. He was released three months ago. I'm not allowed any contact with him "on the outside," but I hope B. is following his calling to be a tattoo artist in Chicago while continuing to teach people about being hurt, hurting others, and the painful, powerful process of coming back to life.

WASTING TIME—APRIL 20, 2020

The mind tends to wander when the body shelters in place. Lately, mine has been returning to Umberto Eco's debut novel, *The Name of the Rose*, a postmodern murder mystery set in a fourteenth-century Benedictine monastery. The main detective, William of Baskerville, tries desperately to connect wildly disparate dots in order to find some pattern, some overarching meaning, among widespread destruction and death. In the end, he fails. No coherent pattern emerges, only coincidence and confusion alongside a few simple acts of kindness.

How much meaning can and should be found in a pandemic that has strewn indiscriminate fear and loss across the globe? Or better—what *kind* of meaning should we be looking for? According to medical doctor and ethicist Lydia S. Dugdale, our country currently lacks a shared story—a "common existential narrative"—that could illuminate the meaning of shared suffering and death.[33] I think that's right, but we should be careful what we wish for. When worldviews make perfect sense of suffering, they tend to explain too much. They treat suffering as a concept that doesn't fit with other concepts—such as the idea that the universe is fair or that God is all-good and all-powerful and therefore could create a world where babies don't die and tsunamis don't ravish coastlines. Theodicists (those trying to solve such conceptual problems) then work over the concepts until they line up. They might thereby solve an intellectual problem, but the "solution" only sidesteps the existential problem of suffering as it is experienced by those in pain. Theodicists sound more than a little tone-deaf if and when they answer screams of "Why?" with explanations, theories, and apologias.

Theological language that speaks of God's relationship with human suffering is particularly risky. German theologian Dorothee Soelle came of age in the wake of the Shoah (meaning "the catastrophe," an alternative name for the Holocaust, which is Hebrew for "burnt offering"). Having seen all the ways that her German nation used Christian theology (including Lutheran theology) as justification for its anti-Semitism, she vowed to write about suffering with eyes wide open to all the risks. Too often, explanations for suffering portray a sadistic God, a God who wants us to suffer because we deserve it, or to test us, or to teach us a lesson. These explanations lead as well to Christian masochism, with believers accepting their lots, like an abused spouse convinced that their cross-carrying is commanded by God and a sign of their faithfulness.

Much of human suffering, says Soelle, should be eliminated rather than comprehended, theologically or otherwise. Writing her best-known book, *Suffering*, toward the end of the Vietnam War, she attends to all the theopolitical justifications for massacre, which must be interrupted and stopped.[34]

Many throw out theological language altogether. Faced with pandemics or proxy wars, they seek only the technical solutions of finding a vaccine or withdrawing troops. They refuse or do not think to ask what our susceptibility to viruses and violence all *means*. In *Suffering*, Soelle argues that such purely practical responses often entail "one-dimensional" thinking that inoculates us from suffering no less than airtight theodicies do. We must find or make some *kind* of meaning within meaningless suffering if we are to learn from it, live well with it, and become more fully human.[35]

When talking about meaning in times of suffering, one must carefully steer between the Scylla of explaining evil away and the Charybdis of ignoring it altogether.[36] My sense is that we, somewhere in the middle of this pandemic, are more likely to talk about technological fixes to our problems. Sure, some apocalyptic preachers try to find hidden connections between Revelation's Great Beast and Wuhan, China. Other people visit online horoscopes (traffic there is up), desperate to receive some indication of their fate from the imminent signs. But for most of us, the virus means only that we've got to find a vaccine, or a treatment, or more competent political leaders. Most prefer the immediate over the metaphysical because it is more manageable, and because responsibility falls on scientists and politicians rather than on you and me.

And yet we become fully human only when we let the cry of "Why?" ring out and then struggle to make sense of what it means to be susceptible to sickness, suffering, and structural Sin. We make *good* sense when we attend to mysteries rather than only explaining and solving problems. A mystery is not a problem that is not yet solved. It is a different kind of phenomenon, requiring a different kind of response. One knows a mystery only as a mystery—with wonder, curiosity, and humility—but one *can* know it as such.

Literature can help. Novels, short stories, and poems enable us to make some sense of suffering without explaining it away. Literature such as the book of Job or Tolstoy's *The Death of Ivan Ilyich* or even Kate Bowler's sassy and beautiful memoir about living with cancer, *Everything Happens for a Reason: And Other Lies That I've Loved*, invites us to wonder more fully and even to suffer more humanly.[37] In his poem "Asphodel, That Greeny Flower," William Carlos Williams suggests that literature, perhaps no less than scientific research or public health, is a matter of life and death. He writes, "It is difficult / to get the news from poems / yet men die miserably every day / for lack / of what is found there."

Of course, most of us don't really believe this. A professor who teaches poetry at California Lutheran University tells of a student who voiced aloud what most were probably thinking after the professor made her case for the critical importance of poetry. The student said, "Well, if the person I love has a heart attack, the paramedics had better not pull out the sonnets of Shakespeare and start reading!" My colleague quickly concurred. But, she said, later that night when you are lying in bed wondering whether your beloved is in pain and whether God is real, Shakespeare's sonnets might just bring you some lifesaving comfort. Poetry, my colleague says, can help us live well in the face of death. It can "reassure us that we are not alone in our pain and suffering, even in times when no one else can be present with us." It can become the way that we "reach out to others when otherwise we might be left mute and isolate."[38]

Last week, I finished my latest rereading of Toni Morrison's *Beloved*, a novel that I first read during the long bus ride home from my college summer job as a camp counselor in Montana. Having finished *Beloved*, I moved on to my used copy of *The Plague* by Albert Camus, which is well worn from being well read (complete with duct tape over the spine), but not by me until now.

The fictional story is set in a depressed town in North Africa on the Algerian coast, which an outbreak of the bubonic plague devastates sometime in the 1940s. It's about an absurd disease that inflicts the innocent and guilty alike, that separates loved ones stranded on different sides of the barricaded city limits, and that leads many to despair and others to the necessity of hope and to simple acts of kindness. Camus wrote it during World War II and published it at age thirty-three. The book was deeply personal for Camus, who suffered from repeated bouts of tuberculosis and was separated from his family by Germany's occupation of France.

Like Eco's *The Name of the Rose*, much of *The Plague* pokes holes in conceptually tight, morally tone-deaf explanations for the absurdity of suffering. The town priest, Father Paneloux, initially comes off as particularly oblivious. He preaches a finger-wagging sermon at the conclusion of the town's Week of Prayer, beginning, "Calamity has come on you, my brethren, and, my brethren, you deserved it." Addressing the town as "brethren" might offset the accusation to some degree, but really, the most important word here is *you*. You (not me) deserve it. You (not we) have brought this on yourselves. He goes on to make what one parish member calls an "absolutely irrefutable" case for plague as punishment for the town's moral laxity.[39]

SparkNotes might suggest that the priest is but a negative foil for the novel's secular heroes, including the narrator, Dr. Rieux, who join in solidarity to bravely fight the plague rather than explain its cosmic meaning. But the novel is too smart to play zero-sum games between apathetic religious speculation and valiant secular pragmatism. The priest eventually joins Dr. Rieux's campaign in caring for the sick. He also preaches a final sermon (addressed to "us" rather than "you") which admits that their suffering, and especially the deaths of children, cannot be understood. The only way to "justify" them is through total surrender of self to God, including the surrender of all intellectual schemes that presume to know God's will.[40]

Camus was also aware that you don't need to invoke God's providence to have Manichaean conceptions of good versus evil, or to position oneself on the side of the good. Writing in the wake of the French Resistance, Camus valued heroism but remained uncomfortable with the "smug myth of heroism" itself. He abhorred some resisters' "tone of moral superiority."[41] It seems that secular stories about fighting the Germans or the plague can also fall into the trap of too clearly dividing good from evil, innocence from guilt, heroes from those who flounder. *The Plague* frames meaning and purpose in more ambiguous, truthful ways. Heroism itself gets redefined. "It may seem a ridiculous idea," says Dr. Rieux, "but the only way to fight the plague is with decency." And what does decency mean to him? "Doing my job," he says.[42]

Soelle claims that all acute suffering—what she (following Simone Weil) calls affliction—is essentially anachronistic.[43] Those of us not suffering try to skip to the end of the story, assuring the sufferers (and really, ourselves) that everything happens for a reason and that it will all work out eventually. Meanwhile, those suffering are stuck in another time, one that moves with agonizing slowness. Reading can also be a painfully slow process, especially when done well. Perhaps, in part, this is why reading can help one attend to the suffering of others, and thereby cultivate compassion.

When I was a freshman in college, my first-year advisor and seminar professor was Dr. B., a former nun turned English professor, who had flowing red hair and oversized eyeglasses. She frequently lamented about the phlegm she would find in the English building's drinking fountain. I came to know her as a joyful person, but she was no-nonsense in the classroom. Faced with eighteen-year-olds slouching in their chairs, asking questions about what will be on the midterm, Dr. B. insisted that we read literature more slowly and with fewer concerns about what we were supposed to be getting out of it. "These books will take time," she said. "You've got to be willing to waste time with them."

HOUSEHOLD MANAGEMENT—APRIL 22, 2020

I forgot that today is Earth Day. Luckily, the various news feeds sent to my inbox quickly remind me. Luckier still, they assure me I haven't missed anything.

For two years, international organizations such as 350.org have been planning a monumental Earth Day celebration for today, the fiftieth anniversary of the first Earth Day, which coincided with the Clean Air Act in 1970. Greta Thunberg and Pope Francis committed to speak. There were to be marches, rallies, protests, teach-ins, lectures, and concerts. They were to demand a global Green New Deal. They sought no less than to "solve the climate crisis," according to one news release. All of it was also, of course, canceled. According to an opinion piece in the *Seattle Times*, the United States has only one day equally if not more important than Earth Day: Election Day. The final line is straightforward enough: "This November 3, vote for the Earth."[44]

I like the sentiment, but rather dislike this way of putting it. Voting for a candidate who will help the United States reengage global commitments to reduce CO2 emissions, bringing global levels down to 350 parts per million (from which 350.org gets its name), is critical in responding to the existential crisis of climate change. Certainly, November 3 matters to the earth's sustainability or at least to human participation in a planet that may flourish better without us. What I don't like is the inference that voting surrogate environmentalists into office comes close to fulfilling my otherwise nontransferable individual responsibilities to work with the grain of the ecosystem. Nor do I like the now common association of environmentalism with liberalism, as if voting made you green, or green made you a Democrat. If we cannot answer our common human calling to till and keep the earth (see Gen 2:15), then being left, right, blue, red, or green has become more important than being *human* (a word related to humus, the decomposed organic compound in topsoil). Is our very humanity eroding along partisan divides?

Hope that the right elected officials will "solve the climate crisis" is no less delusional—and abdicates no less personal responsibility—than the hope that opening up the economy will get us out of the coronavirus crisis. Both cases transfigure real despair into ephemeral fantasies about technocratic fixes onto which we transfer our own liabilities and obligations. The government will fix it. Scientists will find a way. The market knows best.

Our environmental crisis cannot be "fixed" or "solved" technologically or technocratically precisely because it is not a problem out there (notwithstanding the misnomer "environment"). It is a *human* problem—a problem within *us*, as individuals and as a country rent asunder. Why can't the small-town Republican who wants to hold on to local self-government and regional jobs recognize themselves in the urban Democrat who buys their produce through a CSA and boycotts clothing made in sweatshops? Why not also the reverse? The economy and the environment have become totems competing for allegiance rather than the means through which we hang onto humanity.

I think here of the press photo taken by Joshua Bickel on April 13 and circulated widely since, especially among liberals. Covering a coronavirus response update from within the Ohio statehouse, the photojournalist turns the camera toward angry protesters with flags, red Trump hats, and masks outside—freeze-framing their raw rage and shouts of protest over stay-at-home orders. Although the left sees little more than the irony of "law-and-order" conservatives defying local laws and taking to the streets, the president goading them on, the photo subtly captures both sides of the painful divisions of our political and cultural fabric. The doors and windows keeping the protestors out perfectly frame their anger, but they also reflect figures behind the camera, who look like unsympathetic bureaucrats, one standing guard with clasped hands, another in a rumpled dress shirt, walking away.[45] One hopes that these new activists will gain some measure of empathy for more experienced protestors within Black Lives Matter (BLM), Me Too, or immigrants' rights movements. One hopes, too, that liberals who are quick to relish the conservatives' anger can see also the real pain and anxiety underneath it, as well as reflect on their own disdain.

Our larger debate is between saving livelihoods by opening up the economy and saving lives by continuing to shelter in place. That debate, too, is complex and ironic. Complex because livelihoods, the means of securing the necessities of life, also obviously preserve lives, and because the lives saved are qualitative and not merely quantitative, notwithstanding death toll tickers on every cable news channel. Indeed, a now obsolete meaning of "livelihood" is the *quality* of being lively—truly alive. Only the most extreme ends of this debate think that you can disregard wealth or health in pursuit of the other. The vast majority of us want to get back to work as quickly as it is safe to do so, knowing that jobs and lives will ultimately be lost and saved together.

But the debate is also ironic, largely because of the terms that we use for it and the deeply deluded assumptions that lie beneath them. We talk as though the health of the economy and the health of bodies—human bodies, the bodies of other creatures, and the whole body of the earth—were different things. We've forgotten that *economy* and *ecology* come from the same Greek word, *oikonomia*, the management of the household. Worse, we've designed metrics such as the GDP that abstract the accrual of monetary wealth from the larger economy of carbon and water cycles, relegating changes in the latter to mere "externalities." We talk about endless economic growth while, as Wendell Berry says, failing to subtract.[46] We fail to account for the loss of biodiversity and topsoil, rising sea levels and monocultures, precipitous climate change, and—this is *intrinsically* related—deteriorations in human public health, especially among the most vulnerable.

If the endless monetary growth that both neoliberals and neocons fantasize about happened in the deep space of an expanding universe, we might be able to call it good. When it happens on a finite planet with limited resources and a particular carrying capacity, we should call it what we normally call uncontrollable growth that overtakes its host—a cancer.

Nowhere are these ironies more conspicuous than in the negative oil prices that contorted global markets last week. Unable or unwilling to stop our fracking and pumping (in part, because it might be harder to return to maximum capacity), and running out of offshore tankers and other storage spaces, producers *literally* couldn't give the stuff away. For the last two decades, the United States has wanted nothing more than to be energy independent, and (thanks in part to fracking) we have largely succeeded. But because this independence depends on nonrenewable fossil fuels extracted from the earth, it is fragile, abstract, and temporary, if not delusional. To claim that any nation is energy independent while using high-powered machines to blast gas from shale is like saying that able-bodied, employed adult men are entirely self-sufficient, while their mothers cook their dinners.[47]

* * *

I won't teach my Environmental Ethics course again for over a year. Still, I'm beginning to think that all my teaching, like each of my students' callings, needs to consider matters of ecological sustainability in and through our other vocations. I also think that our calling to till and keep the earth is intrinsically related to the central vocation that Christians share with other religious and nonreligious people of goodwill—the calling to love and serve the neighbor in need.

Attending to the fundamental relationship between economy and ecosystem helps us recognize the importance of vocational discernment, as it surpasses other forms of career choice. One can choose a career by matching one's capabilities with interests; interest assessment tests do exactly this. To discern a vocation, by contrast, adds a critical third piece—that of understanding the human and nonhuman communities that have gifted one in the first place, and then responding with one's gifts and passions to work for the community's good. In other words, jobs become callings when they contribute to public health and the common good, including the health of the land itself.[48]

I guess there are some reasons to be hopeful, at least when we look to long-term possibilities. It may turn out that the coronavirus pandemic shines bright enough of a spotlight on injustices that we raise the wages of the workers who should earn a living wage on top of our praise. The bad irony of negative oil prices may inspire countries to use stimulus money to move further toward renewable energy. (Wind and sunlight don't need to sit in offshore tankers while we figure out how to use them.) It may be that we individually pursue and corporately compensate work that leads to happiness and health rather than only to wealth as abstracted from the well-being of the whole. The Gen Z students I teach are often more socially responsible and environmentally conscious than many of us who are called to teach them. We have what we need to learn from one another, as well as from Earth, our home.

Having Been Neighbored—April 29, 2020

This morning, after sleeping later than planned, I am reading a column entitled, "What Will our New Normal Feel Like?" The author draws on the lasting impacts of prior epidemics and sieges to predict some long-term changes in our daily behaviors that might emerge from COVID-19. Some are rather hopeful. We may experience a psychological shift toward emotional growth and prosocial behavior as people more naturally care for the communities that sustain them. Others are more frightening, as a year or more without physical contact beyond nuclear families might make us fearful of handshakes and hugs, even when they are safe. There may be widespread symptoms of post-traumatic stress. People may find it more difficult to manage their anger and more easily fall into panic.

Still other possible effects feel to me like a mixed bag. Studying how war-torn Afghanistan residents continue to get by, one researcher claims that anxiety about the future and memories of past trauma make people live more in the moment, unable or unwilling to make long-term plans, but that they also "cultivate moments of joy" whenever and wherever they can. The researcher has already seen behavior changes in New York, where neighborhoods are founding local support groups and people "instinctively" rely on their local neighbors. Were this to become the norm, would protection of immediate communities be a sign of moral learning, a widening from individualistic self-concern, on which we could look back and be rightfully proud? Or is it merely a survival mechanism—no less instinctual and so no more commendable than when early humans, trapped in a hostile environment, "thrived when they cooperated, typically in groups of a few hundred"?[49]

As these quotations suggest, the author of the article presupposes a kind of biological determinism. The question, for him, is not whether we will rise above instinct to answer a higher calling, but whether the biological instincts hardwired within us will issue self-protections that include or exclude others.

Many of my secular, scientific students assume that I, a theologian, will fight for human freedom over and against scientific determinacy. They're right in intuiting the difference in our worldviews, especially between me and those who have a rather reductive understanding of scientific knowing. But I'm really more interested in discussing whether God-language adds anything to our common calling to love and serve the neighbor.

When I introduce the language of vocation to students, I often defend the category by way of its versatility. If you're a religious person, then you might imagine a personal Caller behind the calling and use the name God. If you're not particularly religious, I say, then you might just feel called by your family, or your community, or your sense of ethics or justice. Such equivocations may be necessary to get the language of vocation off the ground. I wonder, though, whether understanding "your" community or "your" sense of ethics as calling you isn't finally solipsistic and inherently self-justifying—a way of dressing up self-interest in the costume of transcendent purpose, service to others, and ethical responsibility. The same, of course, can be true of religious language. "I hear God calling me to . . ." too often functions as "What I am doing is inherently good, and so you don't get to question it."

Even when vocational discernment, or the experience of what Brian Mahan calls an "epiphany of recruitment" during what Brenda Salter McNeil calls "the appointed time," is clearly distinguished from one's own preferences and desires, some students easily fall back on language of personal choice and self-fulfillment.[50] I think of A., a sophomore student in the Called to Work class that I taught with our director for vocational reflection this past January. In his final paper, A. repeatedly made the case that our lives are not, in fact, called forward by other people and certainly not by God. To understand them as such would amount to a bad-faith relegation of our individual freedom to carve our own paths. A. writes that "one's vocation is ultimately decided by the individual"; each one of us alone "decides who they are meant to be . . . based [on] personal experience." Yes, admits A., many have "the sensation of being 'called' or having 'vocation' . . . but the attribution of that feeling to a God-given purpose seems farcical."

Soon after making his case that callings come only from the one called, A. tells a rather moving story about his experience working with Native Americans from the Oglala Lakota tribe in Pine Ridge, South Dakota. He writes of his encounter with generous and loving people, with whom he felt "a profound sense of belonging." He writes also of coming to know the causes behind their poverty and of working through his anger and disappointment in himself for mistaking his privilege as reward for hard work. He calls the whole experience "the nearest thing to being 'called' I can remember." Perhaps straining to fit the genre of stories about epiphanies of recruitment, he writes that "from that point on, I decided to dedicate my life to serving people like the members of the Oglala Lakota community."

Then immediately after A. tells this story and traces his new worldview and commitments back to it, he reasserts his conviction that the meaning of that moment was generated wholly by him. A. writes, "Essentially, the notion of being called only exists because people are quick to assign meaning to otherwise arbitrary things or events that they subjectively feel are important. . . . We ultimately have the power within ourselves to choose the path that we want to pursue. Although not always clear, we have more control over the course our lives will follow than we generally think we do. Vocation isn't something forced upon us, but rather something we can choose to seek out." A. reclaims his jurisdiction for making something of his life at the very moment that he shares a story about being vulnerable to unbidden others who reveal his privilege and call him toward solidarity. His own descriptions notwithstanding, that moment does not seem to me like a subjective *feeling* or *sensation* of the encounter, but rather the encounter itself, an encounter with people *other* than him who call him toward service and justice. Why it is here—*exactly* when A. is made answerable and vulnerable—that he reasserts full and final control? Perhaps that question answers itself.

A. got an A in the class. If I am pushing hard against his assumptions here (as I did with him on drafts of the paper), it is because I think that there is a lot at stake in distinguishing callings from personal preferences. Between the idea that God or Fate decides your future in advance, on the one hand, and total self-authorship on the other, there are manifold ways to describe hearing a calling and finding a purpose, of being made open, ready, responsive. The debate is not whether the summoning comes from "out there" or "in here," but whether we see ourselves as constituted and called forward by others, as gifted through and through, or as the haphazard product of our own whims and wants.

* * *

To recognize oneself as gifted—perhaps that is a more helpful way to describe the difference between the spiritually and vocationally attuned (whether traditionally religious or not) and those who want to take full credit or blame for the meaning or meaninglessness of their lives.

Six weeks ago, when I started writing these entries, I invoked the work of Emmanuel Levinas in wondering whether the "face of the other" could summon us to neighbor love, even as we shelter in place. I still find that way of thinking useful, especially because it brings together those who see the face of God with those who call it neighbor or conscience. (For Levinas, the best of theological and secular understandings finally converge. In his playful French, *tout autre est tout autre*—"every other is the Other."[51] It's a sentiment rooted in Levinas's own Jewish tradition and that also flowers in Christ's command to serve and know the Divine by serving and knowing others who suffer among us: the hungry and the thirsty, the alien and the naked, the sick and the imprisoned [Matt 25:31–46].)

I still find this way of thinking helpful, but there are limits to considering vocation in terms of what we might call the demand side of moral economics. "What does the Lord require of you?" asks the prophet Micah (Mic 6:8). Requirements, pleas, pleads, and beckonings by others are invaluable. We must carefully discern what the world needs and then respond with courage and love.

But in my musing today—and really, over the past six weeks—I am beginning to see how we ought not overlook the supply side of our callings. I have been gifted. I have been given certain gifts and talents (and limits), and with them come the freedom and responsibility to serve the common good. I have been gifted. My life as a whole is something I receive rather than own. Or rather, I take full ownership only insofar as I humbly receive it and gratefully give it away.

Can we work for the good out of such a sense of giftedness? The real payoff here is that it allows me to see myself as empowered and gifted by others before I am called to empower still others. Without this sense, relatively affluent, white, privileged people like A. and me will assume that we are the ones helping, that we are the doers, that our service can change the world. Lenny Duncan, the Black Lutheran pastor who visited my campus several months ago, told a mainly white gathering of Lutheran professors that we need to read the Good Samaritan story as though we are the ones on the side of the road. We are the ones who need healing. Jesus's final command—go and do likewise—asks us not to become saviors, on the hunt for victims to help, but to come to know ourselves as wholly dependent on the mercy of others, and so to go out and heal as ones who have been healed. To shelter others because one is sheltered. To gift as one who is gifted.

65

PART 2

STRANGE FRUIT

(May and June)

POTATOES AGAIN—MAY 1, 2020

April, indeed, was the cruelest month. Fifty thousand are dead from COVID-19 in the United States, almost all of whom died in April. Thirty million are out of work. More than two hundred thousand are dead worldwide.

How does the cruel April just lived through by those of us who survived compare with the one in T. S. Eliot's poem? For Eliot, the agony of April springs (quite literally) from the contrast between a dull and dead winter and the new, painful growth that disturbs its sedated contentedness: "April is the cruelest month, breeding / Lilacs out of the dead land, mixing / Memory and desire, stirring / Dull roots with spring rain." These stirrings of spring and hope seem welcome, but Eliot suggests that rebirth can be a dreaded thing, especially when compared with the consolation of a life resigned to mere subsistence: "Winter kept us warm, covering / Earth in forgetful snow, feeding / A little life with dried tubers."[1]

In *Beloved*, Toni Morrison puts a similar sentiment into the mouth of a white girl who rubs the swollen, disfigured feet of a pregnant runaway slave, the latter writhing in pain. "Anything dead coming back to life hurts," says the white girl, oblivious of the full truth of her words.[2]

Many would prefer that our April of 2020 had been cruel in this way. We shut down the economy on purpose; unlike the global financial crisis of 2008, this was self-inflicted pain, pain that promised to be productive, like the thawing of frozen land or the healing of human tissue. When, at the beginning of April, the Centers for Disease Control and Prevention (CDC) reversed its original advice and told people to wear masks, many wore them diligently, knowing that the discomfort and inconvenience was a small price to pay for the possibility of "flattening the curve" and keeping one another safe. By the end of April, we were tiring quickly. The curve wasn't flattening. It's easy not to wear a mask when others aren't and difficult to do so when no one else is. As our own memories of normal life mix with the desire to go to a restaurant, see family members, and relax the rules, we seem eager to forget why the pain is needed. To forget it all. Whatever.

And now it's May Day, which is Labor Day (or "Workers' Day") for most of the world. In the United States, the day typically gets observed only by elementary teachers who still have their students fold construction paper into cone-shaped baskets and fill them with flowers for their parents, who vaguely remember doing this kind of thing when they themselves were kids. "April showers bring May flowers," the students are taught to say. That may have been 2020's chosen proverb, lyrics to our walk-out song, were we to hit May having suffered productively, the pandemic behind us. Instead, we will be eating dried tubers for a long time.

And we know it. In the middle of March, 15 percent of Americans surveyed thought that disruptions in travel, school, work, and public events would last through 2020 or longer; today, 40 percent think they will last that long. Then, a third of people thought that disruptions would be over in a few weeks; now, a very optimistic 18 percent think we will back to normal that soon.[3] While some are thus steadying themselves—one tuber at a time—others want to plunge the frozen economy in a hot bath, reopen today, which, if nothing else, is the beginning of a new month and thus should start a new chapter in this slow and slogging saga.

The monotony of each day lived similarly to the one before is not always bad. My family has settled into our everyday vocations—as sons, parents, students, spouses, teachers, ministers—and found some daily rhythms of work and rest. Yet grooves so easily become ruts. A pandemic-free spring would have rhythms and melodies beyond the metronomic downbeat of the day after day after day after day. There would be high school proms and college commencements, birthday parties, spring weddings, March Madness, and the opening day of baseball. Instead, graduation commencements are going online. Kids are celebrating their birthdays with drive-by parties. People are sending out wedding postponement announcements, requesting that friends now "save the date" for some undetermined date in the future. John Krasinski hosted a virtual prom with the help of Chance the Rapper and others. I am told "it was epic," but it was also as easy as tuning into the livestream on YouTube, and if they missed it, they can go back and watch it anytime. Designed to offset the hardship of these days, it had none of the mixture of pleasure and pain that makes a typical prom part of the heartrending process of growing up.

During Lent, I wrote that liturgical time—the time of the church calendar—has so much more variety and complexity than secular clock time. I now think that was unfair. Christians do have the advantage of Advent, Christmas, Epiphany, Lent, Easter, and Pentecost, each with different practices that develop different dispositions and that together gather time itself, rescuing it from flat uniformity. Jews have high holy days (Rosh Hashanah and Yom Kippur), and pilgrimage festivals (Passover, Shavuot, and Sukkot); not least important is the weekly Shabbat, or Sabbath, which enfolds each week into God's drama of creation, rest, and re-creation. But so-called secular communities have meaningful rhythms of their own—cookouts and family gatherings on Memorial Day, the Fourth of July, and Labor Day; the high holidays of Thanksgiving, Black Friday, Christmas, and New Year's Eve. College students observe the liturgy of the academic year as well, which includes not only the official rites of opening convocations, midterms, and finals but also traditions specific to each university: buckethead, orgo night, silent dance parties, pumpkin drops, and campus-wide smoochfests.

By contrast, April of 2020 has felt uniform, one-dimensional, and meaningless—what the philosopher Martin Heidegger calls the vulgar notion of time, time as measured by clocks. We have had little on which to hitch our memories or from which to launch our desires.

Ironically, it is religious monastics who are preeminently practiced at withstanding the monotony of purely secular, one-dimensional time. Whether praying the hours (Christianity) or reciting mantras and meditating (Buddhism), monks and nuns structure each day like the one before. Having renounced distractions and committed to simplicity, their stripped-down lives take time head-on. They face the monotony, developing dispositions of stability, simplicity, and hospitality. Without recourse to distraction, however, they are also more susceptible to bouts of dejection and despair. Christian monastics call it *acedia*. The deadly sin can feel like depression, but it is more like a spiritual despair to which those in close community are especially vulnerable. Nicknamed the "noontime demon," acedia typically arrives as the *ora et labora*, the constant prayer and work and prayer and work, and rolls into yet another afternoon.[4]

The lockdown has made all of us monastics. Even though we didn't vow to live this way and have little of the monastics' discipline, we easily catch their spiritual virus. Acedia—that's what the ancient Christian tradition called going bat-shit crazy when every day resembles the one before.

* * *

Ramadan, the Muslim holy month of fasting, began last week. U. is observing the fast, as he always did in his home country of Pakistan. U. is a student at my college and has had a challenging first year. Intending to go into computer science, he found the introductory classes more difficult than expected. It was hard to know how much the language barrier (English is his third language) contributed to grades that were lower than he wanted. He considered business administration and engineering before reconsidering computer science; to date, he remains undeclared and so still needs to meet with me, his first-year advisor, to make a plan for his sophomore year.

U. is still living in the dorms with other international students who couldn't make it home—or didn't want to risk the possibility of not being able to return. He told me it was hard enough before the start of Ramadan. The international students are spread out throughout the dorms and apartments. They venture out to pick up food in to-go containers or find microwaveable groceries in the college's food pantry. Other than that, and a few pickup games of soccer on the tennis courts, they mostly stay in their rooms in front of screens, FaceTiming with family when they can, rewatching *Game of Thrones* when they can't.

Ramadan would usually be a time when the Muslim students would bond nightly over *iftar*, the nightly meal that breaks the fast. This year, U. has been breaking the fast alone or with his roommate. They eat some dates before pulling to-go containers from the minifridge, but it's not the same. Since his family in Pakistan is ten hours ahead, they resume the next day's fast around the time that U. is breaking his. He checks in nightly (their morning) by video chat, but technology can't bring the times together.

"In fact," said U., having described the monotony of his days, "it's my birthday tomorrow, which means that it is already my birthday in Pakistan." When I asked him how he will celebrate, U. said he won't, really. "It's OK," he reassured me, "missing a birthday is the least of our problems."

A local Muslim leader, Dr. K., added some words of resolve to this shared feeling of resignation. From the kitchen of her home in Bettendorf, Iowa, she spoke to my Encountering Religion students over Google Meets this past week. The Muslim community has never experienced anything like this, she said. The daily fast begins this year around 4:20 a.m. and ends at sunset around 8 p.m. She said local Muslims are used to breaking the fast with a community feast, either in the masjid or in one another's homes. They then typically head to the prayer room for an hour and a half of prayer, followed by conversation, support, and fun. Ramadan is somber in the day but celebratory in the evening. She said that you need those evenings (really, they celebrate well into the night) in order to get through the days. She now misses standing shoulder to shoulder with her Muslim sisters, repeating full body prayers alongside one another. She misses hearing the imam chant one-thirtieth of the Qur'an nightly so that the whole of the holy book is recited by Eid al-Fitr, the end of the thirty-day fast. She misses the community she relies on to "toughen out the month together."

But, Dr. K. said, this year has also given more time to spiritually reflect. Without the rush of hosting or attending gatherings, and scrambling to clean up before communal prayer, she breaks fast alone with a simple meal of rice, lentils, and yogurt; says some prayers; and gets more sleep. "I'm taking the isolation as a gift," she said, turning resignation into resolve. "I'm taking the blessing of this as God's choice for us, and benefiting from it."

I'm a Christian, but admit that I have a bit of "holy envy" (to use Barbara Brown Taylor's term) for the resolve of Dr. K.[5] Getting to gratitude like that will take some sustained spiritual practices, which people from different faith traditions (and secularists too) have available to them. Practicing the art of gratitude for isolation and simplicity may just lead to life abundant. Until our palates develop, it may also taste like dried tubers during a winter that lasts into spring.

RUNNING WITH MAUD—MAY 9, 2020

Yesterday would have been Ahmaud Arbery's twenty-sixth birthday. Instead, he was shot and killed on February 23 by a father-son team of vigilantes who, from their porch, saw Arbery jogging through their southern Georgia neighborhood, armed themselves with a shotgun and pistol, chased him in their pickup truck, and killed him with three shots. They justified Arbery's death by claiming that he fit the description of a suspect associated with break-ins of a nearby construction site. They also said that Arbery had tried to take one of the guns they brandished, and so killing him was in self-defense. A video released this past week suggests that Ahmaud Arbery's crime was running while Black. He was a former high school football star who liked to stay in shape and could often be seen jogging throughout the neighborhood. With the release of the video, the self-appointed vigilantes finally have been charged with murder.

I'm writing this from the safety of my home in Rock Island, Illinois, where all the members of my family walk our dog, go for runs, and ride our bikes without any thought to our safety. Sometimes we go out together, but often one of us is alone, again, without any thought to our safety. We can make our way through neighborhoods that are diverse (like the one we live in), that are primarily white (up the hill from us), primarily Hispanic (just to the east), or largely African American and African immigrant (the West End). We move about freely, with little concern for our safety. Which is to say that I write this from the protection of a white supremacist culture and as a privileged beneficiary of that culture. It's a privilege that I think about frequently, but want to do more to change.

When Asa and Gabe get up this morning, I'll suggest that we pack the picnic and go for the bike ride on the Duck Creek Trail that they were planning for tomorrow (Mother's Day), when chilly weather is supposed to roll in. We'll load our bikes onto the back of our two Priuses, which my snarky colleague with a nose for liberal posturing calls our two "Piouses." Then we'll head over the Arsenal Bridge to the Iowa side of the Mississippi.

From a park in the middle of the bike trail, we'll either head east toward Bettendorf, our area's wealthiest and whitest community, where the smooth bike path winds between Frisbee golf courses and the clear water of the creek, populated by kids in shorts with red anchors on them skipping stones or men in Patagonia caps fly fishing for bluegills. Or we'll head west through Davenport, where the path crosses busier streets filled with fast-food restaurants, taquerias, and auto-parts stores, where the baseball fields have chain-linked fences, and where you are more likely to pass a baller than a Frisbee golfer. Either way, we'll wind along, stopping to eat by the creek when we are hungry, saying hello to others on the trail, being mindful of our face masks and distance from other bikers, but not whether we are properly deferential to those who may be carrying concealed lethal weapons.

After the bike ride, I'll ask them to join me in a 2.23-mile jog as part of the #RunWithMaud movement. (The distance recalls Arbery's murder on February 23.) We will run together, tie a ribbon to a tree, and post a photo on Facebook. All of this will be quite safe—not to mention easy. In fact, several dozen Facebook friends will like our post, make comments, or post their own. We stand with Maud. We say Black Lives Matter. Do we live our lives as though this were true?

* * *

I once gave a Sunday morning adult education presentation on white privilege and Christian discipleship. It was at St. Paul Lutheran Church in Davenport, Iowa, a primarily white congregation in the Evangelical Lutheran Church in America (ELCA), which Black Lutheran preacher Lenny Duncan accurately describes as "the whitest denomination in the United States." A few weeks prior, Asa, Gabe, and I had become members there (while retaining joint membership at Laura's church). Since this particular Sunday was my first adult ed talk since officially joining the church, I put our membership photo on the first PowerPoint slide, intending to use it to announce that I was now part of the congregation. It was not until I clicked to that first slide and looked with forty or fifty attendees at the three gangly figures in church clothes on the screen, readying myself for what was sure to be a controversial forty-five-minute presentation on white privilege, that I thought to say—and did say—this: "These are my two sons, Asa and Gabe, and me. And we are white supremacists."

It took most of the session to explain what I meant. We don't want to be white supremacists. We want to be the opposite of those who claim the title proudly. But we are, in fact, white supremacists in the same way that the rest of the white people in the room (which all but a handful were) are white supremacists. We live in a cultural and political system that has been created for and by people like me. We were raised to "believe ourselves white," as both Ta-Nehisi Coates and James Baldwin have described us.[6] Part of this belief is the assumption that our success is something that we have earned. We see whiteness as neutral and so fail to see the supremacist assumptions that fuel it, as well as the manifold privileges bestowed by it. Often ignorant of the way that the cards are stacked for us and against others, we also assume that we are not racist whenever we don't intentionally act out of prejudice or bigotry. But, says Ibram X. Kendi, this ignores the racist structure into which each of us has been born. The structure is such that it is not possible to be *non*racist; whenever we are not actively subverting the racism of our culture, actively becoming *anti*racist, we are tacitly endorsing and benefiting from it.[7]

Most, if not all, churchgoers I was speaking with that day have deeply seated, unsaid assumptions about a hierarchy of human value, which often puts Black bodies below the property white folks feel "called" to protect. Arbery's killers valued a new home construction site more than the life of a twenty-five-year-old man. The felt duty to protect white property (sometimes including white women) from the imagined threat of Black people (especially Black men) goes back to the time of slavery, when the value of Black lives was recorded on a bill of sale. That felt duty is still at the root of our stand-your-ground culture, which pervades white space and exonerates violence by police, vigilantes, bystanders, and all who do not actively turn from their white supremacy.[8]

In fact, whites have amassed their security and wealth *through* the usually subtle, sometimes horrific policing, regulation, confinement of, and violence against Black bodies. That is to say, white folks like me are privileged not only in comparison with *but also by virtue of* the more limited protections for and violence against people and communities of color. Whenever I am not actively antiracist, I am benefiting from white supremacy. And so are my kids—as innocent as they may appear, smiling for a new membership photo in their Sunday best. Like original sin, structural racism is a condition that each of us is born into and of which we must repent.[9]

But how to repent? Maybe I thought my impromptu blurting out that I was racist would work like a confession, like the one St. Paul Lutheran and countless other churches recite every Sunday, where "we confess that we are in bondage to sin and cannot free ourselves." We confess that we have sinned against God "in thought, word, and deed, by what we have done and by what we have left undone," and that we continuously break the two great commandments, by not loving God "with our whole hearts" and by not loving "our neighbors as ourselves." If my fellow Christians and I could connect the acknowledgment of privilege, racism, and white supremacy to our regular confession of (other) deadly sins, perhaps we would understand that our very identities as Christians are at stake when reckoning with racism. What the culture calls *unmasking*, *dismantling*, and *reparations* is for us a matter of contrition, confession, and penitence.

But the teaching session was in the church classroom, not the sanctuary. I declared my white supremacy rather than confessed it, strictly speaking. It was answered by some shuffling of feet and looks of disbelief (as well as some nods of affirmation, mainly from white women)—not the pastor's proclamation that God has made my sons and me alive through God's Son, Jesus, and forgives us all our sin. Perhaps that's as it should be, since forgiveness without repentance (which is much more than verbal confession) amounts only to "cheap grace," according to the Lutheran martyr, Dietrich Bonhoeffer. The grace of racial reconciliation will cost an honest reckoning.

Today, as I plan to #RunWithMaud and then post photos on Facebook, I struggle to understand my positive, seemingly justice-oriented affirmations just as much as my extemporized admission that Sunday morning. What do any of my proclamations that Black Lives Matter and symbols of antiracist commitments mean? What do they *do*? I've got a BLM sticker on my office door, beside the "safe zone" sticker and the "faith zone" interfaith ally sticker. Who is it for? Does it mean I'm woke? That I'm standing on the right side of history as it bends toward justice? Ribbons and stickers and T-shirts that ask "Got Privilege?" seem too often to be about the one displaying them or, worse, about what others should think about where we stand—like driving a Prius to exhibit my piousness. The lawyer asked Jesus the question about neighbor love as a way to "justify himself." Pronouncements of having been woke or having marched in the 1960s or having Black friends also often work to justify ourselves, saving ourselves from the pain of repentance.

In the first of his Ninety-Five Theses, Martin Luther said that "when our Lord and Master Jesus Christ said, 'Repent,' he willed *the entire life* of believers to be one of repentance."[10] Luther himself came to repent even and especially of his *good* works, insofar as he trusted in their righteousness. He even repented of his endless confession of other sins, insofar as he was desperately trying to save himself through those confessions. I, too, feel called to turn from self-serving confessions whenever they are more about whom I'd like to be seen as, rather than who I've become in our sinful and savable world.

FINDING PURPOSE—MAY 14, 2020

Last week, my college's "Last Lecture" event (through Zoom, of course) took place, where seniors elect three of their favorite professors to bestow on them words of advice as they head out into the "real world," followed by a champagne toast from the college president. Those of us who have never been elected or were only elected once some years ago (yours truly), say that the Last Lecture is only a popularity contest; it has nothing to do with good teaching and deep learning. We're jealous, of course, and feel a little left out.

In our last Encountering Religion session this morning, I give my own parting words, sans champagne. I tell my students how grateful I am to be with them during this time. I say that we were lucky—maybe blessed—to have gotten to know one another in person through the first half of the semester before scattering to Denver, Chicago, Atlanta, rural Illinois, Brazil, and other places. I thank them for their flexibility and grit.

I also remind them of the ways that the various religions we've been studying are sustaining people through the pandemic, even as practitioners reinvent how religion is done. Eucharist is online; Quakers join chatrooms to sit in silence together; virtual Seder meals have set records for the number of Jews and gentiles participating; Hindu *puja* at home is absorbing the role of a priest in the temple; the communal meal (*langar*) in Sikh meeting-houses has ballooned into food banks for the hungry.

Students at Augsburg University in Minneapolis can hear the Muslim call to prayer (*adhan*) amplified from the Dar Al-Hijrah Mosque a few blocks away. With mosques closed down and the huge Somali population confined to their residences, Minneapolis Mayor Jacob Frey approved the sound permit that allows the call to prayer to go public. Muslims are grateful, and many others are supportive. Still others grumble about how Minnesota is starting to feel like Eastern Africa or the Middle East. I remind the students that they now have basic literacy in diverse religions and skills in interfaith negotiations. What would you say at the city hall meeting where such things are being debated? What if your comment followed that of a veteran deployed in Iraq or Afghanistan, who says that the call to prayer might trigger his post-traumatic stress disorder (PTSD)? Interfaith work is tough, I say. Yet our college's mission speaks of being equipped for service and leadership in a diverse and changing world. It doesn't mention ease.

Not wanting to have the last word, I ask the two graduating seniors if they would like to give any advice to the juniors and sophomores. From the edge of her bed in her parents' home, environmental science major M. talks about how difficult it was to depart from campus eight weeks ago. She says that she is a first-generation college student, and it took some time for her to feel like she belonged here. She encourages her classmates not to take their time in college for granted. Say yes to things, she says. Get outside your comfort zone.

J. addresses the class swinging from a hammock on the porch of the house he rents with classmates—making distance learning look a bit too much like an extended staycation. J. is a dedicated student; he will finish his local internship with the US Army Corps of Engineers this summer before heading to Austin, Texas, to pursue a PhD in geological sciences. He waxes philosophical with the class. He says that he used to think college was "just four years that help you get to the next point in your life." He has come to see how the knowledge and relationships he found here "have woven themselves into my life's story."

Students like these epitomize what Tim Clydesdale calls "reforming activists" in his book, *The Purposeful Graduate*. They give high priority to grades and success, but with idealist rather than instrumentalist regard for what education is ultimately for. They live purposeful lives.[11]

Purpose. As a noun, the word means the reason something is done or for which something exists—for example, the *purpose* of higher education is to contribute to the common good. As a verb, it means to resolve or intend to do something, or to set a goal for oneself—for example, she *purposed* to get better grades. The noun form is linguistically more common, but most of us, when pressed, think that purpose is something we do rather than something we find or discover somewhere "out there."

Many in church-related higher education would rather talk about purpose and meaning than vocation or calling. The former terms not only carry less metaphysical baggage; they also sound more inspiring. Evoked in commencement speeches and last lectures, they beckon students to embark on a life of value that they themselves *purpose*. A purposeful life or purposeful graduate suggests something the person intends and makes, if not wholly invents, rather than receives or finds. Many students and educators together likewise assume that to live a purposeful life is to go from being conflicted, torn, and indecisive to charting a clear and single path by way of decisive decision-making. Students are encouraged by a host of career services and parental voices (some rather insistent) to *choose* a major, *embark* on a career, *decide* who you're going to be.

I understand why my colleagues emphasize the intentional activity of making meaning and acting purposefully when showcasing successful students. Indeed, today's job market—even before the deep freeze of this "pancession"—seems to require nothing less than graduates who can actively carve their own paths forward. Positive psychologists Bryan Dik and Ryan Duffy describe a new age of employee "free agency," where career trajectories are highly individualized and "protean"—that is, careers "in which the person, not the organization, is in charge, the core values are freedom and growth, and the main success criteria are subjective." They encourage all of us, from entry-level employees to those at the end of their careers, to actively *make* meaning, to *forge* our paths, and to *craft* our jobs in a way that makes them meaningful and purposeful.[12] In today's economy, many of us (actually, most of us) will need to reassess our chosen paths, repurpose, retool, "reinvent ourselves." Even those of us on traditional career paths with relatively linear trajectories can and should still find new ways to *make* meaning and *purpose* new goals.

Again, this is hard to disagree with, and many Gen Z students need to hear it. Those born from the late 1990s until the early 2010s have grown up in the most unstable, uncertain time in modern history. Following Millennials before them, Gen Z is famous (or infamous) for extending the period between adolescence and adulthood; they spend their twenty-something years in a kind of "elongated adolescence" or "emerging adulthood." Reluctant to take on commitments of marriage or career or religious affiliation, an increasing number lead their lives day to day, working at Starbucks (as the caricature has it) and living in their parents' basements (statistically on the rise). According to psychologist Meg Jay, Gen Z graduates are, like Millennials before them, all too passive when it comes to meaning, purpose, and vocation. In her book, *The Defining Decade*, she stridently appeals to young adults in their twenties to "claim your adulthood. Be intentional. Get to work. Pick your family. . . . Make your own certainty!" This is *purpose* as all verb, no noun. It's something that young people should stop looking for and start making.[13]

Unfortunately, such appeals to choose your own adventure land on those already being told to choose their very identities. The identities of today's young people—their morality, spirituality, gender, sense of belonging, and the whole meaning of their lives—are increasingly contingent on the choices of each individual. Whereas previously many accepted identities as prepackaged and assigned (Christian or female or Asian American), now just as many, maybe more, feel responsible for authoring themselves, for claiming their full autonomy. On the one hand, *autonomy* (literally, "giving the rule to oneself") has freed countless individuals from scripts that were foisted on them in earlier generations. Malcolm X, for example, tells the story of how he needed to shatter teachers' expectations that he would grow up to do the work normally reserved for Black men in a racist world, rather than become a lawyer—a story that demonstrates how essential claiming one's autonomy (and humanity) can be.[14] On the other hand, self-authorship has also created unprecedented levels of anxiety. When everything from a gig economy to self-presentation on social media asks you to reinvent yourself again and again, it is hard not to be anxious, insecure, and exhausted. Incidences of FOMO (fear of missing out) turn inward, transmuting into FOML—the fear of a meaningless life.

Maybe that's a bit bleak. Countless students like M. and J. are thriving, even when they have to take unprecedented responsibility for their learning during the last seven weeks of their senior year. Still, we risk giving too much custody and charge—not to mention credit—to any one human being when we ask them to create their own purpose. It risks obscuring the receptive, responsive dimension of *being* called or *finding* meaning and purpose. Certainly, educators ought to enable students to actively carve a fitting path rather than perpetually wait for a vocational Godot to enter their lives, stage right. And certainly, we ought never to foist biased, unfair scripts onto others, thinking we know their place. At the same time, both educators and students can and often do overemphasize the degree to which passion development is in our control. Perhaps the most active—but also strangely passive—thing that we can do is to pay attention to that which we do not create but which may be calling us toward new ways of life.

The French philosopher and religious mystic Simone Weil writes of the art of paying attention and the transcendent experience of doing so. Attention, Weil says, is the very substance of prayer. While that might sound metaphysical, Weil thinks we develop the capacity for attention in rather mundane ways. When a student is stuck on a difficult math problem, instead of furrowing their brow in concentration and frustration, they need to loosen their grip, submit themselves to the problem, and go back through it with humility and curiosity. The student will find the answer not by hunting furiously, but by allowing it to emerge, by opening up to the solution. Developing the art of paying attention comes by way of listening carefully, suspending one's grasp, opening oneself to the unbidden.[15]

Weil's example of the student stuck on a math problem has an additional truth for these tumultuous times. As I suggested in my previous entry, I, as a beneficiary of a white supremacist culture, feel called to repentance during this time. Weil's student similarly comes to know the truth by attending closely to their error, as difficult as that may be. Perhaps answering the call to repentance by privileged people like me is a way of steering a middle course between wanting to save the world, which so quickly devolves into white savior syndrome, on the one hand, and wallowing in white guilt or passively enjoying privilege, on the other. Repenting, like paying attention and finding one's calling, can always devolve into something one forces, a technique employed to get what one wants. At best, it's a practice in purgation, a burning away of false loves so that the love that remains is purer and more powerful.

CONFESSIONS OF A NOVICE LOVER—MAY 17, 2020

Here's a story about neighbor love, or the lack thereof. I tell it in the spirit of repentance.

A few years ago, I was doing yard work when I saw a Black woman pass through the yard of the W's, a retired couple who live across the street. The woman nonchalantly picked up a bicycle that was parked by the front porch and continued on her way.

I thought that I had seen her before on the side of our house; she had left quickly when I called out to her. And I later learned that the kale growing next to another neighbor's sidewalk was planted for her after they witnessed her picking and eating hostas, which are nonedible yard plants. But when I saw her walking off with our neighbor's bike, I mainly saw a stranger and threat, although certainly a nonaggressive one.

I walked toward her and asked her what she was doing. When she mumbled incoherently, I blocked her pathway, inquiring whether the bike belonged to her. She dropped the bike and tried to continue steadily on, almost pleading in her body language. I'm six foot three, athletic, and white. It was perhaps that assumed physical and cultural power that swayed her to step onto my neighbor's porch with me while I knocked on the door to explain what I had witnessed.

Mrs. W. answered the door. She is a considerate, artistic woman whose grandchild used to walk to school next to Asa. She obviously had had earlier run-ins with the woman. Reminding her with an exasperated tone that she can't take things that don't belong to her, my neighbor appeared less affronted or angry than disappointed and disconcerted. The three of us stared at one another, awkward and powerless. The woman obviously needed help—probably money, maybe a recovery program or treatment for mental illness. Neither of us knew how to help her or whether our help would include punishment for an attempted petty theft.

"Should we call the police?" I asked.

"I don't know," my neighbor conceded.

An additional moment passed, as we stood looking at our feet on the porch. Not knowing what else to do and not knowing how to extricate myself from the civic duty I had assumed, I said that I would be happy to make the call. Later, I identified the tinges of self-satisfaction accompanying that offer with pride of having made the "responsible" decision, even in a moment of ambiguity and uncertainty.

"OK," Mrs. W. said softly, perhaps relieved that I was the one acting out the tough love that neither of us was convinced was loving. I called, and the police arrived and arrested the woman, explaining to us that she had a prior record. I later learned that the perpetrator rented a house on the street behind me. Geographically, she was no less a neighbor than the neighbor whose property I helped protect. Biblically, I should have regarded her as neighbor even if she lived far away. I never saw her again.

Here's a story about the telling of that story:

The first person I told it to (other than Laura) was a pastor I trusted, Pastor T., whom I saw at an ELCA gathering weeks after the incident. During those weeks, I had been thinking about my failure of nerve that day or, more exactly, about my overactive nerves, my inability to be still and endure an awkward situation and respond more carefully and creatively in ways that loved each neighbor. I confessed to Pastor T. that I had failed to act like a Christian that day: I had treated one neighbor as a danger and prematurely saved another neighbor and myself from a sense of powerlessness that we might have endured and from which we might have learned. I involved the police and the law, chief powers of an anonymous state, in what should have been two close, interpersonal relationships between neighbors. Pastor T. swiftly assured me that I had done nothing wrong. I wonder whether that quick word—not of *absolution* but of *reassurance*—did not reproduce my own failure of nerve, my own nervous haste.[16]

I still do not know what exactly I could have done differently. Calling the cops remains, for white people at least, a typical and socially acceptable response to conflict between citizens, even those who are neighbors. It is also rather unimaginative—especially compared to, say, planting kale near the sidewalk if a woman keeps eating your hostas.

Having told this story and the story of its telling, I have reached some realizations about my central Christian calling to love and serve my neighbors.

First, while I grew up in the church, my spiritual and moral formation—the development of my deepest habits, dispositions, and character—owes at least as much to America's liberal society and to white culture as it does to Christianity. I have been formed as a citizen in a liberal democracy, whose chief duty is to protect personal freedoms and property ownership. Formed as such, I felt allegiance to the homeowner, Mrs. W., over the trespasser, my Black neighbor. Given that Mrs. W. expressed her own ambivalence about calling the police, perhaps I even showed more allegiance to her home, or to the abstract right to homeownership, than to her.

Compounding this disparity is the fact that, as many studies show, white folks like me identify more quickly and pervasively with other whites than we do with people of color. When we walk in a room, we gravitate toward other white people, even when the Black and brown folks that we angle away from share our politics, religion, or worldview. In the United States, racial belonging almost always trumps every other connection, including worshipping the same God.

According to leading Black theologian Willie James Jennings, tragedies such as the murder of nine Black church members in Charleston's Emanuel AME Church on June 17, 2015, by another Christian, Dylan

Roof, reveal a white supremacy that is woven into the very fabric of white Christianity.[17] The white supremacy that I *confessed* during adult education at St. Paul Lutheran Church is not the same as the one Dylan Roof *avowed* and acted on at Emanuel AME. And yet beyond belonging to the same denomination (Roof is a member of the ELCA), each of us has been trained to imagine "the neighbor" as the white landowner, "citizenship" as the duty to protect her house, and "faithfulness" as allegiance to a white, American civil religion that masks as Christian faith. Each of us has been shaped in myriad unspoken ways to identify with relatively affluent, white, law-abiding, and landowning neighbors over more transient, darker-skinned, and poorer ones.

Second, I realize from this story—and especially in the way that I have told it—how easy it is to confuse the central Christian calling to love the neighbor with a more abstract, purportedly objective duty to love everyone and to be appropriately color-blind when doing so. It would be easy to conclude from the story that my love of neighbor was too limited, that it admitted only one of two neighbors in my field of concern. Sometimes, Christian love (what the biblical Greek calls *agape*) is distinguished from passionate love (*eros*) and the love between friends (*philia*) in terms of the latter two being exclusive and self-fulfilling, while agape is not tainted by what I get out of it and therefore is universal in scope. These distinctions between universal, self-effacing, Christian love and more self-centered, limited, natural loves make it sound as though the goal is to overcome particularity (loving *this* particular neighbor) in order to regard everyone equally (without regard for color, class, gender, etc.). Certainly, the inability to love those who do not look or act like you is problematic, to say the least. But so is the idea that one should look beyond all the particularities of a person in order to confer on them a fair, objective love. Feminists have questioned whether love that is unilaterally, passionlessly bestowed on another can really be called love. Christian feminists, too, suggest that that image of love looks more like Aristotle's Unmoved Mover than the passionate, suffering love of the God of Jesus.[18]

Especially since the Enlightenment, we have thought about ethical action in terms of abiding by universal rules and regulations rather than engaging messy, particular circumstances and the messy, particular stories that make us who we are. Add to this a reigning political philosophy that emphasizes the hands-off respect for one another's rights, and love starts to look like the tacit agreement not to get into one another's business. Add again a society that sometimes considers itself postracial, where love purportedly sees no color, and the calling to love the neighbor as oneself degenerates into platitudes about not playing favorites and respecting everyone. And yet I didn't fail to love my Black neighbor because I noticed that she was Black. I failed to love her Blackness, her femaleness, her woundedness and giftedness, and all the other components of her particular story.

I stared at my feet instead of asking the woman, "What are you going through?" That's at least partly why I didn't love her well. Her story, if I had come to know it, may have evoked a more passionate and compassionate response. But I didn't know it and so acted out of abstractions such as "duty" and "fairness" rather than responding lovingly to the concrete realities of another.

Third, the story of my Black neighbor raises the question of what it would mean to repent from the sin of white privilege and white supremacy. *Repentance* is the translation of the Greek word *metanoia*, which literally means a change of mind or, better, a turning of the heart. Repentance is fully active and fully passive, both an intentional commitment and an undergoing, something to bear or suffer. It is broader and deeper than the confession of sin. My unabsolved confession to Pastor T. thus barely scratched the surface of the repentance to which I am called. I was looking for a quick return to normal, when I should have been setting off on a journey which, although too long to glimpse the ending, might have just led to love between neighbors who know something of each other's stories.

* * *

A Hispanic family rents the home next door to us. The mother, M., works first shift at a gas station downtown and has raised five children largely on her own, including a deaf young man, D. Jr., who recently moved back in, does their yard work, and always waves to us warmly. The stepfather, J., works at a factory making boxes by night and trains mixed martial arts (MMA) fighters by day. The factory work has been deemed essential, and so it continues throughout the lockdown. It looks like the training has moved mostly into his driveway.

I know what I know about these neighbors mainly through Laura, who speaks to M. with an ease and genuineness that I admire. Today, though, is a beautiful spring day, and when I see M., J., and the youngest daughter hanging out on their porch, I walk over, hand them a bag of lettuces from our garden, and say I need to ask them for a favor. J. stiffens slightly and M. looks concerned; they think I am going to complain about something. "We were given that chicken coop by some friends," I say, pointing to my backyard. "When I finally get it fixed up and make a longer run for the chickens, we'd like to get six—all hens. No roosters waking us up in the morning. Would you be willing to sign this neighbor notification on my application to the city?"

J. quickly signs and M. asks how we are doing during the lockdown. We talk about the fruit trees that I planted between our yards earlier this spring. They like apples, peaches, and plums but not really pears, she says. Please pick whatever you want, I say, adding that it will be a few years before the trees produce fruit. I say that, if all goes well, we should be able to come over with a carton of eggs sometime this fall. We all like eggs, M. says. D. Jr. would eat eggs for every meal, if we let him.

It's not much, but I know a little more of my neighbor's story, and they know something of mine.

BEARING IT—MAY 24, 2020

The only time I tried to hurt my brother—who was older, stronger, and didn't try to hurt me back because it would have been too easy—was in high school when he was living with our dad, and I was living with our mom, and he didn't show up for a reconciliatory birthday dinner that my mother made for him. I found him leaving my dad's apartment, dragged him down a flight of stairs, glanced a fist off his face, and told him that he wasn't my brother. I'm thinking of that episode this morning after Asa and Gabe wrestled in our living room last night. Asa had taken Gabe's notebook, and Gabe pinned him down to try to get it back. Laura and I looked on, refraining from jumping in, silently wondering whether the teasing and tussling were turning into something more dangerous.

An hour after they went to bed, the boys came downstairs, shuffling feet outside our room. I assumed that the fighting had continued into the night, but we came to learn that they had been lying in bed talking about missing school, friends, sports, and especially childhood innocence, although they didn't use that term. When Gabe started to cry upstairs, Asa tenderly, compassionately walked him downstairs to find parents who would help him hold his brother.

After some hugs and solaces downstairs, I walked them up to their room to retuck them in. Asa let me rub his back without recoiling in teenage contempt. From his bed across the room, Gabe held my gaze, eyes tired and red, but alert and almost beseeching.

I wish I were a poet and could put into proper words the depth of that exchange. Gabe didn't seem to be attempting anything with his gaze—not asking for anything or communicating a particular emotion. It was a blank stare, but unconscious of being so, entirely different from the look performed by a child locked in a playful staring contest. His eyes suggested where he was, who he was. They were attentive but not determined to take a stand; they were persistent but quietly so, holding my own gaze as an offering rather than a challenge. He let himself be seen.

In those eyes, I saw an outer layer of anxiety settled into sorrow. Just below was something else—confidence maybe, or restrained hope, or acceptance. The worry and the resolution seemed to be of the same piece. He was submitting to the loss of our normal lives and saying yes to new realities. He was bearing it all, actively and passively, with muted confidence and because there were no other options.

Those few seconds were pure gift. Perhaps moments like these are frequent in children but usually go unrecognized. If we knew where to look, or didn't so quickly look away, perhaps we'd glimpse them between a child's bouts of silliness or in the seconds before a teenager's swing to sullenness. They're moments of acceptance and endurance, of yearning and yielding and submitting to vulnerability.

The gift was ambivalent—or better, a gift *of* ambivalence. I was sorry for all that my children were facing, which includes their own mortality. *And* I was gratified that they were facing it. I was pleased (I'm not sure that's the right word, but I don't know a better one) that they were experiencing some of the solemn freedom that comes from living with the knowledge of death.

This morning, thinking on these things, Wendell Berry's poem "To My Children, Fearing for Them" rises to mind. I memorized it some years ago while walking the trail that passes through fields of fireweed between Holden Village and Monkey Bear Falls. It's an ambivalent poem, a poem about ambivalence. It captures better than I can the painful gift of "loving what I cannot save."

The poem begins with a statement of undeniable fact: "Terrors are to come." The cause is in deeds already done—"The earth / Is poisoned with narrow lives." Berry addresses his children directly, considering "What you will / Live through, or perish by"—all of which "eats at [Berry's] heart." He then describes the "pain of coming to see / what was done in blindness" and, more heart wrenching still, of "loving what [he] cannot save."[19]

The poem suggests the piercing guilt of having bequeathed a world where environmental disasters, pandemics, human hunger, systemic injustices, and an ugliness of landscapes and inscapes will become even more the norm. Our children must live in this broken world. The deepest pain lies in our inability to make things right, coupled with the anguished grief of still loving what we cannot save.

Still loving what we cannot save. That seems to characterize the particularly painful and essential vocation of parenthood. Yet I would bet there are analogs in every calling, every elemental commitment that we make to become people capable of good and needed change, even while realizing—not without grief—that even our most momentous efforts will not begin from or return us to scratch. Those called to medicine will have to connect with patients as whole persons, even within a medical-industrial complex that incentivizes spending little time with them, which increases patient alienation and physician burnout. Those called to education will have to attend to the particular needs and gifts of students whom the educational system otherwise funnels toward detention and incarceration. Those called to parent children in a racist world will not be able to protect their innocence; some will have to have lovingly brutal talks about protecting their Black bodies, while others will teach children to identify the racial scripts that form their bodies, habits, and sense of space long before they can articulate them.[20] To be born into this particular world is to be born into one already overpopulated with systemic racism, cultural disintegration, and irreversible climate change. We go on loving, working, and grieving, sometimes fiercely.

Little good comes when we desperately try to save what we cannot save. Typically, these inordinate quests to save only add to our grief and, at the same time, take away a means of grieving. We know this to be true of end-of-life care. In her new book, *The Lost Art of Dying*, physician Lydia S. Dugdale tells heartbreaking stories about desperate attempts to prolong the lives of the elderly or those with terminal illnesses. Sometimes doctors suggest one more experimental drug or invasive surgery because those heroic efforts are easier to try than telling a family that their loved one will die. Other times, family members, afraid and confused, do not know what to do other than to insist that doctors do everything possible to prolong life. Both sides can be gripped by "the rescue fantasy," as doctors are "hardwired to free patients from the grip of death, and patients are hardwired to seek safety." Trying to save what cannot be saved medicalizes death, postpones grief, and sometimes deprives families of the time and presence of mind needed to let go and say good-bye.[21]

Trying to save what cannot be saved can also lead to violence. Pacifists are those who repudiate, on moral or religious grounds, lethal violence, even when sanctioned by the state, such as with war or capital punishment. The quickest and most common rejoinder to pacifists typically goes something like this: "If a killer were coming after your daughter or sister intending to hurt or kill her, would you stand by and let him have his way?" The question means to be a rhetorical conversation stopper. *Of course*, you would kill someone who is trying to kill someone you loved. It then follows that love of neighbor, consistently personified with paternalistic images of protecting dependent females, necessitates that responsible people get their hands dirty, using violence to stop violence. Never mind that waging a war to end all war or executing a violent criminal is—to borrow the colorful language of Christian ethicist Stanley Hauerwas (borrowing it in turn from George Carlin)—a bit like trying to screw your way to virginity. Fighting our way toward peace is the last resort that we choose rather quickly whenever we tell ourselves that there is no other way to save the vulnerable ones we love.

Add systemic racism into the mix, and lethal violence follows paternalistic and protective love all too easily and often with impunity. Until
two weeks ago, the father and son who killed Ahmaud Arbery were not
charged. The district attorney who refused to do so said that the two car-
ried their guns legally and that Georgia's citizen's arrest law, which goes
back to the Civil War era, permitted the two men to pursue Arbery in
their pickup, guns ablazing. The neighborhood-watch volunteer in Florida
who killed Trayvon Martin in 2012 likewise invoked his right—or even his
duty—to stand his ground and protect the property of the neighbors he
loved.

Today, the FBI announced that it has opened an investigation into the
death of Breonna Taylor, the twenty-six-year-old Black EMT worker who
was fatally shot by multiple plainclothes police officers after they broke into
her apartment with a no-knock warrant. The man they were searching
for, believed to be selling drugs, lived ten miles away and was already in
custody. The police claim to have announced their presence (even with the
no-knock warrant), but Taylor's boyfriend thought they were intruders and
used his own legally purchased firearm to shoot at them. The police fired
twenty rounds into the apartment in return; three officers struck Taylor
eight times. She was pronounced dead on the scene.

Police answer the call to serve and protect. Some argue that the
vast majority of good cops fully hear and faithfully heed that call. That
may be true, but the problem is systemic, inscribed into the very duties
that cops are made to perform. We know, for example, that the modern
police force evolved from night watches and slave patrols, which were
designed to control Native American and enslaved populations and to
protect the property of those deemed white. We also know that when
the US military unloads military-grade weapons and riot gear on police
departments, the latter find ways to use it. Today, the frequently invoked
difference between good cops and bad cops is nowhere close to being
as important as the difference between those who own property and
want to protect it, on the one hand, and those whose property has been

confiscated and who have *been* property and are now seen as a threat to it, on the other. This latter difference is systemically inscribed into the responsibilities and offices that good cops alongside bad cops, as well as good politicians, teachers, and other citizens, take on when they answer the call to serve and protect.

I know the violence that comes by way of misdirected love—that is, by trying to viciously save rather than painfully bear. I see it when I look at invasive medicine, interventionist foreign policies, and militarized and racialized police forces. But I recognize it out *there* because I also see it *here*, in my own predilections to violence, which arise from and try to cover over my inability to bear what I cannot change.

When I pulled my brother down the stairs of my father's apartment building, hitting him in the face, I did so because I couldn't put the broken family I loved—with cracks between brothers as well as between parents—back together again. Living that brokenness was too painful to bear, so I thrashed about in the stairwell instead. When I called the cops on my Black neighbor, the embarrassed silence of two adults who should have been asking the third what she was going through was too much to suffer, although we didn't try for long. I stepped into the role of neighborhood watchman with the resolve of Georgians getting into their pickup, even if my particular violence was outsourced to the state. I yell the loudest at Asa (who, I confess, bears the brunt of my anger) when I most fear that he is growing up with as much white, male, upper-middle-class privilege as I did, and may turn out to be the kind of person who hits his brother, calls the cops on his neighbors, and yells at his kids.

In another colorful phrase, Stanley Hauerwas, who calls himself a Christian pacifist, frequently declares that he is too damn violent *not* to be a pacifist. The feminist theorist Judith Butler concurs—nonviolence is a practice belonging to those already "disposed to violent retribution" but who learn nevertheless to admit their fears and struggle against their own anger.[22] This excessively long time of COVID-19 seems too much to bear. Its gift to me and others is training in bearing it, endurance, long-suffering.

It's the gift of spiritual education in saving what can be saved, in continuing to love all that we cannot, and in discerning the difference between the two. It's the gift of love between neighbors, once paternalism and protectionism are purged, and fear, named and admitted, becomes a path toward wisdom.

FRAMING FIRE—JUNE 1, 2020

Yesterday was Pentecost. One week ago was Memorial Day, the day George Floyd cried out for his mother with his final breaths after a Minneapolis police officer, Derek Chauvin, knelt on his neck for eight minutes and forty-six seconds.

Today, the day after Christians commemorated the movement of the Holy Ghost through raging wind and tongues of fire, fires burn in Minneapolis and protests rage throughout the United States. The uprisings are cries of pain for over four hundred years of slavery, disenfranchisement, de jure and de facto segregation, lynchings, mass incarceration, and a carceral state that wields lethal violence largely to protect the property of white people like me. The death of Floyd is just one grotesque example of death at the hands of white supremacy. Since 2015, 1,252 Black people have been shot and killed by police—a rate twice as high as that of whites.[23] Some names are well known—Eric Garner, Tamir Rice, Michael Brown, Philando Castile, Atatiana Jefferson, Freddie Gray. So many more become hashtags for a time and then drop to the back page of newspapers, if they make it into them at all.

I watched George Floyd die. Like everyone except those who happened to be outside the Minneapolis grocery store, some pleading with Derek Chauvin to stop, I watched the death on video. I don't know whether viewing it is morally defensible or whether repeatedly circulating videos of Black death at the hands of police does anything other than retraumatize those already traumatized and desensitize those who are not. Floyd's desperate cries for breath and for his dead mother, together with the image of eyes moving from fear to almost puzzlement and then slack with the loss of consciousness, should decidedly *not* be framed by a computer screen. You shouldn't be able to pause the footage, studying the position of hands and the tenseness of muscles, as jurors will be asked to do. Uncanny to watch it here, just a few clicks away from the easily digestible deaths of *CSI* episodes or *Fortnite*.

I would say that watching the video was hard, which is true, if that didn't accentuate just how painless watching the brutalization of Black bodies is for people like me, compared to those whose bodies are brutalized or who live in fear of such. In her tremendous essay from the late 1930s, "The Love of God and Affliction," Simone Weil describes the difference between those of us who see the affliction of others and then can look away and those for whom the horror is incessant, "like a butterfly pinned alive into an album."[24] Weil's image may suggest that some of us who are not traumatized see the afflicted as specimens bound for books.

I wonder what the white audience members sitting in New York's first integrated nightclub thought of "Strange Fruit," the protest song with which Billie Holiday closed each performance. The agreement was that the song always came last and no encore would follow; waiters had to stop serving food and drink while the spotlight was on Holiday alone. Over a few soft piano notes in the background, her raspy voice bore witness to the painful history of lynchings. She begins the first verse at an agonizingly slow pace, each word accentuating the terrible metaphor: "Southern trees bear a strange fruit / Blood on the leaves and blood at the root / Black bodies swingin' in the Southern breeze / Strange fruit hangin' from the poplar trees."

The song was written by a white, Jewish schoolteacher, Abel Meeropol, after he viewed a photograph-turned-postcard from the 1930 lynching of Thomas Shipp, Abram Smith, and James Cameron. The photograph shows two of the young Black men dangling from ropes, below them a crowd of white onlookers posing for photos in what one historian called a "carnival of white supremacy."[25] Not being able to get the grotesque image out of his mind, Meeropol wrote a poem, "Bitter Fruit," which he later set to music and renamed "Strange Fruit." When Holiday began performing it in 1939 (recording it that same year), her bare voice only accentuated the horror clad in rhyming couplets. She allowed her audience no embellishment, prettification, outer frame. With sparse piano behind, and outer darkness beyond, the spotlighted Holiday told the truth of America's brutalization of Black bodies so directly that the audience couldn't look away. The song is awful and sublime. It leaves the listener without recourse to mediating factors or rationalizations. Our stomachs churn and knees feel weak, as though standing before a vast and violent sea.

Weil says affliction always includes physical pain but never physical pain alone; psychological distress and social degradation distinguish affliction of the soul from other forms of bodily suffering. Writes Weil, "Affliction hardens and discourages us because, like a red hot iron, it stamps the soul to its very depths with the scorn, the disgust, and even the self-hatred and sense of guilt and defilement that crime logically should produce but actually does not." Weil suggests that those not suffering attack the afflicted with the necessity of animal instincts or the laws of physics: "Men have the same carnal nature as animals. If a hen is hurt, the others rush upon it, attacking it with their beaks. This phenomenon is as automatic as gravitation. Our senses attach all the scorn, all the revulsion, all the hatred that our reason attaches to crime, to affliction."[26] In other words, distinguishing guilt from innocence is (or should be) the function of reason; those who have perpetrated crimes are tried and punished through rational deliberation. By contrast, when faced with images of affliction—Floyd taking his final breaths, strange fruit hanging from poplar trees—we feel the scorn and disgust at this senseless death far below the level of reason. Our revulsion before police brutality is not a conclusion to deliberation. It is immediate in time and space. It follows the spectacle spontaneously. It is felt in bones and blood.

This partly explains why video footage of Black men and women dying at the hands of police divides people from one another and even individuals from themselves. Those of us not traumatized by the fear of white supremacy watch, and we are spontaneously, suitably disgusted. But we are also told not to let our visceral judgments get the best of us. If we study the footage objectively, take a different frame of reference, and see things from the police officers' point of view, we might just rationally conclude that the use of force is "objectively reasonable." Such was the final verdict about the deadly force used against twelve-year-old Tamir Rice, who in 2015 was playing in a Cleveland park with a toy gun and was justifiably—"reasonably"—perceived as a threat.[27]

Two things seem different when it comes to the death of George Floyd and the anger and fire and resolve and uprisings that follow in its wake. First, the almost nine minutes of prolonged agony is much too long to be able to neatly frame and explain by considering other points of view. Unlike the recording of a split-second shooting, there is no place to pause and "more objectively" reconstruct the point of view of the police officer. Chauvin's face is right above Floyd's. He sees and hears everything we see and hear and still remains calm, cool, and unsympathetic. No one can tell us to reframe and reevaluate a split-second decision enacted in a moment of adrenaline and confusion.

Even if Floyd had, a few minutes before, refused to get into the squad car, or resisted arrest, or was slow to show his hands, for eight minutes and forty-six seconds Chauvin, the eyewitnesses, and now millions more see a handcuffed man face down in the street, hear him crying "I can't breathe" at least sixteen times, hear him murmuring "Mama I love you—tell my kids I love them" before breathing his last and giving up the ghost. There is simply no objective, reasonable frame that could or should qualify our natural, human response to this. To suspend our judgments would feel like suspending our humanity.

Second, as people take to the streets in Minneapolis and throughout the world, their cries for justice are burning hot, and the heat feels hotter than in years past. True, protests that started in Ferguson following the shooting of Michael Brown Jr. (2014) or in Baltimore following the death of Freddie Gray Jr. (2015) also sparked nationwide demonstrations that lasted for months. Still, something feels more tempestuous, infectious, and unbounded this time. Maybe more propitious.

Like standing before a furious sea, the excessive nature of the aftermath is unnerving. Its sparks have erupted into violence, including state violence wielded by the National Guard and police in riot gear. The violence from protesters is also frustrating, especially for organizers and relatives of the deceased. "My family is a peaceful family," Terrence Floyd, the brother of George Floyd, said today when he visited the corner of Thirty-Eighth Street and Chicago, which now is blocked off with a circle of flowers. "I understand y'all are upset," he said, "but I doubt y'all are half as upset as I am. So if I'm not here wilin' out, if I'm not out here blowin' up stuff, if I'm not out here messin' up my community, then what are y'all doin'?" Three days ago, Breonna Taylor's sister, Ju'Niyah Palmer, said much the same: "At this point y'all are no longer doing this for my sister! You guys are just vandalizing stuff for NO reason."[28] Despite their pleadings, cries and shouts at organized rallies continue to give way to the battle cries of warring factions. Violence should be condemned; especially that of militarized police forces, whose response to—and provocation of—low-level street violence both fans the flames and frames them as civil war.

But beyond fires, rubber bullets, and tear gas, the protests themselves are unleashing a spirit that is hard to describe or contain. As they spill into each new day and spread like Pentecost across the globe, the legion of vigils, chants, protests, sit-ins, rallies, and marches mean more than morality and language can get a handle on. Again here, the unrest following the deaths of Freddie Gray, Michael Brown, and many others suggests that the situation now is not unprecedented. Yet we do seem to be reaching a tipping point in our racial reckoning. Jennifer Cobbina, a criminology professor and author of *Hands Up, Don't Shoot*, repeatedly describes the killing of Floyd as "egregious" and so "pretty much impossible to justify." Given the egregiousness, the senselessness, "you see a number of people horrified and outraged—people who typically weren't in the cases of Michael Brown or Freddie Gray or many others."[29]

To decide whether any one protest is good or bad seems like a category mistake, like defending or condemning the sublime. We argue over how to frame it. Is this a riot, with people caught up in opportunistic looting and arson? An uprising, with people swept up in the winds of justice? Both may be true. The point is that there is much more here than the indictment of police officers or the personal responsibility of others involved in violence, as important as each may be. There is a kind of transcendence—the whooshing up of the spirit of a people and others who ride the wave.[30]

Before ascending into heaven, the risen Jesus told his followers to wait in Jerusalem for the coming of the Holy Ghost (Acts 1:4–5 KJV). It happened at Pentecost, when believers from around the world together heard a "sound from heaven like the roaring of a mighty windstorm" (Acts 2:2 NLT). Tongues of fire descended on them, they were filled with the Spirit, and then they began to speak in other languages. People from around the ancient world were together swept up. They could all hear in their own languages "the wonderful things God has done" and yet remained perplexed (Acts 2:11–12 NLT). Too much meaning, excess on all sides. Nothing to name and frame it. "What can this mean?" they asked (Acts 2:12 NLT). Others had a quick explanation for the wildness: "They're just drunk, that's all" (Acts 2:13 NLT). That tries to pin it live in a book, where certainly it cannot stay.

EVOLUTION OF EMPATHY—JUNE 7, 2020

Yesterday, Laura and I biked to the Seaford Building, an old clothing plant that has been refurbished to house Closet-2-Closet, a nonprofit that distributes clothes to foster kids, and The House—a Local Church, a nondenominational church pastored by Gregg Hampton. (Laura hopes that the remaining third of the building, currently unfinished, will become NEST Café, the pay-what-you-can restaurant she plans to open next spring.) In the parking lot under the hot sun, we joined an event for religious and civic leaders aimed at unifying the community to protect and cherish Black bodies.

The organizer was Pastor Daniel Teague Jr., a Black minister who leads New Life Kingdom Ministries as well as "Boots on the Ground," a community-organizing program addressing racial justice. Pastor Teague and others spoke of uniting churches across our community to address systemic injustices, food deserts, police brutality, and other sins. A Black woman performed a spoken word poem that lasted eight minutes and forty-six seconds—the length of time that Derick Chauvin pinned his knee to George Floyd's neck. A city council member implored the crowd to call the mayors of our cities first thing on Monday to inquire about how the area's police are held accountable for protecting the most vulnerable. A Muslim imam recited verses from the Qur'an and prayed for justice. A scholar-activist recited some of the ugly history of the intimate relationship between the white church and white supremacy, including how white ministers reconfigured salvation to mean the salvation of disembodied souls in heaven so that Black bodies here on Earth could continue to be owned, flogged, raped, bred, lynched, and patrolled by Christians.

Pastor Gregg, who is white, was invited up to the mic to speak as well. I've known him since he and I coached little league together five years ago. An evangelical Christian devoted to relationship building, Gregg's sincerity first struck me as all too carefully cultured. His eye contact lasted just a bit too long. He'd give out a game ball to a player after the game while giving a talk that, to my ears, was always just about to mention Jesus. I say this to confess my own prejudices against a certain brand of Christianity, which Gregg represented to me, and over and against which I have carefully crafted my own religious identity. Perhaps my misgivings about Gregg's way with me and our players (did it show?) confirmed Gregg's earliest assumption that a religion professor teaching at the local Lutheran college is more concerned with respecting the neutral, secular space of classrooms and ballfields than he is in spreading the gospel. A year later, this low-level, mutual apprehension gave way to more important things.

Gregg's son (Gabe's teammate) contracted a rare and mysterious virus that eventually led to the paralysis of half his body. Laura and I followed each misdiagnosis, airlift to a new hospital, and consultation with a new team of specialists over social media. When I saw Gregg writing a sermon in a local coffee shop after his son finally returned home with a tracheostomy, wheelchair, and diagnosis of acute flaccid myelitis (AFM), I told him that my family had been praying nightly for their family, which we had. Sitting across from Gregg, the same interpersonal intimacy that used to make me uncomfortable now seemed like clear windows into the rich faith of a Christian. I assume that faith was sculpted by the undulations of suffering and prayer that had rolled over the last half year of his life. He had been loving what he could not save; his eyes softened on account of it.

Gregg stepped up to the microphone yesterday with a shaky voice and folded face, already taking in the story he was about to share. He spoke about an early visit to the hospital, after his son lost full use of his arm. The family had been told that there was probably a simple explanation for the strange symptoms and that life would go back to normal soon enough. Father was helping son go to the bathroom in the hospital when the boy began mumbling, "I can't breathe." Gregg ran into the hallway. "My son can't breathe," he shouted. "My son can't breathe. This is not normal."

Gregg said that any parent would run into the hallway when their son or daughter couldn't breathe. He said that half of Liam's body still isn't well and that half of America still isn't well. That is not normal, he said, and we shouldn't pretend that it is. It's not normal when any of our sons and daughters cry out that they can't breathe, as did Eric Garner, as did George Floyd, as do protestors in cities throughout the world. We need to run out into the hallway, into the streets, into police precincts and city halls, and cry out that our sons and daughters can't breathe.

I don't know what the other participants standing on the hot asphalt thought of this white preacher recalling the time when his white son gasped for air, using it as a way of relating to George Floyd and BLM protestors. Having already seen Gregg go on loving what he cannot save, having seen him go on witnessing to Christian hope, I was convinced and convicted by his words.

* * *

Since yesterday afternoon, I've been wondering about how empathy evolves. How does a father so embroiled in fear for his own child come to fear for other children? Or more difficult still, how does interpersonal care and concern, one that has already evolved from being directed at my child to your child, then also make the evolutionary leap to think and act in terms of systems and structures?[31] This is the question of whether and how people can find solidarity in shared suffering. It is perhaps the most important question for our nation in times of crisis, when we seem to be anything but "in this together."

Simone Weil says that people flee from the suffering of others as predictably as gravity or turn on them as naturally as hens pecking at another's blood. Compassion, she says, is something of a miracle, and one for which we should pray. Naturally, we flee and fight; only by the light of supernatural grace can we see what another is going through, and so stand and wait for God with them.[32]

Martin Luther agrees. For him, the entropy of the heart turning in on itself becomes our second nature. This sin-sick, turned-in heart will not and cannot love another for the other's sake. So strong is the ego's vortex, in fact, that even the strongest, most willful love remains motivated, at least in part, by what the lover can get out of it. *Caritas* becomes mere charity, a material down payment on spiritual reward.

Only God can silence the ego's storm. When God does so, justifying the person "by grace through faith," God loves them gratuitously, without kickbacks, with a love without a why or wherefore. Trusting this, the person is finally free to love another the same way. Completely, miraculously loved, they spontaneously look around and finally see what another is going through. How can I help? they ask. Idle and blessed, they have nothing else to do. True love of neighbor follows grace as naturally as a fruit tree blossoms in spring. That's Luther's favorite metaphor for neighbor love—the fruit of grace. Negatively construed, he means you can't force it, at least when left to your own stormy heart. Positively said, empathic attention and agape love quite naturally bloom out of the gratitude and joy of those who know they are loved by God.[33]

I believe this—or want to. I also think that it begs the question of how Pastor Gregg can pass from protective fear for his own son toward the same for the sons and daughters of others. The story of transformation he tells pivots on a learned solidarity in suffering. Can pain, like grace, bring people together? Again, this, for me, has become the central question of these pandemics. Can we build community on loss, come together in solidarity of suffering? It is also a question of how the pandemic of COVID-19 comes to include, or passes into, or seems to be giving way to (at least by way of our focus) the pandemic of structural racism and the social unrest that has followed. I wonder whether *compassion*—literally, suffering (*passio*) with (*com*) another—can emerge from one already in pain. If it cannot, is compassion then only available to the sheltered, who unilaterally bestow it on the needy? If, alternatively, those already suffering can also suffer with others, then by what miraculous transformation does pain added to pain issue in something other than increased pain?

The book of Job tells the story of an innocent and righteous man, Job, who loses everything after God accepts Satan's wager regarding whether Job will still praise God when his life is stripped of everything and he is left to lament on a dung heap. Job's friends bestow their quiet compassion for a full seven days, longer than most would last. But the compassion gets old, or doesn't really seem to be doing much, and they resort to explaining why Job's suffering is just. You, Job, must have done something wrong, they say. Perhaps God is teaching you a lesson. What doesn't kill you makes you stronger.

The back and forth between the friends' explanations and Job's lamentations goes round and round for thirty-five chapters. Nothing seems to happen, at least at first glance. According to Gustavo Gutiérrez, the father of Latin American liberation theology, Job does in fact undergo a subtle, critical transformation, which is discernible when one reads from the perspective of the poor. Job goes from defending himself and blaming God to defending the poor and scrutinizing unjust social and economic factors that ensure that they remain poor (see especially Job 24). Somehow, the acuteness of his own affliction enables him to see the plight of the poor, the alien, the outcast, and all those on the underside of history.[34]

Perhaps if we could read the hearts and minds of those who have taken to the streets in the last two weeks to protest police brutality, we would see a similar transformation. Perhaps they are chanting "I can't breathe" and demanding the defunding of police not despite but because they first felt the pain of the other pandemic; they came to see the structural injustices that determined who is most susceptible and so now respond by attending to the injustices that lie beneath both tragedies. Perhaps those with plac-ards and milk to pour on teargassed eyes are also frontline workers. Theirs would be a transformation similar to that of the Good Samaritan, who, despite suffering—or again, *because* he suffers—from prejudice against Samaria and the legalized injustices inscribing it, attends to another in pain.

Weil says that all an afflicted person can do is to resist and to love. People can resist the "poison of inertia" that accompanies affliction, an inclosing that prevents them from seeing both the suffering and the salva-tion that others bear. Resistance, itself, is by way of that love. "Through all the horror," writes Weil, the afflicted one "can continue to want to love."[35]

DEAR AMY—JUNE 15, 2020

Dear Amy,

I am writing to you from my mother's apartment in the northeastern suburbs of Minneapolis. Perhaps I should be writing this letter to her. My mom has been isolated in her apartment near White Bear Lake for months now. This past weekend my family and I made the six-hour trip up north, eating fast-food in the car and peeing in gas stations with our masks on. We fished in the lake and took turns paddling her kayak and went for walks and argued about the looting of Target, the burning of Minneapolis's Third Precinct police station, and all the unrest over the past two weeks. My mother says she agrees with the protests and that Black Lives Matter, but that the looting and senseless violence cross a line. I remind her that we are talking about the destruction of property and not of human life and that difference gets blurred in news reports. She calls it a riot. I call it an uprising. I'm not sure either of us is optimistic that needed reform will come out of it.

I am grateful for a mother with whom I can discuss such things. I know very little about you, Amy, but have reason to think we could understand one another. The video of you threatening to call the police on Christian Cooper—the Black bird-watcher in Central Park who asked you to put your dog on a leash and then filmed you concocting distress—and then telling the 911 dispatcher that an "African American man" was threatening you and your dog went viral just hours before George Floyd died in Minneapolis, fifteen or so miles from where I safely sit now.

Perhaps I should be writing a letter to my mother, or my sons, rather than to you. James Baldwin writes *The Fire Next Time* as a letter to the nephew who is named after him on the one hundredth anniversary of the Emancipation. Ta-Nehisi Coates writes *Between the World and Me* to his fifteen-year-old son, explaining, "I am writing you because this was the year you saw Eric Garner choked to death for selling cigarettes" and that "you know now, if you did not before, that the police departments of your country have been endowed with the authority to destroy your body." Imani Perry begins *Breathe: A Letter to My Sons* scrutinizing the crude pity and sadistic curiosity of people who say offhandedly, "it must be terrifying to raise a black boy in America." She addresses her boys directly: "My sons, you are not a problem. Mothering you is not a problem. It is a gift. A vast one. A breathtaking one, beautiful. One that makes me pray for an unmercenary spirit about what I am here to do, never considering it a burden or worthy of particular praise."[36]

My children—like my mother—are white and privileged, besides being beautiful, gifted, and loved by God. I may find the words to write to family members about privilege and grace and how easily they are confused in America. But today, Amy, I am writing to you—another white adult beneficiary of a white supremacist culture who, in a moment of stress or impatience, surrounded by a cloud of racist scripts that neither of us invented but which we know verbatim and readily employ, marshaled authorities to save yourself from the fabricated threat of a Black man and, more to the point, from your own unfounded, underlying fears. You and I can have Black people arrested. That's near the heart of our white privilege. They will be assumed guilty, and we will be assumed innocent. People surround us who know the script as well as we do. That includes armed police, as well as Black people themselves. Christian Cooper knew all too well the script of a white woman in Central Park calling 911 and saying that a Black man was threatening her. He also—I find this amazing—had such presence of mind that he began filming early in your encounter, knowing that the presumption of guilt against him would need hard evidence to overturn. In a flash of misunderstanding (such as the flash of bird-watching binoculars that could be seen as a gun), you or I can have a Black person killed. That's white privilege at its base—repulsive and shameful but true.

I have also called the police when I didn't need to do so. For me, too, it was a way out of a conflict that I should have endured and that could have been reconciled in interpersonal ways. Did you make the call not only because you could, or because you felt threatened, but also because, when Christian Cooper pointed his camera at you, you already saw what others would see? Did you feel the script exposed and so try even more frantically to incant it? Is this why your phony accusation climbed to a feverish pitch when you screamed into your phone that an "African American man" was trying to assault you?

Sure, our particular scripts diverge, often where gender intersects with race. Yours is the well-worn tale of the Black rapist versus the white woman in distress, hysterical with unbounded fear. Mine is the white man all too coolly making the seemingly rational, responsible, and defensible decision to involve the authorities, tragic as the case may be. The scripts overlap more than either of us might want to admit. In your public apology to Mr. Cooper, you asked that he (and we) not let a few seconds of fearful misjudgment overshadow an otherwise ethical life. When I named my sin to a pastor, it was also, at least in part, a way to contain the guilt, to set it aside as the exception to the rule. You and I know that what we desperately want to be peccadillos are essentially revelations of how whiteness works in our country and lives.

The Black social ethicist and priest Fr. Bryan Massingale wrote about us in his essay for the *National Catholic Reporter* last week. He says that you, Amy Cooper, "hold the key" to understanding what happened not only to Christian Cooper but also to Ahmaud Arbery, Breonna Taylor, and George Floyd, as well as to all the Black, Hispanic, and Indigenous people who have disproportionately suffered and died from COVID-19. (They, too, are tacitly assumed to be guilty of their "choice" to be unhealthy, poor, or dirty and so deserve to suffer more than those who are "right-because-white.") Those sixty-nine seconds of cell-phone footage reveal what you and I won't say aloud and yet know to be true and can invoke when need or convenience warrants. In Massingale's terms, you and I assume that the frame of a Black man threatening a white woman will be clearly understood by the police, the press, and the public. You and I assume that we can exploit the deeply ingrained white fears of Black men—or, in my case, the perceived sacredness of white property and the expendability of a destitute Black woman. We assume that we will be believed and will have the presumption of innocence *precisely because* those deemed Black will not. (It has taken me some time to get to the *precisely because*, and I admit that I still only understand it abstractly. It is one thing to say that some are underprivileged and others over-privileged; another to say that the very benefits I enjoy *burden* people of color.)[37]

Even if we explicitly call on the scripts only rarely, we live with and within them whenever we do not actively choose a different story. What's unique about the present moment is just how exposed our scripts have become. There are revelations all around—the cell phones of bystanders record them—and each is a window into the others. I'm guessing that you have watched the video of Officer Derek Chauvin, under whose knee George Floyd cried out for breath, mercy, and his dead mother. I have watched it only once. Above the sickening sight of a dying man, I saw the face of another fanatically and fiercely—and all too stoically—adhering to the script that we know. Chauvin's cold and collected posture resembled mine more than yours. I will say it: I see myself in him.

I know that you have been fired from your job, and maybe that is just. You've also been harassed on social media, which isn't just, at least not according to Christian Cooper, who is uncomfortable with the frenzy his video put in motion. Again with the composure of someone who reads what's going on, Cooper says, "If our goal is to change the underlying factors, I am not sure that this young woman having her life completely torn apart serves that goal." Now you have also received death threats, and again it is Cooper protecting you, protecting us, from the very violence we've conjured. The threats against you are "wholly inappropriate and abhorrent and should stop immediately," Christian Cooper said. "I find it strange that people who were upset that she tried to bring death by cop down on my head, would then turn around and try to put death threats on her head. Where is the logic in that? Where does that make any kind of sense?"[38]

The logic is perverse, but it does make sense. For as soon as the script of white supremacy is brought to light, recorded for all to see, people will, out of shame that shape-shifts into righteous anger, do whatever they can to cover the revelation right back up. If we can scapegoat you, if you and Chauvin and others like you can be properly stereotyped and bear the sin of us all, then we can banish you through legal means and with our cancel culture. And if that doesn't work, we can always threaten violence. We can get rid of you, you who reveal and bear our sin, and so come back together, our presumed innocence fully restored.

The portrayal of you as beyond forgiveness and reconciliation with the community (there is talk of prohibiting you from Central Park), this canceling of solitary sinners, is itself of exactly the same script, the very one you called on when you cried wolf in Central Park. Black people typically pay the price so that white people can believe they are innocent. The fact that your role has shifted from damsel to demon hasn't changed the script; it hasn't, says Christian Cooper, "changed the underlying factors."

Where on Earth do we go from here? I don't clearly know. I have been writing about repentance when I thought I would be writing about neighbor love. I thought that I would be finding ways to reach out to others during this time of crisis, but as COVID has done its own shape-shifting to reveal structural sins underneath, I find myself remembering backward and reaching inward—confessing sin in lieu of outwardly loving. Equally as surprising, there turn out to be as many barriers within as without—logjams where the currents of my confessions turn to eddies, churning in on themselves.

But repent we must. There's no other way forward. As C. S. Lewis wrote in *Mere Christianity*, "We all want progress. But progress means getting nearer to the place where you want to be. And if you have taken a wrong turning, then to go forward does not get you any nearer. If you are on the wrong road, progress means doing an about-turn and walking back to the right road."[39]

I don't know if you, Amy, call yourself a Christian or what that means if you do. To me, it means that the road toward love of our neighbors necessarily winds through places we don't want to go. We've got to repent from the sin of wielding our whiteness. It will be hard to see that sin exposed, especially if you believe that, at some point here or in the world beyond, all of it will be *utterly* exposed, a time when all our usual strategies of hiding from one another and from God are made *utterly* useless.[40] Lewis says that, at that time, only two options will be available—to suffer the truth of who we have become and the pain of being born anew, or to cling to our privilege, hellishly hoping that it can somehow shield us from truth and joy.[41]

I am a Christian and so believe that all our loves can be redeemed. I believe that the joy of what King called the beloved community and what Jesus and the prophets call the kingdom of God will be much better than the spoils afforded by whiteness. In the meantime, says Adam Clayton Powell, the Black Baptist pastor from the Harlem Renaissance, repentance will be painful: "No one has ever turned from sin until he has felt the evil effects of sin so keenly that he [or she] cries with Isaiah: 'Woe is me for I am undone.'"[42]

May our pain be productive.

Yours truly,
Jason

MINDING THE GAP—JUNE 18, 2020

Before returning from Minnesota, I was able to spend a couple nights alone at Lake Hattie, camping and fishing at the Tuck-A-Way Resort, where my family vacationed when I was young, and where we returned with my aging father after doctors gave him a few months to live. Being there alone was quiet and peaceful and also a bit uncanny. The tranquil outdoors and memories of my childhood collided with all that has weighed on my heart these past weeks. I read a collection of essays examining Ta-Nehisi Coates's work on the same deck from which my father watched his grandchildren swim. Lying uncomfortably in the tent at night, I thought back to a day five years ago when I was lying face down in my college's coffee shop.

It was a Black Lives Matter die-in, organized by students of color—including D., a Black, nonbinary graduate of my college, who helped organize much of the students' activism work. I was supposed to be reflecting on Michael Brown, Eric Garner, and others who were killed at the intersection of white supremacy and state violence. Alas, I found myself wondering what other faculty were doing and whether the news cameras were pointed in my direction. I experienced the same self-conspicuousness some months later when I joined a rally and march organized by Latinx United students. In the wake of Trump's anti-immigration executive orders and while passing predominantly white, non-Hispanic alumni who were on campus for homecoming weekend, we chanted, "WHOSE HOME IS IT, ANYWAY?" I don't always know whether I am best positioned to shout out that cry, to silently support the students who do, or to hear it and respond.

I know that some of my anxieties about activism stem from inexperience. Before the BLM protests on campus, it had been fifteen years since I participated in marches in DC and Atlanta, and those were large and sanctioned. I had attended an "Anarchism and Christianity" gathering in Minneapolis, but only as a participant-observer and curious outsider. (I sat next to a fellow Christian who wore a T-shirt that read "Fuck the Police—but Love the Police Officer.") I have Catholic Worker friends who are currently awaiting trial after breaking into an Enbridge site to manually shut off the flow of tar sands oil, having prayerfully concluded that "it was necessary to take urgent action to address the severe and imminent threat posed by climate change."[43] When I bring my Environmental Ethics students to meet with the Catholic Workers on their farm in Wisconsin, I am a fellow student who is learning right beside other students about the nonviolent civil disobedience of others.

My anxieties also arose from the place and scope of my vocation as a professor of the college. In their protests, D. and other student leaders were, after all, publicly demanding that my college make institutional changes that would increase the sense of belonging of its nonwhite students. I didn't know, and still don't always know, how to live out my paid vocation as a religion teacher while also responding to the unfamiliar, powerful call to stand in solidarity with those critiquing the institution that pays me.

I've been thinking about this a lot this past week. I connected by phone with D., who attended Union Theological Seminary after graduating from college and is now back in their hometown of Chicago, working with Alternatives Youth and Family Services as a restorative justice coach and educator. They have helped me see that the very ways other educators and I often talk about vocation may be inconsequential or even a barrier to the deepest passions of some of our most courageous students. We need to rethink frameworks to better enable students to hear and heed the call to activism and social justice.[44] At the same time, students who feel called in this direction (and their numbers are multiplying) also have work to do. Often, when they consider the slow change that comes by working through established positions (e.g., going into politics in order to reform the police rather than insisting that it be defunded), they dismiss that work as uncourageous pandering to "the system." Admittedly, working through established roles and the system often *is* too slow, if not self-defeating; it sometimes only bolsters a system that needs to be dismantled. But just as often, political, economic, ecclesial (church), and other systems—including that of higher education—can harness, hold, and guide a person's passion for justice.

The mismatch between standard accounts of vocation and the passions of our most radical students can be seen in who is and is not helped by vocational exploration programs. The programs educators design for exploring vocation don't attract those most inclined to work for structural change through direct action, civil disobedience, and other forms of activism. This is so even if those engaged in *advocacy* work—work that uses established governmental and nongovernmental organization (NGO) positions to support and give voice to (*ad + vocare*) underrepresented groups and justice issues—are the *most* likely to participate. According to sociologist Tim Clydesdale, such advocates, or what he calls "reforming activists," are the first ones to volunteer at food banks, to attend discernment retreats, and to consider their work as a response to the needs of others.

Meanwhile, those students who have moved from advocacy to activism, for whom reforms to the system seem overly cautious or even amount to selling out, are perhaps the hardest to find in conversations about callings. Such radicals (or "rebels," as Clydesdale calls them) may not go to college at all or may quickly drop out, convinced that higher ed amounts to another bureaucratic institution that warrants rejection rather than reform. According to Clydesdale, "these students reject mainstream culture for its superficiality, academia for its hypocrisy, and reform as unattainable." If they do stay in school, they often inhabit the margins of campus life.[45]

For their part, educators need to support activism work, as well as respond openly and creatively to charges leveled at their own institutions in ways that bring such rebels into our schools, keep them enrolled, and move them in from the margins. This may entail reimagining the way we lead vocational discernment. Many colleges root their understandings of vocation in religious traditions that connect callings to official roles and offices rather than to the work of critically questioning those establishments. Ironically, this may be especially true for *Protestant* colleges and universities, whose name carries only distant echoes of sixteenth-century *protests*. Martin Luther wrote of a person's vocations in terms of the various positions within three "orders" or arenas of activity—that of the household, the state/government, and the church. (Today, we would add paid, nongovernmental work as a fourth sphere.) His driving question about vocation was whether soldiers and hangmen (his examples) are doing the work of God when they responsibly assume their prescribed duties. (His basic answer was yes.)[46]

Those questions tend to leave out our questions about whether people with or without sanctioned positions can still use their bodies and voices to abolish prisons, shut down oil pipelines, give sanctuary to undocumented people, or defund the police. The discrepancy shows up when we explicitly lead vocational reflection exercises, which, especially when too closely linked to career interest inventories, presuppose that we live within systems that generally work to serve the common good. Many colleges help students discern whether they should be a nurse or a doctor, a schoolteacher or social worker; we thus help plug students into the market, the nation-state, or other established spheres that can and do serve the common good. Except when they don't. Our discernment sessions will need to change in order to include critical consideration of who benefits from such systems, as well as who is left out, upon whose exploitation the systems are built in the first place.

The work before students is perhaps even more challenging. It is a good deal easier to discern whether or not to be a police officer, or investment banker, or pharmaceutical sales rep than to consider the systemic injustices of mass incarceration, global neoliberalism, and privatized health care. Doing the latter requires you to pay particular attention to moments when the injustices and suffering of the world are laid bare, which call you beyond employability to advocacy and even activism, beyond the use of established positions to the unsanctioned use of your voice and body.

Brian Mahan calls these powerful, disorienting moments "epiphanies of recruitment."[47] They typically include exposure to one form of suffering or another, followed by the summons to do all that one can to alleviate that suffering, often by personally accompanying those who suffer or mounting resistance against the systems that cause it. Meeting orphans in Guatemala or the working poor of Appalachia moves students to want to stay in those places, devoting their lives to works of love. Seeing bleached coral reefs in Australia motivates students to organize a climate strike on campus. I, too, know how powerful and important such epiphanies of recruitment are; I have experienced them while handing out teddy bears on a weekend retreat for people living with AIDS, and while listening to incarcerated students tell stories about their brokenness, repentance, and healing. The student A. had his in Pine Ridge, South Dakota, where he met members of the Oglala Lakota community and "decided to dedicate [his] life to serving people like them."

We should cherish these moments, moments when the meaning and purpose of our lives fall into place, when we know we are doing exactly what we ought to be doing and can imagine doing nothing else. However, Mahan also reminds us that the experience of being summoned and the resolve of our initial response typically fade, giving way to business as usual. We need to be honest with ourselves about the gap that inevitably exists between cataclysmic moments of recruitment and the work-a-day world of writing papers, getting to class, clocking into a work-study job, and being a good son, daughter, teammate, or friend. Standing in the gap is painful because we always feel that more is being asked of us than we are able to give right now.[48]

It is tempting to close the gap altogether. Typically, we do this by downplaying or even trying to forget the moments of recruitment, aware that they can distract us from our pressing daily obligations or lead to feelings of guilt. The most idealist, activist students alleviate the tension from the other side. They drop out of school or quit jobs that do not directly tap into their deepest passions (which would be most jobs). Some who are able may move to Guatemala to work with orphans or join Catholic Workers in their nonviolent civil disobedience. But for many of these students, getting out of the tainted systems of college, work, church, or politics is a whole lot easier than tapping into new roles and accepting new responsibilities. Too many of them are left with a purely negative sense of freedom, where nearly every official organization or conventional role (student, son, daughter, employee, citizen, church member) is rejected in the quest for a life of pure purpose. In wanting all or nothing, some are left with very little. Many of them are lonely.

Realistic students who too quickly forget their epiphanies of recruitment while settling into everyday duties need to actively remember and narrate what draws them forward, lest passing a class or building a longer résumé becomes an end in itself. Idealistic students who too quickly reject traditional roles and offices in the hopes of an authentic, uncompromised life need to recognize that change can come through imperfect structures, and that very little change happens without them. Both sides need to remain in the gap, learning how to move into and out of official roles, both using them to do good work and criticizing them for not working well enough. This is a delicate dance, and one that is never comfortable. I feel it when I use my official position at a college to amplify the voices of students protesting the ways of that college. Students feel it when they do homework in order to pass a class that they also walk out of during a climate strike.

Barbara Brown Taylor ends her book, *Holy Envy*, with the story of a protester who interrupts an outdoor worship service with an angry rant against organized religion. The congregation listens rather than silencing her. She eventually moves to the back of those gathered for worship, standing under a tree throughout the service, talking quietly with a member of the community. Taylor ends the story by asking whether remaining there put the woman "at the outer edge of the inside or the inner edge of the outside."[49] Those of us who critique institutions we love—whether a church, a college, or a democracy—and do so because we love them, are called to the margins, where we can move from the outermost inside to the innermost outside and back again, doing good work where it can be done while calling out injustices that must be undone.

Letting Go—June 29, 2020

In the two weeks following George Floyd's death, American support for Black Lives Matter has increased more than in the previous two years. By a twenty-eight-point margin, a majority of registered voters say they support the movement, up from a seventeen-point margin before the recent wave of protests. Over two-thirds take Floyd's death as revealing systemic issues; a *Washington Post* poll found that 69 percent of respondents say that his death is "a sign of broader problems in treatment of Black Americans by police" rather than an isolated incident. Another poll found that 76 percent of Americans now say racial and ethnic discrimination is "a big problem" in the United States.[50]

Four years ago, when Colin Kaepernick became a symbol of what the NFL could do to you if you didn't show proper allegiance to the country (and to the white-owned league), only 28 percent of Americans considered his nonviolent, silent protest of kneeling during the national anthem appropriate. Today, 52 percent of citizens agree that it is "OK for NFL players to kneel during the national anthem to protest police killings of African-Americans."[51] The NFL is quickly following the popular opinion. Two weeks ago, Commissioner Roger Goodell declared, "We, the National Football League, believe black lives matter. I personally protest with you and want to be part of the much-needed change in this country."[52] The NBA, trying to stay further ahead of the curve (and, really, to convince its activist players to return to the court), has said that it will allow players to display racial justice slogans on the back of jerseys. Today, it announced that "Black Lives Matter" would be printed on the courts in Orlando, where teams are scheduled to resume the 2019–20 season next month.

It is easy to be cynical about the NFL's ostensible change of heart or the NBA's need to defend its restart season as a valuable platform for social change. Being perceived as progressive and self-aware is important to each, as it is to countless companies who have been publicly declaring their support for BLM. Businesses must appear woke without appearing as if they only want to *look* woke. There are now branding consulting companies declaring that #BlackLivesMatter is not a trend but a movement, followed by a list of things your brand can do to stay relevant, be authentic, and successfully link products to the said movement. Likewise with the hashtags, likes, hearts, and black squares posted by individuals on Instagram, Facebook, Snapchat, and Twitter. In the open market for identity capital on social media, people present themselves as having reckoned with race almost as quickly as they call out the "performative activism" or "slacktivism" of others. Has there been a change of heart when it comes to Black lives, or is the race to wokeness simply trending right now?

My concern is how easily this burgeoning support might shrink in numbers, or more likely, fade in intensity when the next disaster strikes or the novelty simply wears off. It happens in the weeks that follow each school shooting and the initial uptick in support for gun safety laws. In terms of our present crises, I wonder whether some white people's new embrace of racial justice may already be a way to get beyond it. If we declare that Black Lives Matter, perhaps we can release ourselves from the painful, interminable process of repenting of our supremacist culture and personal privilege. Perhaps, too, our alleged emergence from prejudice is so clear and quick precisely because our emergence from COVID-19 has been muddled and protracted. In this summer of problems on problems, here finally is one where we can declare ourselves fixed and move on.

The common response to the inevitable entropy of compassion for any one issue (terror, oppression, and death are not, of course, "issues" for Black America) is to try to muster more political will to enact legislative change before the moment passes. That is certainly important. My musing over the past two months about feeling called to repentance indicates a different, more personal response, one that will seem like going backward, or worse, going nowhere at all.

Admittedly, when I think about white supremacy and my responsibility for perpetrating it, and then imagine repentance as a response, the sentiment nearly falls into the trap of wallowing in white guilt. Audre Lorde, speaking to white women in 1981, warned that "all too often, guilt is just another name for impotence, for defensiveness destructive of communication; it becomes a device to protect ignorance and the continuation of things the way they are, the ultimate protection for changelessness."[53] I take these words to heart. If getting on a racial justice bandwagon is no solution, neither is the unchanging continuation of the status quo under the banner of a more thorough reckoning.

Ideally, repentance for sin would be the way one moves forward in hope. Of course, the spatial metaphors of *forward* and *back* are here limited. They are also weighted in favor of the forward and future, and so personal introspection and remorse cannot but appear a bit backward. By contrast, when Jesus begins his public ministry by saying, "Repent, for the kingdom of heaven is at hand" (Matt 3:2 ESV), he links the imminent in-breaking of a radically new future with the commandment to turn around. Exactly because a new dawn is rising, one needs to go back through one's sin. Repentance is a turning inward and around—a reconfiguring of one's mind—so that one can see where God is breaking into the world.

We repent not only because we have done things and left things undone but also because the topsy-turvy reign of God, where the poor and marginalized are blessed and inherit the kingdom, requires that everyone with traditional understandings of power and implicit hierarchies of human value turn them inside out. For the oppressed, repentance may mean turning from hatred of the oppressors, which bears its own "deadly and bitter fruit," according to Howard Thurman. For those of us who benefit from the way things are, repentance means loosening our grasp of all the false security and pillaged spoils that privilege and power secure.[54]

Jesus embodied this ethic of repentance, this letting go. According to the early Christian hymn that Paul quotes in his letter to the Philippians, the very incarnation—God becoming flesh in the person of Jesus—is God's own turning around, God's letting go, God's emptying Godself of all power that is not the power of suffering love (Phil 2:6–11).

The life of Jesus continues to model this letting go. According to Kelly Brown Douglas, Jesus repeatedly "departs the space of the privileged class." He "fully divests himself of all pretensions to power, privilege, and exceptionalism." Determinative is his "free and steadfast identification with crucified bodies." Jesus enters Samaritan space. He leaves his own cherished male Jewish space to be with the bodies of Samaritan women (see John 4:1–25). He lets go of anything that would compromise absolute allegiance with those whose marginalization and exploitation would otherwise fuel his privilege.[55]

Jesus's death is the culmination of this life of letting go. Despite popular images of Jesus flinging himself toward death in heroic resolve to ransom sinners or appease an angry God, the gospels testify that Jesus wants to die no more than the rest of us. Only after a life so well practiced in letting go is he able to let go of his life as well. He submits to torture and death by crucifixion, which is essentially the Roman Empire's preferred method of lynching. He does so to expose the so-called power of empire and supremacy in all its fear and terror, and to witness, by contrast, to the power that comes through friendship and compassion. What Luther calls theologians of the cross will find God fully, paradoxically revealed especially here, in Jesus's solidarity with "the crucified class" (Douglas), even unto death on a cross. "God can be found only in suffering and the cross," says Luther. "God is where the crucified are," says Douglas.[56]

It can be hard to know what letting go of privilege and living a life of repentance look like on the ground. Douglas says that white Christians need to physically leave their cherished white spaces to be where God is, with the poor and oppressed.[57] The higher education leader Darby Ray says that colleges need to develop more immersive community engagement experiences, experiences that "challenge us to be radically open to those whose life stories are often dramatically different than our own and to allow our own story to be re-made under the impress of that connection."[58] Whether it is church members leaving their sanctuaries or college students leaving their campus bubbles, letting go of and turning from traditional understandings of knowledge and power will take practice.

For me, writing out these reflections has been part of that practice. My writing has felt like paying attention and thus like prayer. But I also know that introverts like me who find sanctuary in leather-bound journals need to give up that security, too, in order to be with others more practiced at loving neighbors and to try to learn from them, as awkward and humbling as that is. Compassion—literally, suffering with others—cannot be learned except by committing to be with others and remaining there, even when it is painful to do so. I, like everyone else, continue to long for the end of COVID-19, of this summer of racialized violence and political unrest, and even (on some days) of my commitment to reflect on it all. I—and we—need to remain, to let go of our fantasies about just moving on, so that compassion and hope can take root exactly where we are.

PART 3

THESE THREE REMAIN

(July and August)

LAND OF THE FREE FOR OTHERS—JULY 4, 2020

The prophet Joel declared that in the last days, when God pours out God's spirit on all flesh, young men will see visions, and old men will dream dreams. I'm still middle-aged, but last night I had my first COVID dream.

I am on a bus that turns out to be an amusement park ride inside the Mall of America with Asa, my older son. The ride is packed, and I am painstakingly explaining to Asa why it is safe to be on it, even without masks; we are all facing the same direction, and the Mall of America is so big that it is almost like being outside. Besides, the ride has so many twists and turns that respiratory droplets are thrown from the car in every direction other than toward the person in the car behind.

The ride must have brought us to Chicago, because we are now in a coffee shop on the North Side, where I ask the interfaith leader Eboo Patel (a real person I respect immensely) whether he and his wife walked there. Yes, he says; it took twenty-five-and-a-half minutes from their house, but they walk everywhere because it is the only safe way to get around. I am self-conscious of the fact that we arrived on a crowded roller coaster and wonder whether Eboo knows this. It dawns on me that we are sipping hot cocoa inside a coffee shop, so it must be winter, except it isn't, and the pandemic must be over, except it's not. Eboo introduces his wife, Shehnaz, who dons a fake multicolored mustache and beard. I slowly realize that her flamboyant facial hair is really a stylish *niquab* (a Muslim face covering) and then that it is really just a face mask for the safety of us all.

The dream ends with Eboo and Shehnaz putting my bike (I had a bike?) on the back of their black van with red racing stripes that looks like the one from the 1980's TV show *The A-Team*. They let me drive and we are catching up to Asa, who is either fleeing or leading the way on his own bike, bobbing up and down on the side of the road like a snowmobiler in north country. We stop the van so that Eboo can drive, but while he and his wife are taking my bike off the rack, the van starts rolling backward. I am pumping the brakes, but to no avail; the van is picking up speed. As it is about to roll over Shehnaz, I can only think to scream, "It's not my fault!"

Call it the subconscious, or soul, or any other name for the faculty by which young men see visions and old men dream dreams; a corner of mine seems absorbed with explaining why we can't go on acting vigilantly forever and why I am not responsible if amusement park riders or the spouses of interfaith leaders happen to get hurt from my actions. (The real Eboo Patel and his family are faring OK, which he let me know when I recounted this dream to him.)

Reading back over what I have written this summer, I realize that much of it oscillates between minimizing human control in the wake of tragedy and maximizing individual responsibility, even for that which one didn't choose. Earlier entries worried that we would try to fix and solve a pandemic rather than learn how to bear and endure it. When a second pandemic of systemic racism fully manifested itself, I saw more clearly the opposing risk—namely, that white people like me might chalk up unnecessary death and despair to the bad luck of tragedy, or relegate responsibility to a few bad apples in comparison with which the rest of us can consider ourselves innocent. I fluctuate between fearing a false sense of control and trying to own my sinful desire to be lily-white innocent. If my dream is any indication, the oscillation continues. Responsibility is hard. I want some time off. Maybe Shehnaz was just unlucky to be run over by the A-Team van. It's not my fault.

Perhaps this back and forth between emphasizing that which exceeds our control (like death) and taking responsibility for that which we do not necessarily choose (like the sin of racism) amounts to flip-flopping. An ethicist or psychoanalyst might have me more carefully consider who and what are within my sphere of ethical responsibility. But that's easier in principle than in practice, especially during public health crises and in the wake of other "natural" catastrophes, which we know are also influenced by climate change and other factors related to human choice. In our Anthropocene age, there simply isn't a storm, flood, fire, or drought that is not both natural and influenced by the decisions of humans, especially by those living in the most prosperous countries. We are now almost always responsible, at least in part, for the tragedies responsible for hurting us, the coronavirus included.[1]

*   *   *

It's July 4, Independence Day, the day that we celebrate the freedom of our country and the individual liberties of its residents. Having more freedom is almost always better than having less. For me, though, the crises that we are living through reveal just how burdensome freedom can be, as well as how much responsibility and accountability individuals with the freedom to make decisions must bear. Many of us long for others to bear the freedom and just be told what to do. We want to maximize individual choice while minimizing responsibility for others—especially now, when every decision we are asked to make is potentially fraught with life-and-death consequences.

The desire to maximize individual liberty and minimize the responsibility for that liberty characterizes almost every negotiation that I see, hear, and participate in these days. For example, when the mayor of my town canceled the "Red, White, and Bomb" fireworks display for the Fourth of July, the mayor of the city across the Mississippi announced that they would host their own fireworks display ("Star Spangled Extravaganza"), saying individuals—not city leaders—should decide what is best. "If you think it's too much, don't come," the mayor said. "We encourage everyone to socially distance. If you want to sit in your car, sit in your car. Do what you think is best." Alas, a week or so later, he announced, "the City has determined it best to postpone the Star Spangled Extravaganza." He seemed sheepish about having to decide what is best for others, admitting "that this decision will disappoint some people."[2]

Business owners have to decide whether to enforce local or state rules about mask wearing, social distancing, capacity limits, and so forth, merely to post them and let patrons make their own decisions, or ignore them altogether. Families like mine with school-aged children are now being surveyed by school districts about our "preferences" and "levels of comfort" concerning a possible return to in-person school in a month.

College students and their families used to sit in front of financial aid packages with calculators and charts about projected earnings and decide whether college was worth it. Now the options have grown, and the question of worth is taking on existential weight. The stakes couldn't be higher. Students recognize all that they may be giving up if they stay online or drop out; residential liberals arts colleges are about immersive, in-person learning, learning that entails holistic growth (in "mind, body, and spirit") and requires whole persons to live, work, study, play, and eat beside other whole persons. Yet if the students return, they risk exposure, illness, and loneliness. They may not be able to go home when they want to or return to campus if they do. Enrolling may feel like enlisting.

I thought that this weighty decision whether to put lives at stake for the sake of education was unprecedented for all except some international students who risk so much to study in the United States. One domestic student, A., who grew up in the Chicago suburbs, corrected me. "Our generation has grown up with school shootings," she said. "Each time we show up for school following a shooting, we are talking with friends about whether it is worth it." That question—is it really *worth* it—is not the same as the utilitarian calculus that typically characterizes decisions about getting a degree. Whatever the answer, it is less a conclusion than a leap of faith.

Even seemingly small decisions, such as participating in youth sports, can involve intricate and principled deliberations about what is best, followed by a decision simply to let each person make their own decision, avoiding the responsibility (and blame) for either canceling a season or getting others sick. When the baseball team of my younger son, Gabe, received permission to have something of a season this summer, our online deliberations with other parents began with sharing concerns, followed by some rather deep listening and an agreement to do what was best for the most vulnerable (at least one parent has a severely compromised immune system). But rule by consensus is extremely difficult, and we are all rather unpracticed at it. As of now, the team will participate to the full degree that it is permitted to do so, and each family gets to opt in or out—and then sign liability waivers.

I think of the second great commandment, or "the Golden Rule," shared by Jews and Christians and (with some differences) by other religious traditions as well: You shall love your neighbor as yourself (Lev 19:18; Mark 12:31; Matt 22:39; Luke 10:27). The key word seems to be *as*. To love the neighbor as yourself is to take personal responsibility for those who are "outside" one's own personhood. While many of us long for more consistent and clear governing by authorities, that calling is, in principle, shared by all within a democracy, or a team, or a campus. It is becoming painfully clear that curbing this public health crisis depends on making decisions based on the health and safety of other people and the whole community, above and beyond one's self-concern.

For example, if and when a vaccination for the coronavirus is found, each individual will have the right to decide for themselves whether they will get vaccinated or not. That is as it should be. Still, both the benefits and the burden of those individual choices are experienced by the whole. Eula Biss, author of *On Immunity*, reminds us that immunity is not an individual shield that covers the borders of a person's body. We rather need to "think of vaccination as a kind of banking of immunity. Contributions to this bank are donations to those who cannot or will not be protected by

137

their own immunity." Unvaccinated people are protected when they are surrounded by those who are vaccinated, just as vaccinated people are made more vulnerable when they are surrounded by the unvaccinated. According to Biss, "we are protected not so much by our own skin, but by what is beyond it."[3] When my wife and I are asked about our preferences and comfort level in surveys about in-person school for our kids or are trying to decide whether Gabe can play baseball, we should also be thinking of the health of the whole. We should be making deposits into a common trust from which others draw their health, even as we draw ours from the health of the whole.

That's not easy—for any of us. The foundational myths of our country portray humans as essentially discrete individuals who first of all try to maximize and protect their possessions and power.[4] Add to this the privatization of what used to be public, shared goods,[5] and the work of reimagining freedom *as* responsibility for the whole will seem counterintuitive, or even paradoxical.

Martin Luther takes advantage of exactly that; he uses paradoxes to break open our habitual ways of understanding personal freedom and its place in our deepest responsibilities, duties, and callings. Five hundred years ago, he began his treatise "The Freedom of a Christian" with this paradox: "A Christian is a perfectly free lord of all, subject to none. A Christian is a perfectly dutiful servant of all, subject to all." For Luther, personal liberty and responsibility for others are two sides of a single paradoxical truth.

I appreciate this vision of the way wholesale liberation (freedom *from*) so naturally and inevitably redoubles as the freedom *for* mutual aid in the community. The problem, though, is in Luther's expectations that the redoubling will happen as a matter of course—as naturally and easily as a fruit tree bears its good fruit. I think it will take a whole lot of time and practice not only to imagine but also to put into play this alternative understanding of freedom for others.

Fortunately, the various crises we are living through offer some clear opportunities to practice freedom for others. The mutual-aid networks that have popped up throughout our country and world are essentially training grounds for developing a different habit (or virtue) of freedom—the freedom to take responsibility for the well-being of neighbors. Protestors in the wake of George Floyd are much more racially diverse than they were at the start of the BLM movement five years ago; they recognize that everyone becomes freer and safer when no one is enslaved or endangered. More and more humans are coming to realize that their personal health and our public health depend on the health of interdependent ecosystems. Strangely, the more time and care I invest in growing our own food, the easier that food is to give away. (I've been dropping off small boxes of produce on neighbors' porches, and giving others away through the local elementary school's drive-by lunch pickup.)

Finally, if there is college this fall, the students and teachers who return to campus may think of their learning in less individualistic and commodified terms. Enrolling may turn out to feel like enlisting, and this may be a good thing. Each of us may make a commitment to be part of something bigger than ourselves, like students enrolled in upper-level seminars, where the success of the class depends on everyone doing the reading, listening carefully, contributing to the conversation, and otherwise taking responsibility not only for their own learning but also for the learning of others. Best-case scenario: the whole campus this fall takes on the seriousness, accountability, trust, and fun of a giant special-topics seminar. We should hope for no less.

TURTLES ALL THE WAY DOWN—JULY 8, 2020

When I started writing these entries four months ago, I thought that there would be a clear climax to the story. I thought the coronavirus pandemic would hit like a hurricane and that we would soon be rebuilding from amid the rubble. Now, I'm not sure whether we are still in a first wave, already in a second, or if the idea of waves has misled me and many others into thinking there would be something in between. A second pandemic of racial violence erupted ferociously last month, and that one has been raging far longer than the novel coronavirus (in this country, by about four hundred years). A third crisis—what Jim Kunstler calls "the long emergency" of environmental degradation[6]—goes back to the Industrial Revolution, picked up speed with the consumerism following World War II, and is now manifesting itself in climate change, glacial melting, rising sea levels, cataclysmic storms, and loss of biodiversity—all of which, with tipping points and feedback loops, are quickening at a rate beyond even the most fearful predictions. With the planned 2020 updates to the Paris Accord postponed for a year, and with news cycles and the average person's attention focusing on other crises (or their children's hunger or safety), many of us try to forget about the planetary crisis we are living in. Reminders are coming—scientists at Colorado State University predict that this hurricane season will be a dismal one, while NOAA predicts that the historic drought will worsen in the Southwest, and with the heat, the likelihood of more ravaging fires.[7]

I have said that discovering one's vocation depends on understanding one's life experiences in terms of a story and oneself as a character within it. Yet it is hard to tell stories when we are out at sea, caught between simultaneous storms and converging catastrophes, without a sense of beginning, middle, and end. To understand one's life as having a plot enables one to act purposefully and meaningfully, as one pushes past conflict and toward resolution. These days, however, many of us have the existential version of writer's block. Meaning and purpose seem like luxuries. We are caught in absurdist plots that are not of our choosing and that don't promise to end well. We aim merely to survive them.

I think of Professor O., a creative writing instructor at the Lutheran college I attended and one of my favorite professors there. He had a handlebar mustache, a deep Texas drawl, and a fine-tuned bullshit detector. He was known to sit with each student at the end of the term to discuss the grade they thought they deserved. "B???" the student would say, the rising voice already acknowledging that the opening bid was too high.

The lesson that Professor O. repeated most often was about the economy of words and the tightness of literary structure that writing short stories demanded. He was paraphrasing the Russian author Anton Chekhov, and probably said as much, but I thought the words came straight from the folk wisdom of his Texan homestead. He repeatedly told us, "If you describe a gun that is hanging over the fireplace at the beginning of a story, that gun better damn well go off before that story is done!" In other words, don't set something up and then not follow through. For a detail to be important, it must move the story toward resolution.

With all due respect to Professor O., there's a big difference between making up a story, in which you get to put guns above fireplaces, shoot them off at the appropriate time, dream up endings and tie up loose ends, and living a story that feels random, if not absurd, and where no good ending is in sight. The intersecting plots we are embroiled in—the coronavirus pandemic, structural racism, the potential loss of Earth as an inhabitable place for humans—feel like we are waiting for Godot (in Samuel Beckett's absurdist play) or, maybe slightly better, accepting our meaningless fate, like Sisyphus (in Camus's interpretation) deciding that he is fine with rolling his rock up the hill again and again and again.

Actually, while an utterly absurd, storyless life is nothing to settle for, Americans and perhaps especially American Christians often err in the other direction. Often not knowing how to endure (or narrate) real tragedy and persistent loss, they tend to clean stories up. They look away from the messy middle of our lives and instead narrate how it all started or, more typically today, how it will be resolved. The neat tripartite stories often fail to capture, or too quickly look past, the ongoing suffering and meaninglessness that many of us experience.

The "problem of suffering" can sound like a different matter, like a philosophical or theological conceptual conundrum rather than a question about how we tell stories. If God were really all-good, God would *want* to prevent tragedies. If God were all-powerful, God would be *able* to prevent them. And yet shit happens, and some of that shit can undo us. Some people, like Job, sit on piles of it.

Ultimately, though, these questions and all the various responses—from theological and philosophical theodicies to folk wisdom about reaping what you sow or pain making a person stronger—are really about how we tell stories. In the West, those stories typically move in a linear fashion and emphasize both beginning and end. The biggest, our foundational national or religious myths, think about ultimate beginnings—about God creating a "very good" world or the Founders setting out to "form a more perfect Union." In Act II, the world falls into exile, sin, and suffering. Depending on who tells the story, that could come from eating a forbidden fruit, or slavery as America's original sin, or the loss of family values or global leadership. The story ends with resolution, redemption, and reconciliation. Jesus saves. We recommit to making an even more perfect union. America is made great again.

These stories, however much they differ in details, together reflect "the Christian story," if indeed it is a single saga. God made the world and it was good. Humans screwed up and now there is pain. God will make a new heaven and a new earth and

will wipe every tear from their eyes.
Death will be no more;
mourning and crying and pain will be no more. (Rev 21:4)

It is a powerful story and rightly so. Christians find meaning in suffering insofar as they look backward and narrate where it comes from or look forward to describe the good that can come of it. Christians of old favored the first method; they traced all human suffering back to human sin, and thus justified it as appropriate and just. There was simply no such thing as unjust, innocent suffering. Christians today—especially in the United States—typically look forward rather than back. They focus on the good that emerges after and from suffering rather than the bad that produces it.

So too with America as a whole, both religious and secular. According to psychologist Dan McAdams, the story that highly generative, talented Americans typically tell of themselves is one of "redemptive suffering"— how they have developed grit and resilience by overcoming pain and hardship. These are inspirational, powerful stories that can help people make the most of a bad lot, when there is something to make of it.[8] When there isn't—when irredeemable loss remains—telling redemptive stories becomes irrelevant at best or, worse, sides with the script over the sufferer. Implicitly or explicitly, the message becomes that pain cannot be *that* bad or go on for *that* long; we blame those who cannot finally get over it.

There are alternative ways to speak of our suffering, indeed, to story our lives in ways that give them a different sort of meaning.

Buddhists and Hindus can help. They tell no fewer stories than do Christians; many redirect attention from ultimate beginnings and final endings to help us deal with our messy middle. If you have been shot with an arrow, the Buddha said, don't spend your time trying to figure out who shot you and why you were shot. Instead, pull out the arrow.

143

Another story, shared by Hindus and Buddhists, describes a novice monk who approaches his master seeking truth, asking, "Master, upon what does the whole world rest?"

"The world rests on the back of a giant turtle," replies the master.

After meditating on this truth for some time, the novice returns to the master and asks, "Upon what does the giant turtle rest?"

"An even larger turtle," explains the master. When the student approaches him a third time, asking the predictable question about what the two turtles rest on, the master puts a stop to it: "You have misunderstood me. *It's turtles all the way down.*"

That's a meaningful story about the interrelatedness (or ecology) of everything and about the absurdity of searching for ultimate meaning in primordial beginnings and otherworldly endings. It clears the space to focus on the penultimate, reality as we know it here and now, and how to develop compassion and care for our interdependent, fragile whole.

There is nothing wrong with happy endings. We should celebrate them when we experience them and acknowledge the redemptive suffering that enables us to grow in mind, body, or spirit. The problem is when we try to shoehorn all suffering into that which makes sense, whether because deserved in light of sin or redeemable without remainder, because it brings about a greater good. We need to speak of the suffering that remains.[9]

Christians are not left without scripts here, either. In her book, *Resurrecting Wounds*, Christian theologian Shelly Rambo attends to the resurrection stories, and in particular, to the wounds that are resurrected within the literal body of Christ, around which Christians (also the body of Christ) might gather to speak of their own pain, stitching together healing. Her last chapter attends to ways that hero scripts emphasizing the sacrifices of soldiers—their redemptive suffering—do damage to veterans suffering from PTSD insofar as they fail to make space for the ongoing woundedness of trauma. Still, other stories can and do step in; veterans engaged in healing circles hold one another's pain like Thomas, the disciple of Jesus, touching the hurting and healing wounds of his crucified savior.[10]

Theologian Deanna Thompson, who has lived with stage IV cancer since 2008, lifts up the psalms of lament, the story of Job, and Jesus's cry from the cross—*My God, My God, Why have you forsaken me?*—as "spaces within" otherwise neat sin-to-salvation stories, spaces that give some room for these stories to breathe. What seem like subplots or excursions within Christian triumphalism offer ways to "resist solvability." They enable us to hear and hold the stories of those living with tragedy and trauma.[11] By telling such stories, or even by naming the silences that ensue when we don't know how to talk about them, we may discover meanings deeper than explanation and a purpose more delicate—and also truer—than those spawned by fears and fantasies.

THE ART OF BEING NEIGHBORLY—JULY 15, 2020

I read this morning in the *New York Times* that the largest retail chains are quietly ending the temporary raises—dubbed "hero pay"—that they extended to essential workers last spring.[12] While many still hope to give out bonuses, most of the record-setting profits from grocery store chains and online retailers are going to shareholders instead. Companies explain that the hero pay raises were intended to sustain workers through the craze of stockpiling last spring, which has now ended. But the name "hero" was always meant to mark the risks and sacrifices that frontline workers took on—and continue to take on, with record numbers of COVID cases in dozens of states as well as belligerent customers threatening, hurting, and occasionally killing store employees who try to enforce mask-wearing policies. And now, with the $600 weekly supplemental income checks due to run out at the end of July, low-wage workers (many of them Black, Hispanic, and female) are even more exploitable. They work more hours for less pay, even when they themselves feel sick. Many suspect that "hero pay" was really a self-serving way for companies to retain their workforces while stimulus checks were in hand. Now that workers need the work more than employers need them, their heroism and selfless sacrifices depreciate in value.

This all points to how dangerous the language of heroism, sacrifice, and selflessness can be. As feminists have long argued, too often that language simply masks the exploitation of those who do surrogacy and direct-care work for men, often at the expense of their own well-being. These feminists regard mutuality, a balance of self-care and "other regard," as more just and life-giving than is the goal of self-sacrifice.[13]

That has got to be right. However, the ideal of mutuality can also degenerate into the idea of tit for tat, in which self-care and "other care" are only tenuously balanced, if balanced at all. Mindy Makant, my friend and director of the Living Well Center for Vocation and Purpose at Lenoir-Rhyne University, has been thinking along similar lines. She recently shared with me her misgivings with the airline oxygen mask analogy that countless people have used to illustrate the importance of self-care this summer. Like fastening one's own oxygen mask before assisting others, self-care is said to take priority over other care, lest we—depleted or dead—have nothing left to give. For Makant, the analogy misleads because it doesn't go far enough. We do not take care of ourselves before, and in order that, we additionally care for others. Rather, self-care and care of others should be of a piece, as each of us flourishes in and through the well-being of the whole.[14]

I am reminded of the article that E., the graduate of my college living now in Boston, sent me back in March about the mutual-aid networks that he helped get going. The young adults who start these networks typically volunteer their services rather than request help; they are the ones running errands, walking dogs, shoveling walkways, and sometimes helping pay the rent for others who need their help. The author of the article, however, insists that the aid really is mutual, even for those who seem to give more than they get. "There's also a selfish component to joining a mutual-aid network," he writes. "In a moment of deep uncertainty and anxiety, helping those in need is one of the few pure pleasures one can still partake in while social distancing. If you're feeling powerless these days and have the means, [join] your local mutual-aid network."[15]

I think also of the reasons that critical whiteness scholars such as Tim Wise give for why white people like me should get involved in antiracism work. While it may seem that whites like me commit to the work to help Black people, since they suffer the most from racism and presumably need our help, that, says Wise, is a recipe for paternalism. White folks should become antiracist because racism is *their* (*our*) problem. It damages us, and we are in need of healing.[16]

The lawyer who asks Jesus how to get eternal life (who is eventually told the parable of the Good Samaritan) knows the two great commandments by heart: "Love the Lord your God with all your heart and with all your soul and with all your strength and with all your mind" and "Love your neighbor as yourself." Jesus tells him that he has got it right. Simply do this "and you will live" (Luke 10:25–28 NIV). The second commandment seems pretty doable. Especially compared to loving God with *all* your heart and *all* your soul and *all* your strength and *all* your mind, to simply love another *as* yourself—no more or less—sounds rather easy.

Too easy, for some. Søren Kierkegaard notices this, and predicts that some will want to do more, especially for "the needy." "Would it not be possible to love a person *more than oneself*?" Kierkegaard imagines us asking. This ostensibly righteous desire to love another even more than myself, he says, is really more about *my* heroic attempts to prove *my* capacities than it is about actually, humbly loving. So too when we seek out the needy and bestow our charity on them. For Kierkegaard, to love someone who is under you *because* they are under you is, ironically, still too much about you.[17] Theologian and ethicist Samuel Wells adds that while we typically praise selflessness and service that does good work *for* neighbors in need, these works don't go to the heart of our deepest problems, which is alienation from one another. Nor do they go to the heart of the Christian story, which does include sacrifice for others but is more centrally rooted in God being *with* us and the calling to be with others, even when there is little one can do for them.[18]

* * *

When I began these reflections months ago, I thought my calling, and our collective callings, would push past fear to love the stranger and even the enemy, making them neighbors by treating them as such. I am realizing that commitments to love the hitherto unlovable actually undershoot the more difficult, humbling vocation of showing up and being present (often virtually), even when I cannot really *do* anything.

Asa, my older son, is learning this right alongside me. At breakfast this morning, he talked about playing an online game last night with friends, including E., who tested positive for COVID-19, as did her grandpa, soon before he was airlifted to a hospital in Peoria; he is now in critical condition. We had urged Asa to invite E. to the online game in order to break up her time quarantining and to keep her mind off things. "We didn't really do anything for her," Asa reported this morning, wondering why we told him to hang out with her. Exactly, I thought. It may have been easier to try to help E. than to be with her in this difficult time. Playing online games with a girl whose grandpa might die is humbling, awkward, faithful work.

Love is a verb, as the saying goes, but it is also a virtue that characterizes a person, a person's enduring disposition or character, which is formed through practice. As with other virtues (central for Christians are faith, hope, and love), to become the kind of person who loves others as oneself is a refined art or practical wisdom that steers between two extremes—in this case, between self-infatuation and self-abnegation. Those most practiced in the art of neighborliness will not have to weigh self-care against service to others, taking a little off one scale until they balance each other out. The two will come together intuitively and gracefully—like a painter tacitly knowing how much oil to mix with the paint, or a firefighter knowing through muscle memory which risks can or must be taken.[19]

I am a novice at neighbor love. That is humbling for a forty-seven-year-old religion professor to admit, but so be it. Indeed, I consider some students and recent graduates of my college as more experienced mentors from whom I can learn.

Take N. for example, a public health graduate who became a registered nurse. When my colleague in public health reached out to her recently, she spoke about moving from doing to being: "When I started as a nurse, I always assumed 'helping' patients meant improving their health. I have learned, unfortunately, that this is not always possible. . . . Some patients are managing their illness fine physically but have a hard time grasping the mental and emotional side of being ill, like being scared and secluded from their family. Talking to these patients, making them laugh, or holding their tablet during a Zoom call is as important as monitoring their oxygen saturation."[20] N. is learning to be present to patients who are learning to deal with the state of being ill. These are virtues, and loving ones at that.

Or take G., the student who had two brothers die of cancer right before and after she graduated from college, whose poetry I quoted on Holy Saturday. G. now lives in the Powderhorn Park neighborhood of Minneapolis, where hundreds of homeless people have set up tents after the unrest following George Floyd's death displaced them. She has been volunteering for the Minneapolis Sanctuary Movement, which supports the homeless encampments. The volunteer position sounded official (her shift was from four to eight o'clock in the morning), so I asked her what her work entailed. Not much, she said. Once in a while she'll hand out some food or find a first aid kit, but mostly it is just being there, becoming friends with the homeless.

* * *

Late this afternoon, I am out biking on the Mississippi trail and pass a guy holding a cardboard sign at an intersection, asking for help in front of cars waiting for the light to turn green. I circle back and ask if he has eaten lunch. He hasn't and says he wouldn't turn down ham sandwiches; he could probably eat two, and yes, tomatoes and lettuce from our garden are fine—mayo if I got it. I return a half hour later by bike with enough sandwiches and Gatorades in my backpack for the two of us.

I ask him if I can eat with him, and he tells me it would be OK. As he struggles to sit on the base of a construction pylon and I unpack our roadside picnic, he tells me he's got some really good stuff for us as well and begins unwrapping something from the plastic bags that he fishes from his backpack. I think it might be something to take a pull of or smoke up. It is trail mix—peanuts, raisins, and pistachio bits. As I eat my share of it while he has a third sandwich, we talk about Minnesota, where each of us grew up, and the high school that, coincidentally, he, my father, and Jesse Ventura all attended. He actually reminds me of my father, who also slicked back sweaty hair, had bad knees, and was sure to pull his weight when it came to sharing food or knowing where people came from.

We only spend twenty minutes together before I get back on my bike and he makes his way to the number 10 bus that will take him to the MLK Center downtown. We were nothing more than polite, kind, and neighborly with one another. Also, nothing less.

DOWN TO ROOTS—JULY 28, 2020

Much of my work this past week has entailed hacking away at the roots of the last of our overgrown bushes to make space for our new fruit trees. My hands are calloused and blistered, and I've broken the handle of a shovel and the blade of post-hole digger. My neighbor D. has offered to teach me how to make a pergola around the fruit trees once the bushes are all out. Today he stood on the sidewalk for a minute to watch me wrestle with a root ball. There has got to be an easier way, he said, and then sauntered happily away.

My other work consists of teaching a one-credit summer school course called Interfaith Understanding to incoming students. Without summer registration and programming on campus, my college decided to offer these courses as a way for incoming students to acclimate to our college community before the school year starts, if and however that happens. I know the fifteen incoming students in Interfaith Understanding only as they populate their Zoom squares. Later today, they will get to meet Dr. K., the local Muslim leader who also spoke to my Encountering Religion class back in May, during Ramadan. The hopeful resolve that she expressed then has stayed with me throughout the summer. She said that she was going to try to accept her stripped-down, lonely Ramadan as a gift from God. There were opportunities to grow, she said, even amid and through the pain.

Dr. K's cultivated hope is a full octave deeper than optimism, deeper even than courageous resolve. She was speaking from a hope that comes to light only as wishful thinking and human willpower come to grief. Her openness to learn from suffering did not have a worked-out theory (a theodicy) behind it; she didn't *comprehend* (grasp onto) something and then explain it to the students. Rather, she spoke the truth as she herself *under-stood* it—literally, stood under it. In her Muslim parlance, she submitted to God's will. Remaining hopeful was not a way out of the pain, but a way to stand under it, to bear it—like roots that grow down so that the plant can grow up and out.

Since Dr. K. and I last talked, our country and world have had to bear not only a global pandemic but also the hemorrhaging of the economy, a gruesome exposure of the plague of white supremacy, along with un-precedented political division and culture wars, which have moved from online backbiting to actual violence in the streets. For many, the multiple hardships seem unrelated. We deal with one the best we can and then ready ourselves for the next. Others personify the year 2020 itself as a single evil agent who wields his manifold hardships. Still others, perhaps fewer in number, seek to understand what is at the root of them all so that the cumulative weight can be faithfully borne. That sounds good, but get-ting to the bottom of anything is never politically or technologically expe-dient. It often seems to rob us of what hope we have of getting out from under a crisis. At least when we are dealing with one problem at a time, we can consider solutions and chart the way forward. Find a vaccine. Issue governmental checks. Defund the police. Be sure to vote. Those seeking to understand fundamental failures cannot help but appear pessimistic and thus rather unhelpful during crises that call out for solutions.

* * *

I've been rereading Wendell Berry's *The Hidden Wound*.[21] As he was begin-ning his public vocation, Berry felt called to return from a prestigious Gug-genheim fellowship in New York to the Kentucky farm that birthed him and to spend his life writing and farming from the same plot of land in

Port Royal, Kentucky. *The Hidden Wound* is Berry's early attempt to grapple with racism and friendships across racial differences as a white farmer living in the American South. The book was scrutinized carefully, as any book about race from a white man should be. Some took Berry as defending his own white racial privilege or romanticizing Black agrarian experiences. I, however, am helped by Joshua Hochschild's judgment that *The Hidden Wound* is a lament and confession—"an exercise in atonement," rather than defensive apologia. The passage from Berry featured on the dust jacket of the original publication said just that: "If the white man has inflicted the wound of racism upon black men, the cost has been that he would receive the mirror image of that wound into himself. . . . I want to know, as fully and exactly as I can, what the wound is and how much I am suffering from it. And I want to be cured."[22] Black writers from the likes of W. E. B. Du Bois, Lenny Duncan, James H. Cone, Austin Channing Brown, and Martin Luther King Jr. have also said that white people suffer from their own white supremacy and so also need deep healing. Berry agrees and wants to find salvation from his and others' sin.

Most profound and controversial about Berry's book is his insight that the wound of racism stems from a more fundamental, underlying disorder of modern culture as a whole. We glimpse this disorder in what we revere and reward, and what we despise and denigrate. Take, for example, the way we reward upwardly mobile individuals who (often by way of higher education) are freed from working with the land and their hands, and who see bodily work (farming, sewing, slaughtering animals, cooking, caring for the young and the old, building, repairing, and so forth) as disparaging work best outsourced to the poor, women, more "primitive" peoples, migrant workers, prisoners, the ubiquitous machines in our everyday lives, and nameless children in the Global South. Berry understands the wound of racism, America's original sin, to have an even deeper, or at least wider, cause. Human alienation from the land, from other creatures, and from the work of their care and cultivation, manifests itself in the alienation of one race from another, alongside alienation between genders and classes.

For some, Berry's wider lens (or deeper digging) will only blur attention to the wound of white supremacy, and especially to the suffering of Black people. Hochschild thinks Berry's diagnosis is more incisive and rightfully makes healing harder: "What if Berry is right, that racism is the epithelial layer of a deeper wound, that a more primal human tendency to exploitation is the cause of racism, not the effect? Then to heal racism, we must address exploitation, and to address exploitation, we must recognize our common humanity—not in the abstract, but in concrete relations of mutual dependence and care."[23]

One upshot of this otherwise gloomy prognosis is that it makes sense of the redemptive suffering to which faithful, grounded people (such as Dr. K.) are open. Those of us who are privileged, comfortable, relatively invulnerable, and often apathetic have become so not by being blessed, or even by being lucky, but by ignorantly exploiting other people and financing our lifestyles through the suffering of future generations. We will learn to be humble and human only by doing the difficult work that machines and other people have done "for" us. We will suffer, as most of the world has been suffering, so they might suffer less. Most of our suffering (like theirs) will be unwilled and unwelcomed—the suffering that follows the water shortages, famines, civil wars, and global migrations that themselves follow the end of oil, rising sea levels, and unpredictable weather chaos. But we first-world consumers might also get to some of the suffering before we have to and do so with an openness to being reformed.

Weaning ourselves from the convenience of disposable stuff won't be easy; no addict's recovery is. And yet the hope beyond wishful thinking is that we will come to see our pain as labor pains begetting new life—life together, in communion with one another and with the whole of creation.

I'm not sure it matters whether we consider human domination of—and thus alienation from—the natural world as more primary than the colonization by white Europeans of Indigenous peoples and the enslavement of Black people. Digging at one root will find others interconnected, like the shared root system of aspen groves. W. E. B. Du Bois saw white supremacy and the exploitation of Earth as connected already in the years following the First World War; to be white, he noticed, fanatically means "the ownership of the Earth forever and ever, Amen!"[24] Ta-Nehisi Coates also describes whiteness as an artificial abstractness, an alienation from the vulnerability of life as it is lived in bodily form alongside the bodies of other creatures.[25]

Most developed is the case that the influential African American cultural critic bell hooks makes in *Belonging: A Culture of Place*. She there connects the exacerbation of supremacy with the "great migration" of Black people from the agrarian South to the industrialized North and salvation with their homecoming. Alienation from place experienced by persons of color makes "it all the more possible for black people to internalize white-supremacist assumptions about black identity." By contrast, learning again to work the land and reroot in particular places can provide a mode of resistance. Bodily work helps "imbue black folks with an oppositional sensibility." When this humanizing connection with nature was severed, "racism and white supremacy came to be seen as all powerful, the ultimate factors informing our fate."[26] hooks writes from experience. She, like Berry, grew up in rural Kentucky before spending much of her long, distinguished (and yet exiled—as she describes it[27]) career in California and at Yale and Oberlin. In 2004, she returned to Kentucky to live out her teaching vocation at Berea College, a homecoming that she reflects on throughout *Belonging*.

hooks and Berry's shared vision is helpful primarily for the depth at which they find both the problem and the redemptive resistance work that we are called to. By comparison, treating a virus in isolation from the systemic injustices that make some more vulnerable than others, or treating the domination of people of color or women as though it were unrelated to the domination of nonhuman nature, or even trying to solve climate change while ignoring habitat and topsoil loss and the erosion of sustainable rural communities—all these fail to get at the root of the problem. That root is the human heart, a heart turned in on itself, a heart that craves freedom from suffering at any price, even by magnifying the suffering of others.

Ecological thinking is primary—the deepest root—insofar as it names how our problems are interconnected, as are the paths toward healing. Read carefully, the myth of Genesis 2–3 is less about a first cause and more about the interdependence to which we are called, and the pain that ensues when we try to be independent. Adam is from *adamah* (*soil* in Hebrew) and is called by God to till and keep it. Eve, the "mother of all living" (Gen 3:20), is, like the earth itself, a fecund matrix. Their primary vocations to serve and keep, to protect and care for one another and every other animal, plant, and the earth itself, are interrupted by the sin of refusing to be the creatures they are. Death, alienation from nature, and alienation from one another quickly follow suit. Returning to some semblance of wholeness will entail the *humbling, humanizing* work of reconnecting with the life of the soil (*humus*) and with the whole of creation.

* * *

My son Asa, who is incredibly perceptive and smart but not what you would call handy, wonders aloud whether filling the holes with water would soften the roots of these God-forsaken bushes, making them easier to pull out. He's right, it works, and it is all a blow to my ego, but the blisters on my hands are healing.

THE WHY OF WHIRLWINDS—AUGUST 13, 2020

While I write this, Asa and Gabe are on our neighbor's porch, attending their online school via our neighbor's internet. Our power went out three days ago in the derecho (straight-line wind) storm that swept over eight hundred miles of the Midwest in fourteen hours, from South Dakota to Ohio. Winds reached over one hundred miles per hour. Early reports suggest that the storm damaged nearly half of Iowa's corn and soybean crops. The 133,000 people living in Cedar Rapids, Iowa, to our north, lost power, almost without exception. The majority of businesses and homes there were damaged, and at least four people have died.

About half the power on our street has been restored. A massive Eastern cottonwood fell at the end of the block, taking out power lines and our friends' peach tree on the other side of the street. Our tree-lined backyard also took a casualty. A one-hundred-foot Scots pine snapped in two while we huddled by flashlight in the basement; it now leans still, but ominously, against a red maple, the edge of our house a few feet away and power lines buried below.

Still, there's a communal feeling of goodwill and care on our street that typically follows shared hardship. I sense it whenever there is a bad snowstorm, and neighbors push one another's cars out of snowbanks or shovel the sidewalk clear down the street. A number of years ago, when there was a house fire a few days before Christmas, we took up a collection for the family (*literally* by passing an overturned hat) while watching the firefighters battle the flames. This week, neighbors we otherwise don't interact with linger on the sidewalk in front of our house, asking if we have heard anything from the tree removal company. In the hours after the storm, when I finally found a gas station with power and purchased ice to pack our refrigerator, I bought extra bags and handed them out to neighbors. As I attach and reattach the chain on my chainsaw, my neighbor A. makes sure I know that he has a bigger one (his words, delivered with a smirk) and would be happy to help clear branches. Many on our street are asking one another how each is holding up and whether they can help. They do so with the sociability and kindness of an extended family or local parish. It's all so helpful and feels so good. Why do we become neighborly only in the wake of pandemics, infernos, and raging storms? Could we keep it going after the debris is cleared?

Public school was canceled for two days following the storm but is back online today. Our neighbors, D. and D., who don't wait for crises to pick up trash along the road or mow a neighbor's yard, offered their porch and internet connection. Asa and Gabe thus left home for school for the first time this fall. They packed their water bottles and backpacks, put on their masks, and walked down the street to D. and D.'s front porch, where they sit attending their online classes before they will head home for lunch. They brought a bouquet of beets, onions, carrots, and greens to leave on the porch as a thank-you gift. I hope D. and D. don't think we are trying to pay them. Their kindness is a gift.

The derecho storm has been called "otherworldly" in its size and intensity.[28] Any violence that is not directly caused by humans—storms, wildfires, floods, and plagues—is still sometimes called an "act of God," but these days only with air quotations. As a straightforward descriptor, the language has all but disappeared. It seems quaint; meteorological language such as "mesoscale convection weather systems" (which are responsible for derechoes) seems so much more explanatory. I agree that when we want to *explain* natural phenomena, supernatural causes don't seem to help. But the inverse is also true. When a person who has lost home or family to fire or storm cries out "Why?" that metaphysical question ought not to be answered with scientific or other explanations. Science gets at the how. We need the humanities—Greek tragedies of classics, the existentialism of philosophy, and the scriptures of religion—if we are to grapple with the why.

Not that our whys are often or wholly answered. When they are, when people actually *explain* why the innocent suffer—typically, by questioning their innocence (you actually deserve this) or finding a silver lining (look on the bright side)—they play the role of Job's friends who, after practicing silent accompaniment for seven days, begin to proffer theories about his affliction. Theories that cannot be disproved make for bad theories. (Job's insistence on his innocence cannot disprove the theory that he is lying, and thus being punished also for the sin of lying.) They make for worse pastoral care. *Explanation* might bring a kind of comfort to the explainers, but it does not slake Job's unbearable thirst, which is for God and justice, not a theory about either.

From a whirlwind, the God for whom Job cries out finally shows up. God's response to Job provides no sure answer to Job's "Why?" and yet may still offer an evocative response—an "infinite why," as Kierkegaard once put it.[29] God offers no reason for Job's suffering. Instead, God responds to Job's questions with another seventy-some questions, beginning by inquiring into where Job was when the foundation of the world was laid (Job 38:4) and ending by asking whether Job thinks he's able to catch Leviathan, the ancient sea monster, with a fishhook and parade it around like a pet (41:1–5). Together, the rhetorical questions are meant to remind Job of all he cannot know and control. Job finally admits that he has uttered what he did not understand and "repent[s] in dust and ashes" (42:3–6).

Such repentance shouldn't suggest that Job finally confesses to some hitherto undisclosed sin. It probably means that his stance toward God "turns around" as his lament gives way to wonder and hope. Liberation theologian Gustavo Gutiérrez suggests that the Hebrew *naham* (repent) even allows that it is the "dust and ashes," symbolic of Job's near despair, that he is now abandoning.[30] Hebrew Bible scholar Walter Brueggemann sees a similar turning throughout biblical wisdom, where people in intense pain somehow "make the leap from the preoccupation with self to an imaginative acknowledgement of the primacy of the other."[31]

What does Job find in God's whirlwind revelation that enables him to turn from his self-preoccupation? Besides seeing God's raw power, Job comes to know a God whose cosmic justice is less predictable, calculable, and anthropocentric than Job had assumed. Whereas Job has been crying out for justice on a scale he can know (and the friends think that they know it), God's justice is deeper and wilder. God makes rain fall in places where no one lives (Job 38:25–27). God is the God of wild oxen and hawks and monster hippopotamuses, none of which Job controls and all of which God relishes. Admittedly, God's tone can sound derisive and taxing: "Do you know the ordinances of the heavens? / Can you establish their rule on the earth?" (38:33). But it is also magnanimous, playful, and teasing: Do you *really* want a wild ox sleeping beside you? (39:9); could *you* have thought up something as strange as an ostrich? (39:13–18). This is a God who takes special delight in all that is superfluous and useless by human standards. In other words, this God of whirlwinds and derecho storms is also a God of freedom and gratuitous grace—a God whose untamable love will offend all who keep score while surprising those who, like Job, can learn to wonder and hope.

The environmentalist Bill McKibben finds in God's speech a radical broadening of the horizon of our moral worldview. Job learns that God's free grace sustains the whole creation and that creation needs our humble awe as much as our resourcefulness. Trees are much more than wood. We are called to care and attend to nature beyond all utilitarian calculation.[32] That is an ecological ethic, or "deep ecology"—a way of knowing the nonhuman world as having its own awe-full integrity, apart from human innovation and consumption. It is also a deeply religious ethic. After all, religious faith, like funny ostriches or the desert rains and the God who delights in them, is not a means to some other end, including an eternal reward. Rather, it is, as Meister Eckhart says of love, without a why or wherefore.[33]

To me, today, such gratuitous grace and selfless love look a lot like a borrowed chainsaw whose chain stays on, a red maple catching a falling Scots pine moments before it hits the house, and children logging onto social studies and math courses from a neighbor's porch. Each is a gift that shouldn't be explained and so seems without a why or a wherefore.

But again, why is it that neighbors are just so neighborly after storms and fires, circulating gifts without concern for what they will get out of it? With help from people like Walter Brueggemann, I've come to think that our neighborliness emerges quite instinctively once the cultural expectation to satisfy one's own desires has been interrupted. That expectation is untrue; only humans seem tempted to cut themselves off from the web of interdependent relationships that sustain the lives of human and nonhuman creatures. But our consumeristic culture has, in the words of Brueggemann, fooled us into keeping "*us* as the agenda, an excuse for not ceding life beyond the self, an inability to transfer attention beyond our needs and appetites."[34] The trick is to wean ourselves from the self-enclosures of individualism and consumerism, even after the lights come back on.

THE ART OF FAITH—AUGUST 17, 2020

For the last week, my family has been—by necessity—practicing the art of minimums. We are on our eighth day without power following the derecho storm that funneled through our Mississippi River Valley a week ago. A number of tree-removal crews, summoned to the Midwest from other parts of the country, have come by, studied the tangle of trees and power lines in our backyard, come up with plan, and said they'd be back, only to have a different crew show up with a different plan and promise of return. The rest of our block is up and running. Neighbors continue to check in on us, offering generators, battery-operated cell-phone chargers, and room in their deep freezers.

In truth, the burden of this past week has been light, and bearing it has been rather satisfying. I learned that you can make biscuits on the grill between sheets of aluminum foil; my kids say they are the best they've ever had. We eat food from our garden with every meal: blueberries on cold cereal; squash, beets, carrots, and onion roasted on the grill; salads of kale, arugula, lettuces, and cherry tomatoes. The boys continue to attend school using our neighbor's Wi-Fi, sitting on their porch. Without electronics, our play gets more hands-on: kick-the-can in the yard before dusk, card games by lantern light on the porch. This weekend, Laura and the boys gathered storm-strewn branches in McCandless Park and wove them into a teepee-like structure. And even if I try to make it look like cutting branches, bundling them, and dragging them to the curb is painstaking, I am taking joy in it. The hardest part has been falling asleep in the summer heat without an air conditioner or ceiling fan. Still, putting a mattress on the floor below open windows brings its own rewards. Each small draft of outside air is mercy, the larger ones close to delight.

In her poem "To Be of Use," Marge Piercy pays tribute to the "people who submerge / in the task, who go into the fields to harvest / and work in a row and pass the bags along." They "move in a common rhythm / when the food must come in or the fire be put out." Most of us who are college educated have mistaken our expertise and credentials as a ticket out of such meaningful, ennobling work. It sometimes takes a violent storm to get us back to our shared, basic vocation of tending and keeping, work that "has a shape that satisfies, clean and evident."[35]

Wendell Berry, following Thoreau, describes the art of minimums—of knowing what you can do without—in terms of the self-sufficiency or independence we gain when we cease to rely on far-away corporations for all our food, entertainment, work, and energy.[36] I prefer to think of it as local interdependence or acknowledged dependency. We who are college educated or otherwise successful by American meritocratic standards (i.e., those of us who don't have to work with our hands when we are not in the path or wake of storms) already consider ourselves as self-sufficient, at least while the gadgets continue to obey to our clicking, flicking, and swiping. Doing without a small fraction of what I don't need, as I've done this week, doesn't only inch me toward self-sufficiency, but also acknowledges all the gifts of others on which I depend. *Grateful* is a fitting synonym for the simple joy I have felt this week.

* * *

Religious faith, too, is an acknowledged dependence. My colleague E. from the religion department tells students that when they come across the word *faith* in New Testament passages, they should swap out that word for *trust*, which is more reflective of the Greek *pistis*. Faith is not a pronouncement of belief, but an abiding sense of the giftedness of life, come what may, and an awareness of how every life depends on the lives and deaths of others. In his famous ode to love in 1 Corinthians 13, Paul professes that "[love] believes all things" (1 Cor 13:7). The word rendered "believe" is *pisteuei*, which is from *pistis* or trust. "All things" typically renders *panta*, but the word simply means "all." Paul is not saying that love believes every claim or promise (or conspiracy theory) that comes about, as if it were easily duped. Rather, love trusts the all. It depends on the interrelated whole, which it knows like it knows its own garden.

Given how religious faith and ecological awareness at their best closely cohere, I take it that those who buy factory-farmed meat in plastic wrap may have trouble cultivating gratitude, since they are disconnected from that on which they depend. Those who buy clothes made in Mexican *maquiladoras* or Bangladeshi sweatshops do not want to know who produced it and so stumble with gratitude as well. Some of us—maybe most of us—with personal cars, personal computers, and personal phones easily forget (or try to) that precious metals from the earth make them; ancient sunlight in the form of oil, coal, and gas power them; and future generations will pay the real cost of them. Many of these same people pray, but to explicitly thank God for that which—and those whom—actually sustains our privileged lives is extremely difficult and sometimes self-defeating. Maybe this is just me, but when I have given thanks before vegetables that we have grown and grass-fed beef that we've purchased at the farmer's market, those prayers feel real and tangible—like the farmers, cows, soil, sunlight, seeds, and spouse on whom I depend, as well as the Matrix/ Creator who interweaves them all. I have also tried to pray over Little Caesars pizza and microwavable mac 'n' cheese. It feels like lip service at best, or worse, a pious diversion. All of this is to say that authentic faith in God depends on the acknowledgment of, trust in, and gratitude for some measure of all the human and nonhuman creatures that bear God's gifts.

At the start of the coronavirus pandemic, people reported an upsurge in faith. Pew Research found that only 2 percent of US adults said that their faith had become weaker because of the coronavirus pandemic. The majority (47 percent) said their faith hadn't changed, while a quarter (24 percent) said that their faith had become stronger through COVID.[37] Some will wonder whether this isn't really an uptick in *bad faith*—faith that is *merely* a coping mechanism or crutch to lean on during hard times. Like praying over food that you don't want to know the origins of, to have a bad faith (*mauvaise foi*) is to hand over one's responsibilities in the world here and now for the false assurance that things will work out in the end. In Christian circles, bad faith takes flight from the everyday earthy world, fixating on the spiritual bliss of heaven instead. Of course, an uptick in faith in times of crisis is not necessarily a way of mentally or spiritually detaching from a difficult situation. The test, I suppose, is whether the increase in self-reported levels of prayer actually makes us more mindful of the giftedness of life and its dependence on death, or whether it prompts people to skip over each in wishing for life without limits. Do we pray to get back to a normal that is predicated on a consumerism that, in turn, preys on ingratitude? Or does prayer attune us to a new heaven *and a new earth* (Rev 21:1), which will have fewer gadgets and more work, although the saved will learn to delight in it?

The more I think about it, Berry's art of minimums could also be called the art of faith. Berry and Thoreau ask us to make do with little rather than quest after more, trusting that we are given all that we need. It begins with renunciation, but it is artful not only in giving up all that we don't need but also—and especially—in coming to know, trust, and be grateful for all that remains. Faith, too, is an art. It relies on asceticism—a giving up. But the point of asceticism (from *askesis*—the shaping of desire) is to love properly. To love more fully, knowingly, and trustingly that which one receives as gift.

* * *

The tree service arrived at dusk today. The foreman had promised that they would work us in before ending their long day, but I admit I was surprised to see them. The workers were visibly tired, but they scaled the maple, wielded their ropes, and cut out the pine entangled up there like "people who submerge / in the task."[38] As the foreman gave a play-by-play over the phone, two climbers disappeared into the debris above while the groundsmen reined ropes from below. Before they were finished, the power crew was here as well, restringing a line where before there were branches. I am grateful for each of them and for this past week (and also for lights and a ceiling fan).

DARK HOPE—AUGUST 26, 2020

First Corinthians 13 declares that love believes (or trusts) all things and that love hopes (or expects) all things (1 Cor 13:7). With such forward-looking confidence that all will be well and love will prevail, you can see why the chapter is the go-to for couples planning their wedding ceremonies.

What's not always noticed is the dark side of this ode to love and its coconspirators, faith and hope. On either side of Paul's declaration of love trusting and hoping all things, he says that love also bears all and endures all. The Greek word for bear is *stegei*, meaning to cover or shelter, as in a roof that keeps the storm at bay. The Greek for endure is *upomenei*, meaning to stay behind, weathering the imminent storm. This ode to love enumerates the many human gifts that will be swept asunder in the End—prophecies, speaking in tongues, and human knowledge itself. When faith, hope, and love remain (*menei*), as the final verse announces, they do so by having taken shelter. They survive the apocalyptic storm by riding it out, bearing all to the very end.

* * *

For students at my college, the end of summer is five days away. Monday is the first day of the fall semester. As I write, they are moving futons and throw rugs into their dorms at their appointed hour, walking up one stairwell and down the other, while masked parents wait on the sidewalk. The students have signed agreements to remain on campus for the first fourteen days and to abide by distancing, testing, masking, quarantining, and other protocols, which the college hopes against hope will weather the inevitable outbreaks on campus. Outside their dorms, grounds crews are clearing the last of the tree limbs from the derecho storm that struck over two weeks ago. It's a tempestuous time on campus, as it is in the rest of the world.

Today, the National Hurricane Center says that Hurricane Laura is on the verge of becoming a Category 4 storm, with winds in excess of 110 mph, before making landfall this evening. Half a million people have been ordered to evacuate. The hurricane is expected to bring an "unsurvivable storm surge" when it hits southeast Texas and southwest Louisiana, which also have been hotspots for the coronavirus. Mercifully, the number of COVID hospitalizations has fallen in the past two weeks, vacating beds for the expected influx of hurricane victims. Nevertheless, those victims will be followed by other victims of other catastrophes. NOAA predicts that there will be as many as nineteen tropical storms this season; ten or more will reach hurricane status.[39]

A little over a week ago (on August 17), Death Valley, California, recorded the hottest temperature ever measured on earth—130 degrees. Last week, a dry lightning storm produced nearly eleven thousand bursts of lightning, setting off a flurry of fires across that state, which have so far burned over two thousand square miles. In 2019, 4.6 million acres of land burned through the American West. As a historic drought and record-breaking high temps in California have rolled into 2020, scientists predict that the fires will burn even hotter and longer this year. Meanwhile, there are both flooding and drought in the Midwest, each exacerbating rather than alleviating the other. The full devastation from last week's derecho storm is only now making national headlines, and it is worse than people thought. In the nearby city of Cedar Rapids, Iowa, almost every home sustained damage, food distribution lines are long, roads are still unpassable, and the city expects to lose half of its oldest and biggest trees, perhaps including a 170-year-old ginkgo on the Cornell College campus, which is trying to hold on in the arboreal version of an ICU.[40]

It seems like the end of the world is coming, and coming soon. There is no shortage of apocalyptic preachers interpreting the signs, telling us to repent for various sins. Others stay with pragmatics; pack a backpack full of survival gear, they say, or (if you're rich) consider purchasing a condominium in the underground complex in rural Kansas, complete with volcanic ash scrubber, a decontamination room, and waterslide.[41] Jesus also urged immediate repentance (but offered no waterslides). That summons, too, was in light of the End: "Repent, for the kingdom of God is at hand." The question in our case is what "turning around" (a literal translation of *repentance*) can look like when we can't walk back prior action and inaction.

Even if today we double or triple down on reducing emissions of greenhouse gases, eat lower on the food chain, rejoin the Paris Accord, convert to renewable energy, ban fertilizers and plastics, convert monocultures into polycultures, plant perennial grasses, and take other overdue steps, this will only *mitigate* the suffering in store for us and millions of other species. We will not be able to return to the stable climate that we and they have enjoyed for the past ten to twelve thousand years. Like a midflight arrow already shot from the bow, the trajectory of environmental disasters is irreversible, and much of the damage is now unavoidable. Forest fires will worsen. Prolonged droughts will intensify. Storms will get more intense more rapidly. Weather patterns will fluctuate and become less predictable. Conflicts over water supplies will increase. Coral reefs and the ecological diversity therein will die from bleaching. Glaciers will continue to melt. Sea levels will rise. More people will be exposed to more pandemics. Species of plants and animals will become extinct. The human species will be more vulnerable and more fearful. Environmental refugees will be more common. Civil wars will ensue. Landscapes will become barren, as will the inscapes of those made to live in them. Creatures of all kinds will suffer and die.

That's a best-case scenario. I don't enjoy typing it out. First-world peoples who have benefitted the most from industrialization and its labor-saving machines are most responsible for getting us into this mess and should be most responsible for getting us out. The problem is that there is no *out*. Indeed, the quest to get out of our vulnerable place in a vulnerable ecosystem is the very thing that got us into this apocalyptic scenario in the first place. There is only mitigated and unmitigated suffering in our future, and we can only (but still!) decide how much to mitigate. We must do everything we can *not* to do more damage than we have already, irreversibly, done. That's not a rallying cry that you'll find on bumper stickers. It doesn't exactly rouse hope.

What does practical, sustainable hope look like in these days, and how might we awaken it? It's easier to consider what hope cannot and should not entail during these final days of human reign on Earth.

First, hope is not optimism. *Optimism* was first coined by the modern philosopher, Gottfried Wilhelm Leibniz, in his early eighteenth-century work, *Theodicy* (1710). Leibniz argued that our world, despite all evidence to the contrary, must in fact be the optimal one—"the best of all possible worlds." Otherwise, an omnipotent and omnibenevolent God would have, by definition, created a better one. For Europeans, a massive earthquake in Lisbon, Portugal, severely wounded this optimism, as it killed some fifty thousand people on the morning of November 1, 1755, many of whom were attending Mass in observance of the Feast of All Saints when it struck. God could surely do better than this.

Today, optimism typically entails not a philosophical defense of the world as it is but our confidence that with enough technological ingenuity, neoliberal markets, or political revolutions, the future will get progressively better. Optimism is a deeply seated faith that the future will be better than the present and past. It comprises something of the civil religion of the United States, among other postindustrial countries. Civil *fanaticism* may be the better descriptor, given that there is no real reason to believe in the progressive betterment of the world other than our desperate desire that it be true. The laws of thermodynamics, the carbon cycle, and the carrying capacity of Earth downright count against it. Any hope worthy of the name has got to be forged with eyes wide open to present and future suffering. Wishful thinking too easily collapses into utter despair.

Second, hope is not for some alternative world other than the one we inhabit. It is not an exit strategy for those who cannot bear this ordeal any longer. Escapism is often confused with hope, most of all by Christians. Many American Christians connect ultimate hope with heaven but disconnect that new creation, light years away, from the first creation that requires our care and hope here and now. The ecotheologian Norman Wirzba poses a troubling question to those who long for heaven because Earth is going to hell: What makes you think we won't ruin another world in the same way we've ruined this one?[42] The same could be asked of secular and commercial versions of religious otherworldliness, which seem to me to be even more fanatical. Elon Musk, founder of Tesla and SpaceX, the aerospace transportation company with the stated goal of colonizing Mars, cloaks the ambition to flee Earth with a buoyancy worthy of its mass marketing. The landing page of SpaceX is called "Mars and Beyond: The Road to Making Humanity Multiplanetary." Below a photograph of the Martian horizon, we find these words from Musk: "You want to wake up in the morning and think the future is going to be great—and that's what being a spacefaring civilization is all about. It's about believing in the future and thinking that the future will be better than the past. And I can't think of anything more exciting than going out there and being among the stars."[43] To "discover" unspoiled lands (or planets), colonize them, and market that colonization in terms of a clean start, new dawn, or final frontier is not a thing of the future. Europeans and North Americans have done it before, with limited returns for the colonizers, and next to none for the land and people colonized.

Third, hope cannot be in human willpower and ingenuity, nor in the products they produce. Human measures are bound to become fanatical, escapist, and self-defeating as long as we are trying to answer, fix, engineer, innovate, and invent as a country and world without also stopping, waiting, giving up, going without, enduring, grieving, and weaning ourselves from delusions about saving the planet as individuals and local communities. This is the hardest distinction to make, in theory and especially in practice. We do need to act, and act now, if we are to mitigate the most painful effects of biodiversity loss, topsoil erosion, pollution of air and waterways, and climate change. But "we" often just means "they" in such campaigns—world leaders, corporations, scientists, and engineers who the rest of us believe will find fixes to the problems that first-world consumers have created, while we wait to consume those solutions.

Paul Kingsnorth, an English writer, ecologist, and author of *Confessions of a Recovering Environmentalist and Other Essays*, describes the unabashed confidence in new technologies that characterizes today's "neoenvironmentalists," which he contrasts with earlier environmentalists' attention to limits. According to the neoenvironmentalists, "Civilization, nature and people can be 'saved' only by enthusiastically embracing biotechnology, synthetic biology, nuclear power, geoengineering and anything else with the prefix 'new.' . . . The traditional green focus on 'limits' is dismissed as naive. We are now, in [one leading neoenvironmentalist's] words, 'as Gods,' and we have to step up and accept our responsibility to manage the planet rationally through the use of new technology guided by enlightened science."[44] Jews and Christians have stories about what the desire to be "as God" really gets us (alienation from one another, the earth, and God—see Gen 3). For Kingsnorth, the problem with this impulse toward human engineering is its failure to assess losses against the gains. Borrowing from Ronald Wright, he describes each promising innovation as a "progress trap"—a technological solution that helps in the short term but also introduces unforeseen problems and, in the long term, turns out to be a step backward.[45]

If we conducted a wider and longer audit, we'd find that progress often turns out to be a series of interlocking traps that combine to form a ratchet: "Every turn [forces] us more tightly into the gears of a machine we were forced to create to solve the problems created by progress."[46] People notice this on a smaller scale when it comes to the newest and most promising medical procedures, which often beget other problems, additional procedures, and so forth. According to the physician and medical ethicists, Lydia S. Dugdale, many ratchet up the medical interventions anyway, not knowing when and how to stop, especially when in fear of death: "Doctors are hardwired to free patients from the grip of death, and patients are hardwired to seek safety." Each is gripped by "the rescue fantasy."[47] I wonder whether our collective confidence in technologies that promise to save our species turns any less on collective fears.

Kingsnorth is not alone in seeing escapist, fear-driven fantasies for what they are. I think of Ta-Nehisi Coates, whose analyses of the "comforting myths" of "the Dream," including the myth of progress, are so penetrating and dismantling that people will take them to be hopeless, or even cynical. Coates explicitly demurs, writing this to his son in *Between the World and Me*, "I am not a cynic. I love you, and I love the world, and I love it more with every new inch I discover."[48]

The Black cultural critic Cornel West distinguishes hope from optimism similar to how Coates distinguishes interminable critique from empty cynicism. For West, hope is participatory, whereas optimism is "spectatorial." Optimism is a (rather unfounded) way of seeing things positively—often by ignoring present and future suffering. By contrast, hope comes into being through the resolve to attend courageously to suffering and change what can be changed, no matter how small. In this sense, "hope is as much a consequence of your action as it is a source of your action."[49]

The historian and activist Rebecca Solnit adds that pessimists assume perfect clarity and closure no less than optimists. Both think that events inevitably unfold as a matter of course—either climbing upward toward a final utopia or spiraling down to sheer and certain hell. Becoming hopeful is distinct from both insofar as one acts in light of and from a sense of instability, uncertainty, and humility; one hopes precisely because one does not and cannot know how change might happen. In this sense, all hope is "in the dark." In the very "spaciousness of uncertainty," there is room to act.[50]

Kingsnorth explicitly calls the question that remains at bottom, once all false hopes and premature pessimisms have fallen to the floor: "Is it possible to observe the unfolding human attack on nature with horror, be determined to do whatever you can to stop it, and at the same time know that much of it cannot be stopped, whatever you do? Is it possible to see the future as dark and darkening further; to reject false hope and desperate pseudo-optimism without collapsing into despair?"[51] He admits that some despair will follow an honest accounting, adding that "if you don't feel despair, in times like these, you are not fully alive." Yet he writes of something that keeps the despair from closing shut, "something that accompanies it, like a companion on the road."[52]

Kingsnorth suggests a number of ways to cultivate hope during this too-long time of crisis. A person can withdraw from mainstream society, refusing to tighten the ratchet further. They can choose contemplation over action, convinced that "action is not always more effective than inaction." A person can commit to preserving nonhuman life, rewilding a small plot of land so that other creatures might flourish. They can learn a practical skill, some physical work that doesn't try to save the world by intervening but that works along with the grain of the planet, and then preserve that skill like librarians in monasteries preserved books during the Dark Ages.[53]

All of this sounds so small and simple. None of it will save the world. And yet I, for one, feel summoned to follow this path, precisely because it is a path that I *can* follow, acts of hope I *can* take, and ways I *can* calm my own anxious fears, rather than projecting them onto scientists and politicians and fantasizing about Final Solutions (history has tried that one as well). Any hope that will not wash away in imminent storms will need to be rooted in local landscapes and the cultivated dispositions of individuals, families, and local neighborhoods. It is a hope we can only glimpse darkly, as through a tarnished mirror. But the darkness is also durable and can be prolific, like underground seeds hiding from fire or ice, waiting to shoot up into vast prairies or search out small cracks in the pavement.

SACRIFICIAL LOVE—AUGUST 30, 2020

It's Sunday, the day before my college begins what will certainly be one of the strangest and hardest school years in its 160-year history. Church today for me will be this evening with returning and incoming students at an outdoor blessing service. We are between campus pastors; in the meantime, I've been asked to help sustain campus ministries beside some dedicated students and other faculty members. At tonight's blessing service, I will lead the song of blessing that I sang at Camp Omega when I was a kid. We'll close with Holden Village's famous "Prayer of Good Courage": "Give us faith to go out with good courage, not knowing where we go, but only that your hand is leading us." The blessing and prayer are normally to send people forth as they depart from community. It is odd but fitting that we will evoke them as we come together for this extraordinary year.

I like to help with worship. I get to use primary, performative language that I don't often use when teaching *about* religion—phrases such as *I am sorry, You are forgiven, God bless you, There is hope, You are loved*. This is not to say that I never say such things in the classroom—I do, especially now that I have tenure. One example is when I have taught incarcerated students at our local prison, where conversations about C. S. Lewis on salvation or Bryan Stevenson on restorative justice pass over into pronouncements that all of us are worthy of healing. Another is the language that I used with college students after they were sent home with the onset of the pandemic last spring: "You are loved and we will get through this," I said in a video message. "May you find peace and hope." Tragedies have a way of boiling down talk to that which does the needed work.

Words like *trust, hope*, and *love* can sound so simple, or even naive, especially when we use them loosely and unreflectively. We say that we love Whitey's ice cream or Bent River beer right alongside saying we love our grandparents. That we have faith it won't rain as well as faith in God. That we hope to lose weight and hope to go to heaven. Maybe the similarities between the everyday and metaphysical senses are as they should be. Kierkegaard suggests that authentic religious faith (and, by extension, devout hope and agape love) will no doubt resemble more immediate confidences, wishes, and desires. In his book *Fear and Trembling*, he describes a run-of-the-mill citizen of a town who works long hours and comes home joyfully, hoping that his spouse has prepared some special hot meal, maybe even "roast leg of lamb with vegetables." He might actually possess a deeply spiritual faith that manifests itself in this everyday joy and anticipation and that won't be crushed even if they have to eat potatoes yet again. Alternatively, he might just be a "bourgeois philistine" who is hungry. It is hard to tell from the outside.[54]

If we could look from the "inside," Kierkegaard says, we might be able to distinguish what he calls the "first immediacies" of anticipating, wishing, and desiring, on the one hand, and the cultivated virtues of faith, hope, and love, on the other. What distinguishes immediate wishes and wants from the "second immediacy" of faith is not that faith is explicitly in God or has heaven as its ultimate goal. No, says Kierkegaard, even Abraham, the paramount "hero of faith," had faith in *this life*—in Abraham's case, faith in the promise of a son, even in his and Sarah's old age.[55] What distinguishes religious faith, hope, and love from more immediate longings is that the former only *return* to the place where the latter begins and ends. Between everyday wants and the love to which we are called is a letting go or a giving up—in Abraham's case, quite literally a sacrifice. According to Genesis 22, he is called by the God who has gifted him with Isaac to travel to Mt. Moriah and sacrifice the boy. The story turns out well, but Abraham doesn't know that yet. In Kierkegaard's graphic language, Abraham has "to draw the knife before keeping Isaac."[56]

* * *

I've expressed some reservations about "sacrifice" and "hero" language in earlier entries. We honor the sacrifices of frontline workers but often continue to exploit them. We declare a war on the coronavirus but do not always commit to the less heroic, everyday work of caring for the wounded. I have learned these reservations from feminist and womanist colleagues, who point out how language about self-sacrificial love for others is often wielded by white males as a roundabout way of justifying the subservience of women, and especially women of color.[57]

I've also learned from Christian pacifists, many of whom are rooted in the radical reformation ("peace church") tradition or in Catholic social teachings rather than in Lutheran or other mainline Protestant traditions. When discussing the duties and sacrifices to which Christians are called, these pacifists see the language subverted by patriotic appeals of nations with standing armies. When Americans talk about "the ultimate sacrifice," they strangely overlay the image of an armed soldier with the one who disarmed Peter and refused to fight, accepting death on a cross instead. To equate love with sacrifice is risky, at best. It is ideological and idolatrous, according to some of the most perceptive critics.

Now is probably the right moment to express what I haven't yet said—which is that I find language of sacrificial love not only dangerous but also inspiring and indispensable (when properly used) in order to find and follow one's calling. Indeed, there have been moments over the past half year when I have found myself questioning caricatures and easy dismissals of sacrificial love during these times of crisis. The caricatures are typically proffered by political progressives, with whom I otherwise identify. (Republicans have far fewer reservations about stories of sacrifice, as they demonstrated throughout their national convention in Charlotte this past weekend.) Whereas metanarratives on the right suggest that true patriots and real men make sacrifices while liberals want something for nothing, caricatures from the left suggest that sacrifice always or necessarily perpetuates self-serving ideologies and privileges the status quo. They sometimes even suggest that there is nothing more valuable than human life, and so there is nothing to die for. I find myself demurring.

One example early on in the coronavirus pandemic occurred when Dan Patrick, the Texas lieutenant governor, said that he and other older adults might need to be ready to sacrifice their lives for the good of others. Appearing on Fox News on March 23, 2020, Patrick said that "no one reached out to me and said, 'As a senior citizen, are you willing to take a chance on your survival in exchange for keeping the America that all America loves for your children and grandchildren,'" but, he continues, "if that's the exchange, I'm all in." Tucker Carlson, the host of the show, pressed him: "So, you're basically saying that this disease could take your life but that's not the scariest thing to you, there's something that could be worse than dying?" To which Patrick responded, "Yeah."[58]

Many news reporters jumped on him. One headline stated that Patrick declared that "old people *should* volunteer to die to save the economy." Yet Patrick didn't prescribe self-sacrifice; he only described how he and some other senior citizens are in fact willing to die if it came to that. The same report described his response as "sociopathic," even though his words suggest care for others, at least at face value.[59] (I should clarify that sacrificing for the sake of "the Economy," "the American way of life," or other abstractions exposes the ideology that accompanies Patrick's resolve. I am only suggesting that the willingness to sacrifice for something bigger than oneself ought not be dismissed out of hand.)

Most would admire someone who stayed in the path of Hurricane Laura up until the last minute in order to help others evacuate. One Louisiana evacuee wondered—as though cast in the final scene of *Schindler's List*—whether he had done enough, saying, "Those [left behind] are the ones that haunt me because we didn't get them all." Yet fewer would understand this man's expressed unease about leaving at all. "It doesn't feel right leaving my city like this," he said, as he finally drove toward personal safety.[60] Those of us with fewer attachments to place wonder about those who risk their lives for land. And yet Indigenous communities living in those same Louisiana flood zones need to decide whether to accept yet another governmental relocation package that would permanently remove them from the land that they love, or stay on their land, come what may. Either option entails deep sacrifice.[61]

In my experience, many young people in particular want to give themselves over to something bigger than themselves. Many come to these passions while in college or go to college to live them out. Protestors taking to the streets this summer were overwhelmingly young and college-educated. Their passions subjected them to various forms of suffering, from exposure to COVID-19 to being teargassed or shot with rubber bullets after being corralled by police. Educators do passionate young people a disservice when we talk about interest surveys rather than what sets them on fire or their skill sets rather than their deepest gifts and the debts of gratitude that haunt them. Students want to make sacrifices. Some are overly eager to do so, but most want to be safe, happy, and employed and yet have loves that run deeper than these.

I think of M., the recent graduate of my college who first introduced me to the "dark ecology" of Paul Kingsnorth. My Environmental Ethics course was discussing the catastrophic environmental crises that await future generations. M. declared that she didn't think that it was ethically defensible to have children. (No offense, she added while glancing toward me, having met my kids.) At the time, I took M. to be saying that suffering should be prevented at all costs, that we ought to spare the pain of future generations by not birthing them. Since then, however, I have watched M. move into a house and let pollinator-friendly perennials take over her lawn in quiet protest of our city's lawn ordinances. I've heard her describe the rules of the "quaranteam" she formed with other young friends—how they rule by consensus and thus don't take any action (including visiting other family members) unless each member gives their express approval. Having seen her give of herself in these and other ways, I now think that her comment about not having children was about *her* willingness to forgo *her* own present or future desires if that meant other lives—like the pollinators buzzing in her overgrown yard—might better flourish.

I think also of J., who graduated a decade ago, turning down a full-ride scholarship to Yale graduate school to move back to his small Illinois town, convinced that he owed the fruits of his college education to the place from which he came. Six months after his return, his father was diagnosed with brain cancer, a tragedy that only deepened his commitment to give himself over to those he loved. In an email to me after his father died, J. wrote,

> I didn't come home after college to tend to or bury my father. I didn't come home to work a random assortment of jobs that allowed me to shuttle him to his treatments that slowly made his hair gray and disappear. I never intended to move into the basement of his house, where we watched *M*A*S*H* reruns and his beloved Notre Dame Fighting Irish football team in the living room as an almost spiritual practice in his final months. . . . While his illness was indifferent to my presence, I knew that he wasn't—and that made all the harsh realities facing us and our family easier to bear.

No doubt, J. would not characterize the time with his father as a sacrifice. That is because he was already practiced in downward mobility and self-giving love and so knew the deep, heartrending joy of loving what cannot be saved.

Bad things can happen when we don't tell stories of sacrificial love. In his first book, *Acts of Faith*, the interfaith leader Eboo Patel writes of young people's desire to find identity and meaning by joining movements and causes. If those working for the common good do not provide opportunities for youth to fulfill these desires, extremist groups certainly will.[62] I think of Kyle Rittenhouse, the teenager who killed two protestors in Kenosha, Wisconsin, last week with an automatic rifle. Out of habit, I just wrote that Rittenhouse was a *deranged* teenager and then deleted that easy dismissal. When I watch the videos of him from last Tuesday (August 25), I see a composed young man seeing himself in an (untrue) script that elicits his sense of selfless duty. Wearing a backward baseball cap and medical gloves, with medical kit slung over one shoulder and an AR-15 over the other, he speaks of his willingness to "run into harm's way" in answering the call to protect people and property. The problem—a lethal one—is not only that a troubled teen has confused the willingness to kill with the willingness to die; many memorializations of the sacrifice of soldiers do exactly that. The problem, in part, is that those who portray his story as spurious (which it is), but who do not lift up alternative stories of sacrificial love that are more truthful and more loving, hand those stories over to the white nationalist mythmakers.

E., the student living in Boston at the start of the pandemic, tells me that his own sense of safety and well-being comes, in part, when he feels beckoned into something bigger than himself. Recently, when he moved to Chicago, he got work through AmeriCorps tutoring ninth-graders online with their algebra, where he also tries to offer emotional and social support. In his free time, E. supports the movement to defund the Chicago Police Department and loads food and volunteers with Chicago's mutual-aid networks. For him, empathy is about survival. He tells me that his own well-being depends, in part, on staying active in the community.

I hope it is clear that not all so-called sacrifices are honorable or loving. If I value those of graduates such as M., J., and E., it is not only that I happen to love these people—which I do. I treasure their manner of self-giving love because it is for actual people and other creatures rather than for abstractions such as "the American way of life," or "the Economy." Indeed, when sacrifice is meant to uphold a system that demands the death of some so that others can be made to feel less vulnerable—as it is in some patriotic appeals—it may be courageous, but it is anything but loving.

Jesus is a counterexample. He lays down his life for his friends (John 15:13) and wholly gives himself over to the new, nonviolent reign of God. He doesn't die to uphold an empire that crucifies rabbis to show its power. He dies as he lives, by letting go of that so-called power so that "power" will be unmasked and will finally give way to the power of love.

I think also of Tarrou, a character from Camus's *The Plague*. In one pivotal scene, we learn his backstory, as he explains to the lead physician, Dr. Rieux, why he feels called to give so selflessly to the sick in a losing battle against the bubonic plague. At a young age, Tarrou witnessed his father, a judge, condemn a man to death with professional decorum and cool rationality. Tarrou revolted against a social order that was based on the death penalty, which to him consisted of a different sort of plague, one that infected everyone, and was as deadly as the bacillus. He came to feel that the only meaningful work for him was the seemingly humble work of hurting as few people as possible, even as he realized that life as he knew it was predicated on the legalized death of others. As he tells Dr. Rieux, "I have realized that we all have the plague, and I have lost my peace. And today I am still trying to find it; still trying . . . not to be the mortal enemy of anyone. I only know that one must do what one can to cease being plague-stricken, and that's the only way in which we can hope for some peace or, failing that, a decent death. This, and only this, can bring relief to men and, if not save them, at least do them as little harm possible and even, sometimes, a little good."[63] It sounds like an overly modest, or even self-effacing, vision of the sacrifice that he and Dr. Rieux feel called to. Their work, at base, involves the heroically human renunciation of a life that feeds off death. That's real sacrifice. And might just bring new life.

* * *

Perhaps the goal of any true sacrifice cannot be sacrifice per se, but rather the new life—the new reign of God—into which one lives, one where untimely and unjust deaths are required of no one. Jesus's sacrifice was an end to all sacrifice (see Heb 10). Only thus did it count as such.

Kierkegaard, in fact, thinks that this sacrifice of systems that demand sacrifice—this sacrifice of sacrifice—is close to the heart of heroic love. In order to distinguish sacrificial love, a hope beyond hope, and a faith beyond all human accounting from the stuff of narcissists and militarists, he notes an odd discrepancy between Abraham and other so-called tragic heroes. Abraham had faith *for this life* and believed in the gift-giving of God. He was, therefore, just as ready to sacrifice his sacrifice of Isaac when, having drawn the knife, the angel commanded him *not* to carry through with the plan. Strange but true—what Kierkegaard finds most astonishing about Abraham's faith is his readiness to rereceive Isaac, with even greater joy: "What Abraham found the easiest of all would for me be hard, to find joy again in Isaac!" Through the whole ordeal, Abraham remains ready to receive Isaac back, "with more joy than the first time."[64] It turns out that the real miracle of self-giving love is not the sacrifice per se but to go on loving what we have let go, to cherish it all, readying oneself to be surprised by joy.

Ta-Nehisi Coates renounces "the Dream," teaching his son to face awful truths about being Black in a white man's country. And yet he turns the almost despairing critique against itself, coming back to a place of "unhopelessness": "I am not a cynic. I love you, and I love the world, and I love it more with every new inch I discover."[65]

After Tarrou finishes telling the story of his life to Dr. Rieux, the two of them decide to go for a swim in the sea—the one moment in *The Plague* that we see the two selfless servants enjoying themselves. The joy is not simple or naive, but it is no less powerful for having resignation built into it. Dr. Rieux says that he felt happy and "caught a glimpse on his friend's face of the same happiness." It was "a happiness that forgot nothing, not even murder."[66]

Simone Weil writes that when the most debilitating afflictions set in, when "a kind of horror submerges the whole soul," when even God appears absent—"more absent than light in the utter darkness of a cell"—one must face the truth of all this, and yet continue to wait for God. One must continue to "go on loving in the emptiness, or at least to go on wanting to love."[67] To go on loving an absent God when you've given up every other object of hope—that, for Weil, is the way of the cross, the path toward redemption.

These three remain when all else has been relinquished or removed: a faith beyond optimism, a hope against hope, and self-giving, abiding love. Love—the last and greatest of these—is willing to give up everything and yet delights in new, unexpected gifts that may just rise like fireweed, growing from ashes.

OPENING DAY—AUGUST 31, 2020

This morning is breezy, but not blustery. It's overcast, with a chance of thunderstorms forecast for later, but not dark enough now to be ominous. The kind of weather that could go either way—darkening as the day drags on or the sun peeking out and the clouds burning off. How fitting, I think: the perfect backdrop to my college's reopening.

Eighty-some percent of students filed into their dorms and apartments over the past week and are now off to their first class—most of them "hybrids" between in-person learning and synchronous (live) and asynchronous (recorded) virtual participation. The remaining students elected to take online classes from home. For many high-risk and international students, it was a choice without other real options.

I have a sabbatical leave from teaching this term. *Sabbatical* is from *Sabbath*—the seventh day, the day of rest, taken first by the Creator and then mandated to creation. Traditionally, every seven years college faculty are eligible for what the Bible calls rest but what we call "reassigned professional duties." I am deeply grateful for the time. On this first day of class, though, I do feel a bit left out. I decide to take a walk through campus.

I grab my umbrella and cut through Longfellow Elementary school's playground, up the avenue lined with Victorian houses that a number of visiting faculty rent, across Thirty-Eighth Street, and up the stairs. There I see A. sitting with an unfolded laptop on her beach towel on the top tier of the campus's outdoor amphitheater. She was there again last night for a blessing and prayer service, where students and faculty sang a blessing to one another before reciting the "Prayer of Good Courage."

I ask A. how her first class went. Good, she says; she has been dreading Quantitative Reasoning, but the professor is engaging and the class was in-person, the twenty students spreading out in a lecture hall that would normally hold sixty. A double major in English and Religion, A. says she is excited for her other two courses as well—Writing about Literature and Religions of India—except for the fact that both are online. She tells about her family's fraught deliberations that summer. Her younger brother was about to begin as a freshman at a large state university; two weeks ago, their parents convinced him to take his classes remotely until the pandemic passes. A. was resolute in returning for her junior year, come what may. Thoughtful but reserved, she knows she learns best seated around a seminar table and finds her work as a tutor in the college's reading and writing center deeply rewarding. I wonder whether her resolve to return to campus has been dampened by the bad luck of two online classes. Still, she seems happy to be back. She has a look of quiet confidence, a readiness to take what comes. Perhaps she has already implicitly learned what the Hindu scripture, the Bhagavad Gita, will explicitly teach when she reads it later in Religions of India: One should work without attachments to the fruit of one's work. To remain hopeful and determined even through setbacks and when the results don't match one's efforts—that takes good courage.

I walk past Old Main, stopping to look through the ground floor window at my religion colleague E., and seven students seated six feet apart in a classroom, while the heads of others populate Zoom on the monitor. I continue toward the center of campus, past grounds crews tearing down tents, chairs, and portable fire pits from Welcome Weekend. I arrive at the middle of the quad, marked by a giant circular, concrete plaza. (It is officially named the Viking Plaza, but students refer to the circle with the "A" inscribed in it in their own colorful terms.)

From an Adirondack chair, I study the sea of passing students. They look good: upbeat, friendly, happy to be here. Most walk slowly with backpacks donned loosely; some (they may be first-year students) cinch the straps tightly and lean toward their destination. I see fewer T-shirts branded with the college logo. Perhaps the postponement of Division III Fall sports has put a dent in school spirit. Alas, it looks like 1980s fashion is back yet again, to the amazement of faculty who lived through the original. Young women are in tube tops, with their shorts or jeans pulled above the hips. Young men wear pants pegged above red-and-black Jordans or penny loafers with pastel-colored shorts worn midthigh.

From across the circle, I catch the eye of T., a biology major with philosophy and Japanese minors. I wave, he puts down his textbook and walks over to me, tells me things so far are going well. All four of his classes are in-person or hybrid; he is especially excited for Philosophy of Mind. When I ask how his job as a resident advisor (RA) in the dorms is going, he admits that it is tough. With stricter rules around social gatherings and tighter enforcement, he feels more like a cop than a peer mentor. The upshot, he says, is that normally he is quiet and less confident, whereas now he knows he's got to set a good example and be vocal about expectations and consequences. He's leaning into new responsibilities.

Everyone I see is wearing a mask, and there is only one or two that don't cover the mouth and nose. Many are blue and gold, the ones issued to students by mail, along with thermometers and COVID guidelines. Most are colorful and fashionable but not too ostentatious—accessories carefully selected so as not to look carefully selected. The jet-white piping of one mask matches its owner's canvas Keds. A few are wearing the disposable kind, as if in subtle protest, or like they won't be doing this again tomorrow.

"That's a sick mask," a student with bed-head hair calls out, as he passes a guy with a mask of fanged teeth, fit for a Halloween party. The guy slows and pulls a Bose headphone from his ear.

"What's that?"

"Sick mask."

"Thanks."

A senior student named C. saunters by in black-and-white checkered Vans. I call out to him twice before I realize that he, too, is wearing earbuds. I want to ask him about the men's volleyball team, which has been cleared to practice now but will not compete until spring. With broad shoulders, large biceps, and an explosive vertical, C. hits and blocks around the net like Zion rebounds and gets put-back dunks. Three years ago, in his first year as a student-athlete, C. was featured in our student newspaper after he reported racist comments by the volleyball coach. The coach was asked to resign, and the team largely had to coach themselves for the rest of the season. "I wouldn't have been able to do it if it weren't for the support of my white teammates," C. told me after the fact. "We are closer now than ever." Such painful experiences have built up courage and integrity in this young man, virtues that serve the common good of our not-yet-just society. Really, I want to ask C. about this summer of racial reckoning. I resolve to invite him to meet for coffee in the weeks ahead.

Friends greet each other in the center of the circle. Some fist bump or touch elbows; others feign power hugs from a distance. I hear fake cries of alarm when two female students high-five. Another from their group whips hand sanitizer from her backpack, brandishing it like a cross to ward off vampires.

I need to head home. It's my turn to go grocery shopping, an affair no longer heightened with portents and sweeping precautions. (While our garden keeps gifting us with kale, spinach, tomatoes, peppers, zucchini, butternut squash, and even late summer green beans, we are low on what Asa calls "normal food.")

Retracing my steps, I hear "Hi, Dr. Mahn" as I pass the pavilion. Forty feet away is E., a transgender student whom I first came to know as the female F. I remember the sting of misgendering him years ago and now cannot recall his name. I unhook an ear strap of my mask, let it dangle on the side of my face, smile, say it's good to see him, and ask him how he is.

"Good," he says. "Excited to be back."

I tell him to be well, in the fullest sense of the word.

All these students have stories. Many are learning to tell them in a way that makes sense of their lives. The stories are like mirrors—however tarnished and dark—through which they reflect on who they have been and who they feel called to become. A few years back, the vocation center on our campus gave out T-shirts with "What's Your Story?" printed on the back. The question can sound glib, like when my roommate from college (usually when he had a couple beers in him) would squint his eyes, size you up, and ask, "What's *your* story?" My college asks the question more earnestly, with emphasis on the *story*. Students answer in reflective essays and vocational discernment retreats, but also with the lives they live. In both the telling and the living, they learn to navigate setbacks and tragedies, developing grit and determination to overcome obstacles when they can. They also develop patience, repentance, and compassion for others when those characteristics are truer to difficult chapters in their lives, as this year has been for most.

To ask about and tell stories invites attention to messy, beautiful lives so that those lives can move forward with integrity and hope. Simone Weil says that attention of that sort may just be the form prayer takes for many in our secular world. The poet Mary Oliver echoes Weil in her well-known poem "The Summer Day": "I don't know exactly what a prayer is. / I do know how to pay attention, how to fall down / into the grass, how to kneel down in the grass / how to be idle and blessed." She writes of productively wasting time there in the grass by attending to the particular mystery of a single grasshopper, describing intricate details that bring the creature to life. Oliver ends the poem with these famous lines, which I'm sure you can find on the swag of vocation centers at church-related colleges: "Tell me, what is it you plan to do / with your one wild and precious life?"[68]

* * *

As I continue home, I cross Thirty-Eighth Street. Halfway down the Victorian-lined avenue, a Lutheran pastor I know pulls out of a driveway in his Chrysler Sebring convertible, the top down.

"You know it's going to rain, right?" I ask. He answers felicitously, exaggerating the words:

"Oh, but *I* have *faith*!"

Epilogue
THE BEGINNING OF THE END

January 1, 2021

The bald eagle that has been fishing while I take my daily walk—circling the open water of the Mississippi where a creek runs in, pausing midflight, folding wings to plunge toward fish below—today tucks her beak into feathered chest against the icy sleet and wind as she perches, motionless, on a shard of jumbled river ice. I am spending the week alone at the Tree of Life River Retreat house, two hours downriver from my home. The view today out the window is monochromatic—gray sky, gray river, gray trees. After I wished my family Happy New Year's at midnight by phone last night, I woke up this morning knowing, of course, that not all the gloom of 2020 would magically disappear overnight. Still, it's pretty gray. A bright, sunny first day of 2021 would have been a nice gesture.

The months since I ended these daily entries have been dreary for our country, as is the forecast for the months ahead. Dr. Fauci says the start of 2021 will include "a whole lot of pain." The coronavirus pandemic rages on, with almost 350,000 dead in the United States, the largest percentage per capita of any country on Earth. Black people are still three times more likely than whites to die of COVID; in some regions (such as Washington, DC) that rate is six times. In the week before Christmas, the national daily death count was 25 percent higher than the worst of last spring.[1]

We are deep in the middle of a ferocious third wave. While the first two plateaued in spring and summer, hospitalization and death rates are rising this winter at rates that shatter the record from the day before, only to be shattered the following day. The surge hasn't abided in most regions. It has been fueled by Thanksgiving reunions, and potentially now Christmas gatherings and New Year's Eve parties, many under the banner, "Fuck 2020."

At the same time, there is real hope, and millions of people of goodwill are grounding their hope in precautions and care for others and themselves. Wearing a mask seems less politically polarizing than it did some months ago. Most of the country feels like it can get through the winter, now with the promise of spring. We have an incoming president surrounded by experts in public health science, violence de-escalation, and climate change. Communities around the country have pulled together to accomplish goals and rewrite their collective stories in ways almost unimaginable a year ago. There are hundreds, maybe thousands, of mutual-aid networks and networks of networks that efficiently match humble, compassionate people with the basic needs of neighbors. According to some polls, more than twenty-three million US residents participated in protests since George Floyd died, potentially making it the largest protest movement in our country's history. Millions of nurses, schoolteachers, farmers, postal workers, dog walkers, soup-kitchen volunteers, and others continue to get up and give of themselves, finding hope in small successes and in the people around them. The complete unraveling of political systems means to some that we don't have to stitch them back together the same way; we stand right now in the most perilously promising time for the legal and economic enfranchisement of all America since the Reconstruction era.[2] A whole generation of young adults who, having lived through a financial meltdown as kids and now a near-complete meltdown of public trust in science, political leaders, and human decency as young adults, are finding hope in one another, in their own direct action and care, and in the chance of a lifetime to build democracy from the bottom up.

Not to mention that we have in hand two vaccines with a better efficacy rates than what we thought we could hope for. Two-and-a-half weeks ago, on a Monday morning (December 14) in the third week of Advent (which fortuitously means *coming*), Sandra Lindsay, an intensive-care nurse in the Long Island Jewish Medical Center in Queens, New York, received the first vaccination shot around ten o'clock in the morning. "I feel like healing is coming," she said. "I hope this marks the beginning of the end of a very painful time in our history." Lindsay's witness to a healing that is coming sounds to me religious, almost biblical—as if the advent of a new dawn. As if the trucks and cargo planes carrying millions of doses of the coronavirus vaccine to high-risk health care workers across the country will break in on us, like a Savior "coming in clouds with great power and glory" (Mark 13:26 ESV).

Many who surrounded Lindsay when the "shot of hope" was administered shared her optimism about the beginning of the end and used powerful war language to describe it. The first shot is "opening a new chapter in the battle against the coronavirus," the *New York Times* announced. Although speaking of the vaccination, Governor Andrew Cuomo's comment could have been given outside Los Alamos in 1945: "I believe this is the weapon that will end the war."[3]

Battle language and atomic overtones notwithstanding, we know that the vaccine's shot of hope should not be mistaken for a silver bullet. About five hours after the first coronavirus vaccination, the United States reached the mark of three hundred thousand COVID-19 deaths. Rochelle Walensky, the incoming CDC director, reminds us that, for vaccines to work well, we need to give them less work to do by continuing to wear masks, social distancing, and refraining from visiting indoors with people outside our bubbles. Plus, the real work of public inoculation is still ahead of us, and problems plague the underresourced and understaffed rural regions that are suffering the most from COVID-19 and now will need to store and administer the virus. A quarter of the public is still reluctant to get vaccinated, including many Indigenous and Black communities, who have their good reasons. Most frightening, the virus has mutated into strands even more contagious and which we *only think*—God help us—will be inoculated by the vaccines we have or ones we can manufacture quickly.

It would seem that there are silver linings of hope even among these dark days, but that hope will prove unfounded if we do not remain patient and vigilant, refraining from prematurely celebrating the happy ending of a too-long story that is coming but has not yet come. That, too, is biblical. Christians believe that God will save all that can be saved; the resurrection of Jesus is, like a first vaccine administered, decisive for trusting that the end is near. For Christians, the time between the beginning of the end and the end itself, between "already" and "not yet," has gone on for two thousand years, enough time for Christians to practice lament, vigilance, persistence, and hope, as though it were all one long Holy Saturday. The hope sprouting from this fold in time is more realistic than a confidence in fixes and yet far more expectant than those resigned to fate. It's a hope that I have tried to cultivate over the past year, sometimes with great difficulty, other times surprised to find deep roots and new flowerings.

* * *

The time of God's own unfolding story can help us put secular, historical time in context. It can give us endurance when we would otherwise be impatient or hasten us to act decisively when we might otherwise wait and see. The story of God and of our salvation affords the strength to let go of the untrue stories of white supremacy, American exceptionalism, the strength of the fittest, endless technological progress, necessary poverty, and power bereft of love.

In this book, I've wanted to do justice to the Christian story, with its cruciform hope for healing, alongside stories lived out by Jews, Muslims, Buddhists, and many secular students and friends. Perhaps my early decision to tell snippets of many stories meant that no one story could take center stage, "out-narrating" the others. The upshot—at least for me—has been new insights that can be seen and spoken when narratives collide, or better (and to borrow from Toni Morrison), when we lay our stories next to one another.[4]

And honestly, others (and I) need stories of love between neighbors now more than ever. I still strain to hear what I am called to do, and who I am called to be. Writing about neighbor love comes easier to me than neighbor love. My story gets truer, not to mention more interesting, when I see it within the stories of others. Some of those stories are found in books—those by Morrison, Camus, Kierkegaard, Berry, Weil, and others are dear to me. But they include ongoing stories lived out by my neighbors, family, and graduates of my college, some of whom I am glad to call friends.

Several days ago, my colleague, Sharon Varallo, called me (in more than one sense), asking if I would teach again next fall in the East Moline Correctional Center, this time through a for-credit degree program, the Augustana Prison Education Program, which Sharon is spearheading. The opportunity is pure gift. My calling as a teacher and a Christian is never clearer than when I am thinking about suffering and salvation among incarcerated students, who have so much to teach and learn.

My wife, Laura, continues to be a model in loving the neighbor. Having stewarded the gifts of so many people's time and talents, she and her team should be bringing diverse neighbors to eat together—literally, to become *com-panions*—in their permanent location for NEST Café this spring. Laura is gifted at building community, sometimes under the hardest circumstances: in hospital rooms when people are dying, or when she preaches at their funerals. Her grandfather, Larry French, died the week before Christmas along with a third of the remaining residents of his nursing home in Iowa, after an outbreak of COVID-19. Double-masked, and behind a face shield, she got to be with her grandfather in the end, and also with the nurses, aides, cooks, social workers, and cleaning staff who cared for Larry and mourned his death. Larry was a mechanic, tow truck operator, licensed minister, volunteer firefighter for fifty years, husband for seventy-two, member of the Lions Club, and announcer of his small town's high school football games. He had many stories, which no doubt saints and angels are now hearing.

D., the student who led BLM protests on campus before attending Union Theological Seminary and then moving back to Chicago, will begin 2021 with a new job as the program and impact coordinator at Transformative Justice Law Project of Illinois, a start-up nonprofit that advocates for the rights of transgender persons caught in the legal system.

C., the resident doctor whom I described as a wounded healer last spring, continues to care for herself through her care for others, and vice versa. She is excited for her next two rotations in 2021—a week in Flint, Michigan at a community health center, and then two weeks of geriatrics.

J., who was summoned to serve his rural community and care for his dying father after graduating from college, lives with his wife in central Illinois, where he teaches humanities at a private high school—this past fall, outside, under a wedding tent. Their Christmas letter describes 2020 as a year filled with planting apple trees, building raised beds, and preparing a prairie patch in their backyard, where they camp when they need to get "away."

E., the graduate who helped start mutual-aid networks outside Boston before moving to Chicago, tells me that his mantra for 2021 is to "be like water." That's the principle from Daoism, which E. also knows as the Bruce Lee quotation picked up as a rallying cry in the Hong Kong uprisings. Water always finds its way to the ocean, E. says. It does so not through projects and plans, but by staying responsive, opening itself to internal and external forces.

G. is still living in the Powderhorn Park neighborhood of Minneapolis, where she is completing her masters in social work while interning at a children's hospital and working part time at a group home for people with severe mental disabilities. When we chatted by Zoom a few weeks ago, I ended the conversation by commenting that she looks like she is really flourishing. She tilted her head with a quizzical look—a reminder not to try to pull her out of Holy Saturday, if that is where her story is.

My sons continue to plod along with their online school, having attended class inside their high school and junior high for only a handful of days. Some say that school-aged children are losing a year of education. With more time to wrestle, walk with Gracie, go sledding, draw, feed our new chickens, read *The Chronicles of Narnia* and *Lord of the Rings*, play the piano, take a hike with their grandmother (as we did this Christmas), remember the life of their great-grandfather (also this Christmas), and otherwise be "idle and blessed,"[5] I just can't see this year as lost, or know what that would mean. I hope that they and other young people will be able to look back on this year or years and see real growth in mind, body, and spirit, even if that growth is harder to track with standardized tests.

I have not told many clear success stories or stories of certain redemption in these pages; nor have I narrated the lives of those utterly unmade and cut short by physical illness, human hatred, or climate chaos—of which there are far too many. The lives I know move quietly on. They experience real suffering and often the threat of meaninglessness and purposelessness. But they find their way through them, like stories moving toward an end unseen, or water responsive to the summons of the sea.

ACKNOWLEDGMENTS

Thank you to my students, colleagues, family members, and friends who let me tell these stories about our intersecting callings, shared grief, and burgeoning hope.

My family—children, Asa and Gabe; spouse, Rev. Laura Evans Mahn; brother, Aaron; and mother, Anne—let me know when I misremembered details, offered other input, and gave permission to tell stories that involve them. Graduates and students whom I mention in some detail each graciously read what I wrote about them and offered updates about their vocations. Many were fine to use their full names, but I use initials for the sake of consistency and to err on the side of protecting their emerging stories. I have used names or initials of colleagues near and far, local faith leaders, and neighbors, depending on whether our interactions were public or not. I thank them for their feedback and permission and their ongoing care and wisdom.

Many thanks to those who read early forays into this project—Ethan Conley-Keck, Michelle Crouch, David Crowe, David Cunningham, Richard Hughes, Anne Salo, Deanna Thompson, and Mark Wilhelm. Some identified it as a book before I could and offered sage advice about its form and content; others offered the encouragement I needed simply to keep writing until I figured it out. Dr. Monica Smith, vice president for Diversity, Equity and Inclusion at Augustana College, and Dr. Krista Hughes, director of the Mueller Center at Newberry College, both think carefully about race and justice and offered feedback about the voice and moves of part 2. Augustana student Annelisa Burns read a version of almost every paragraph that I wrote, some that were hardly decipherable and many that never saw the light of day (mercifully). Annelisa reads perceptively and generously, thinks carefully about the intersection of substance and voice, offers feedback articulately, and is not afraid to tell a professor that he can't say that or should find a better way to say it. I am deeply grateful.

Thank you to the Augustana Board of Trustees student scholarship fund, which compensated Annelisa for her work, and to Dr. Wendy Hilton-Morrow, Provost of the College, for granting me a sabbatical leave from teaching during the 2020–21 academic year.

Will Bergkamp and Emily King of 1517 Media/Fortress Press recognized the promise of this project early on and worked to shepherd it through editing and production carefully and quickly. Emily went beyond an editor's typical work by receiving installments of the book, reading and offering incisive comments while I was completing other portions. Will went beyond an editor in chief's typical role by personally reaching out to leaders at Lutheran and other church-related colleges and introducing them to this project. I thank Will, Emily, and the editorial staff at Fortress for their work with the book and with me.

The editors and hosts of various publications and platforms let me try out musings as I came to them: *Vocation Matters*, the blog site of the Network for Vocation in Undergraduate Education (NetVUE), which is professionally curated by Hannah Schell; a summer webinar organized by the Council of Independent Colleges (CIC) and NetVUE, which allowed me to discuss activism and vocation alongside national leaders; the *Christian Century* magazine and its editors, Amy Frykholm and Elizabeth Palmer, and publisher, Peter Marty, who agreed to publish early reflections in the magazine's pages; the Vocation of Lutheran Higher Education conference planning committee, who invited me to speak about being "called to place"; and the Inter-Religious Council of Linn County (IRCLC), which asked me to talk about hope at their annual Thanksgiving service. Finally, Don Wooten and Roald Tweet, hosts of WVIK's *Scribble* radio show, invited me to read and discuss an early chapter of the book on-air. Dr. Tweet was a local historian and beloved emeritus professor of English at Augustana College, where he held the Conrad Bergendoff Endowed Chair in the Humanities—a chair that I now hold. He passed away on November 4, 2020. Our community misses him deeply.

NOTES

Introduction

1 Debates about the reconstructionist history told by *Hamilton* can be found in *Historians on Hamilton: How a Blockbuster Musical Is Reimagining America's Past*, ed. Renee C. Romano and Claire Bond Potter (New Brunswick, NJ: Rutgers University Press, 2018). See also Hua Hsu, "In 'The Haunting of Lin-Manuel Miranda,' Ishmael Reed Revives an Old Debate," *New Yorker*, January 9, 2019, https://tinyurl.com/ykm43pc2; and Mark Kennedy, "Historians Irked by Musical 'Hamilton' Escalate Their Duel," Associated Press, February 4, 2019, https://tinyurl.com/npej9kvw.

2 Ta-Nehisi Coates, *Between the World and Me* (New York: Spiegel & Grau, 2015), 11.

3 Statistics about the disproportionate percentage of Black and brown Americans hospitalized and dying from COVID-19 can be found on the CDC website (https://www.cdc.gov/coronavirus/2019-ncov/), which I use throughout this book for statistics, along with various news reports. When particular stats or perspectives are given, I cite my sources but do not do so when the news is repeated across multiple outlets and readily available through internet searches.

4 David Brooks, "The Summoned Self," *New York Times*, August 3, 2010, https://tinyurl.com/2ekgr2ca.

5 Martin Luther, "The Freedom of a Christian (1520)," in *The Annotated Luther Study Edition*, ed. Timothy J. Wengert (Minneapolis: Fortress, 2016), 1:520 (emphasis mine).

6 Barbara Stoler Miller, trans., *The Bhagavad-Gita* (New York: Bantam, 1986), bk. 2, lines 44–45.

7 *Epiphany of recruitment* is the term that Brian J. Mahan uses for a vocational summons in *Forgetting Ourselves on Purpose: Vocation and the Ethics of Ambition* (San Francisco: Jossey-Bass, 2002), 30–32, 127–28.

8 See Deborah Caldwell, "Did God Send the Hurricane?," Catholic Exchange, September 14, 2005, https://tinyurl.com/yxdtdwnt.

9   The theological phrasing is from John Milton, *Paradise Lost* (New York: W. W. Norton, 1975), bk. 1, line 26. The philosophical rendition—"best of all possible worlds"—was coined by Gottfried Leibniz in his 1710 work *Essais de Théodicée sur la bonté de Dieu, la liberté de l'homme et l'origine du mal*. See Gottfried Leibniz, *Theodicy: Essays on the Goodness of God, the Freedom of Man and the Origin of Evil*, trans. E. M. Huggard, ed. Austin Farrer (New Haven, CT: Yale University Press, 1952), 135–40, 151, 228–30.

10 See, as one example, A. Chapple, S. Ziebland, and A. McPherson, "Stigma, Shame, and Blame Experienced by Patients with Lung Cancer: Qualitative Study," *BMJ* 328, no. 7454 (June 17, 2004): 1470.

11 Viktor E. Frankl, *Man's Search for Meaning*, 60th anniversary ed. (New York: Simon & Schuster, 1984), 42, 60.

12 Dorothee Soelle, *Suffering* (Philadelphia: Fortress, 1975), 15.

13 Søren Kierkegaard, *Journals and Papers*, ed. and trans. Howard V. Hong and Edna H. Hong (Bloomington: Indiana University Press, 1978), 5:35. See Carl S. Hughes's discussion in "Søren Kierkegaard: Protesting the Lutheran Establishment," in *Radical Lutherans / Lutheran Radicals*, ed. Jason A. Mahn (Eugene, OR: Cascade, 2017), 47–48.

14 As cited by Nadia Bolz-Weber, *Shameless: A Case for Not Feeling Bad about Feeling Good (about Sex)* (New York: Convergent, 2020), 189.

Part 1

1   For the philosophical ethics of Emmanuel Levinas, see his two best-known books: *Totality and Infinity: An Essay on Exteriority*, trans. Alphonso Lingis (Pittsburgh: Duquesne University Press, 1969); and *Otherwise Than Being, or, Beyond Essence*, trans. Alphonso Lingis (Pittsburgh: Duquesne University Press, 1999).

2   David Brooks, "Pandemics Kill Compassion, Too," *New York Times*, March 12, 2020, https://tinyurl.com/ylfouk7r. Brooks repeated many of the themes on NBC's *Meet the Press*. See "Meet the Press—March 15, 2020," NBC News, March 15, 2020, https://tinyurl.com/w2m8mvz6.

3   I first came to Chris Hedges's book, *War Is a Force That Gives Us Meaning* (Oxford: Public Affairs, 2002), through Stanley Hauerwas's "September 11, 2001: A Pacifist Response," in *Performing the Faith: Bonhoeffer and the Practice of Nonviolence* (Grand Rapids, MI: Brazos, 2004), 201–10, which has informed my thinking here.

4   Deanna A. Thompson, *Glimpsing Resurrection: Cancer, Trauma, and Ministry* (Louisville, KY: Westminster John Knox, 2018), 4, 57.

5 I write of the need for "passive," pacifist virtues and of war as America's civil religion in chapters 4 and 8, respectively, in my *Becoming a Christian in Christendom: Radical Discipleship and the Way of the Cross in America's "Christian" Culture* (Minneapolis: Fortress, 2016). Basic religious beliefs and practices can be found widely; I use Stephen Prothero's *God Is Not One: The Eight Rival Religions That Run the World* (New York: HarperOne, 2011) in my Encountering Religion course.

6 Simone Weil, "Attention and Will," in *Gravity and Grace*, trans. Emma Crawford and Mario von der Ruhr (London: Routledge and K. Paul, 1952), 116–22.

7 Parker J. Palmer, *Let Your Life Speak: Listening for the Voice of Vocation* (San Francisco: Jossey-Bass, 2000), 97.

8 Luther, "Freedom of a Christian (1520)," 1:520.

9 Descriptions of the "theology of self-reliance," along with an account of his own near-death experience, are in Richard T. Hughes's March 19, 2020, blog post "Finding Vocation in Loss, Suffering and Death," *Vocation Matters* (blog), https://tinyurl.com/hx7ytbw6.

10 My colleague was referencing Tim Clydesdale's *The Purposeful Graduate: Why Colleges Must Talk to Students about Vocation* (Chicago: University of Chicago Press, 2015), who in turn was referencing David Brooks's "Summoned Self."

11 Mark D. Tranvik, *Martin Luther and the Called Life* (Minneapolis: Fortress, 2016), 7.

12 I am quoting from Tranvik's translation of Luther's "Sermon on John 21:19–24," in *Martin Luther and the Called Life*, 33.

13 My concern with the privatization of what were once public spaces and goods is indebted to the work of Michael J. Sandel, especially his *What Money Can't Buy: The Moral Limits of Markets* (New York: Farrar, Straus & Giroux, 2012).

14 Frankl, *Man's Search for Meaning*, 42, 63–65.

15 Clare Hymes, "Federal Prisons Will Confine Inmates to Cells for 14 Days to Prevent Coronavirus Spread," CBS News, April 1, 2020, https://tinyurl.com/ddnqzy4y; Matthew Haag, "40% of N.Y. Tenants May Not Pay Rent This Month. What Happens Then?," *New York Times*, March 31, 2020, https://tinyurl.com/2w8j9wea.

16 See also Maeve Higgins, "The Essential Workers America Treats as Disposable," *New York Review*, April 27, 2020, https://tinyurl.com/1ga0fcns.

17 Nouwen is quoting from the tractate Sanhedrin, a portion of the Jewish Talmud, in Henri J. M. Nouwen, *The Wounded Healer: Ministry in Contemporary Society*, 2nd ed. (New York: Image Doubleday, 2010), 87–88.

18 Nouwen, 45, 87–88, 94–96.

19 Judith Butler, *Frames of War: When Is Life Grievable?* (London: Verso, 2009), 31.

20 Kelly Brown Douglas, *Stand Your Ground: Black Bodies and the Justice of God* (Maryknoll, NY: Orbis, 2015).

21 I am here helped by Susan Sontag's two books, *Illness as Metaphor* (1977) and *AIDS and Its Metaphors* (1988), published jointly as *Illness as Metaphor and AIDS and Its Metaphors* (New York: Farrar, Straus & Giroux, 1990).

22 My claim about the usefulness of stories is an appreciative critique of Susan Sontag's work, which primary serves to demythologize—in her words, "to regard cancer as if it were just a disease—a very serious one, but just a disease. Not a curse, not a punishment, not an embarrassment. Without 'meaning.'" Sontag, *Illness as Metaphor and AIDS and Its Metaphors*, 102.

23 Quint Forgey, Gabby Orr, Nancy Cook, and Caitlin Oprysko, "'I'd Love to Have It Open by Easter': Trump Says He Wants to Restart Economy by Mid-April," Politico, March 24, 2020, https://tinyurl.com/6tkvmtye.

24 See Alan E. Lewis, *Between Cross and Resurrection: A Theology of Holy Saturday* (Grand Rapids, MI: Eerdmans, 2003); and Shelly Rambo, *Spirit and Trauma: A Theology of Remaining* (Louisville, KY: Westminster John Knox, 2010).

25 See Martin Luther, "Heidelberg Disputation (1518)," in *Martin Luther's Basic Theological Writings*, 2nd ed., ed. Timothy F. Lull and William R. Russell (Minneapolis: Fortress, 2005), 57 (theses 19 and 20). A great, short introduction to the theology of the cross is that of Robert Cady Saler, *Theologia Crucis: A Companion to the Theology of the Cross* (Eugene, OR: Cascade, 2016).

26 I am helped here by Rebecca Solnit, *Hope in the Dark: Untold Histories, Wild Possibilities*, 3rd ed. (Chicago: Haymarket, 2016).

27 Simone Weil, "The Love of God and Affliction," in *Waiting for God*, trans. Emma Craufurd (New York: Perennial, 2001), 67–82.

28 Bryan Stevenson, *Just Mercy: A Story of Justice and Redemption* (New York: Spiegel & Grau, 2014), 289.

29 Michelle Alexander, *The New Jim Crow: Mass Incarceration in the Age of Colorblindness*, rev. ed. (New York: New Press, 2011), 178–220.

30 Barbara Brown Taylor, *Speaking of Sin: The Lost Language of Salvation* (Cambridge, MA: Cowley, 2001), 32.

31 Taylor, 38–40.

32 Dan Vergano and Kadia Goba, "Why the Coronavirus Is Killing Black Americans at Outsize Rates across the US," Buzzfeed News, April 10, 2020, https://tinyurl.com/x8vup2e2; Molly Kinder, "Essential but Undervalued: Millions of Health Care Workers Aren't Getting the Pay or Respect They Deserve in the COVID-19 Pandemic," Brookings, May 28, 2020, https://tinyurl.com/1c5z3eei.

33 From "The Art of Dying Well: An Interview with Dr. Lydia Dugdale" through Harvard University's Initiative on Health, Religion, and Spirituality, accessed February 22, 2021, https://tinyurl.com/22kw66y5.

34   Soelle, *Suffering*, 9–32.

35   Soelle, 33–41.

36   See Thomas G. Long, *What Shall We Say? Evil, Suffering, and the Crisis of Faith* (Grand Rapids, MI: Eerdmans, 2011); as well as my "Between Presence and Explanation: Thinking through Suffering with Thomas Long," *Theology Today* 69, no. 2 (2012): 225–30.

37   Kate Bowler, *Everything Happens for a Reason: And Other Lies I've Loved* (New York: Random House, 2018).

38   Allison Wee, "Valuing Poetry," *Intersections* 37 (Spring 2013): 6–11. Wee uses this selection from "Asphodel, That Greeny Flower" by William Carlos Williams as an epigraph to her essay.

39   Albert Camus, *The Plague*, trans. Stuart Gilbert (New York: Modern Library, 1948), 84–92.

40   Camus, 198–202.

41   Tony Judt, "A Hero for Our Times," *Guardian* (London), November 16, 2001, https://tinyurl.com/ry3z2b5s.

42   Camus, *Plague*, 150.

43   Soelle, *Suffering*, 15.

44   Denis Hayes, "The Most Important Election of Your Lifetime," *Seattle Times*, April 10, 2020, https://tinyurl.com/zar1kzk3.

45   For the photographer's perspective, see Michelle Everhart, "You've Seen the Photo of Ohio Protestors. Here's the Story behind It," *Columbus Dispatch*, April 16, 2020, https://tinyurl.com/1gmf80lx.

46   For example, Wendell Berry, *Life Is a Miracle: An Essay against Modern Superstition* (New York: Counterpoint, 2001), 89–91.

47   See Katrine Marçal, *Who Cooked Adam Smith's Dinner: A Story of Women and Economics* (New York: Pegasus, 2016). Thanks to Keri Bass for recommending this book to me.

48   My thinking is here informed by David W. Orr, *Earth in Mind: On Education, Environment, and the Human Prospect*, 10th anniversary ed. (New York: Island, 2004), especially 16–25.

49   Max Fisher, "What Will Our New Normal Feel Like? Hints Are Beginning to Emerge," *New York Times*, April 21, 2020, https://tinyurl.com/3uq2quok.

50   Mahan, *Forgetting Ourselves on Purpose*, 27–32, 126–37; and Brenda Salter McNeil, *Becoming Brave: Finding the Courage to Pursue Racial Justice Now* (Grand Rapids, MI: Brazos, 2020), 31. Thanks to Dr. Monica Smith for introducing my college and me to the work of McNeil.

51   Levinas, *Totality and Infinity*, 180–83; and *Otherwise Than Being*, xlii. Jacques Derrida helped popularize the claim that "*tout autre est tout autre*," or that

"every other is wholly other—is the Other." See especially Derrida, *The Gift of Death*, trans. David Wills (Chicago: University of Chicago Press, 1995), 82–115.

Part 2

1　T. S. Eliot, *The Waste Land and Other Poems* (Overland Park, KS: Digireads, 2016), lines 1–7.

2　Toni Morrison, *Beloved* (New York: Knopf, 1998), 42.

3　For these and other changes in circumstance and public opinion since the virus outbreak, see "Coronavirus Pandemic," Gallup, accessed March 31, 2021, https://tinyurl.com/57b9c7a5.

4　See Kathleen Norris, *Acedia & Me: A Marriage, Monks, and a Writer's Life* (New York: Riverhead, 2010).

5　Barbara Brown Taylor, *Holy Envy: Finding God in the Faith of Others* (New York: HarperOne, 2019).

6　Coates, *Between the World and Me*, 11; for connections to Baldwin, see Reggie Williams, "What Does He Mean by, 'They Believe They Are White'?," in *Between the World of Ta-Nehisi Coates and Christianity*, ed. David Evans and Peter Dula (Eugene, OR: Cascade, 2018), 72–83.

7　Ibram X. Kendi, *How to Be an Antiracist* (New York: One World, 2019), 9, 17–20, 143–44.

8　See Douglas, *Stand Your Ground*.

9　My children's responsibility for becoming antiracist depends on my responsibility to raise them as such. I am helped here by Jennifer Harvey's *Raising White Kids: Bringing Up Children in a Racially Unjust America* (Nashville, TN: Abingdon, 2017), as well as by conversations about this book that my church, St. Paul Lutheran in Davenport, Iowa, sponsored in the summer of 2020.

10　Martin Luther, "The Ninety-Five Theses (1517)," in *Martin Luther's Basic Theological Writings*, 40–46 (my emphasis).

11　Clydesdale, *Purposeful Graduate*, 87–89, 209.

12　Bryan J. Dik and Ryan D. Duffy, *Make Your Job a Calling: How the Psychology of Vocation Can Change Your Life at Work* (West Conshohocken, PA: Templeton, 2012), 217 and titles to chapters 4, 6, and 7.

13　Meg Jay, *The Defining Decade: Why Your Twenties Matter—and How to Make the Most of Them Now* (New York: Twelve, 2012), 201. See my additional response in the blog post "The Tragedy of the Road Not Taken," *Vocation Matters* (blog), March 28, 2018, https://tinyurl.com/rupsxm5r, which draws from my developed essay "The Conflict in Our Callings: The Anguish (and Joy) of Willing Several Things," in *Vocation across the Academy: A New Vocabulary for Higher Education*, ed. David S. Cunningham (New York: Oxford University Press, 2017), 44–66.

14 Malcolm X, *The Autobiography of Malcolm X* (New York: Grove, 1965), 43–44. See also Caryn D. Riswold's discussion in "Vocational Discernment: A Pedagogy of Humanization," in *At This Time and in This Place: Vocation and Higher Education*, ed. David S. Cunningham (Oxford: Oxford University Press, 2016), 72–73, 78–80.

15 Simone Weil, "Reflections on the Right Use of School Studies with a View to the Love of God," in *Waiting for God*, 57–65.

16 I have told a briefer version of this story in *Becoming a Christian in Christendom*, 204.

17 Willie James Jennings, "Baptist Minister: Black Churches Were Safe Spaces, Affirmations of Humanity," interview by Kerri Miller, *MPR News*, June 19, 2015, https://tinyurl.com/4rhlosok.

18 Barbara Hilkert Andolsen, "Agape in Feminist Ethics," *Journal of Religious Ethics* 9, no. 1 (Spring 1981): 69–83. See also Cynthia D. Moe-Lobeda, *Resisting Structural Evil: Love as Ecological-Economic Vocation* (Minneapolis: Fortress, 2013), 169–76. For the connection between eros, agape, and the nature of God, see Rita Nakashima Brock, *Journeys by Heart: A Christology of Erotic Power* (New York: Crossroad, 1988).

19 In Wendell Berry, *Collected Poems, 1957–1982* (San Francisco: North Point, 1985), 59.

20 For the plight of physicians, see Atul Gawande, *Being Mortal: Medicine and What Matters in the End* (New York: Metropolitan, 2014), 191–258; and *Freakonomics Radio Archive*, episode 444: "How Do You Cure a Compassion Crisis?," https://freakonomics.com/archive/. For that of teachers of students of color, see Dominique DuBois Gilliard, *Rethinking Incarceration: Advocating for Justice That Restores* (Downers Grove, IL: IVP, 2018), 76–94. For the naming and interrogation of racial scripts, see Harvey, *Raising White Kids*, 172–210.

21 Lydia S. Dugdale, *The Lost Art of Dying: Reviving Forgotten Wisdom* (New York: HarperOne, 2020), 8, 79–81, 188–90.

22 Butler, *Frames of War*, 171.

23 Niall McCarthy, "Police Shootings: Black Americans Disproportionately Affected," *Forbes*, May 28, 2020, https://tinyurl.com/1g4vg30e.

24 Simone Weil, "The Love of God and Affliction," in *Waiting for God*, 68, 81.

25 Eva Schubert, "The Story of Strange Fruit—Billy Holiday + Lyrics," YouTube, https://www.youtube.com/watch?v=9wnV89qo21A; "Strange Fruit:

The Story behind 'The Song of the Century,'" *WFYI Online*, https://www
.youtube.com/watch?v=EZUoYgPe1Y4.

26 Weil, "Love of God," 70–71.

27 "Tamir Rice Shooting Was 'Justified'—Experts," *BBC*, October 11, 2015,
https://tinyurl.com/4rdzvx65.

28 Max Nesterak, "The Place Where George Floyd Was Killed Is Hallowed
Ground," *Minnesota Reformer*, June 1, 2020, https://tinyurl.com/yn32xljk;
Ju'Niyah Palmer, "At this point y'all are no longer doing this for my sister!,"
Facebook, May 30, 2020, https://tinyurl.com/v2xrsak9.

29 Cobbina is quoted by Zack Stanton, "How Ferguson and Baltimore Explain
Why It's Different This Time," Politico, June 11, 2020, https://tinyurl.com/
y5r6lrow.

30 I am drawing the language of whooshing up, and more generally the concept
of being swept up in sublime meaning, from Hubert Dreyfus and Sean Dor-
rance Kelly, *All Things Shining: Reading the Western Classics to Find Meaning in a
Secular Age* (New York: Free Press, 2011), 198–202.

31 Brenda Salter McNeil tells the story of her own transformation from working
for racial reconciliation to working for racial justice in *Becoming Brave*.

32 Weil, "Love of God," 68–69.

33 See Luther, "Freedom of a Christian (1520)," 1:514–15.

34 Gustavo Gutiérrez, *On Job: God-Talk and the Suffering of the Innocent*, trans. Matthew J. O'Connell (Maryknoll, NY: Orbis, 1987), 31–49.

35 Weil, "Love of God," 71, 81.

36 James Baldwin, *The Fire Next Time* (New York: Vintage International, 1993),
1–10; Coates, *Between the World and Me*, 9; Imani Perry, *Breathe: A Letter to My
Sons* (Boston: Beacon, 2019), 1–2.

37 Bryan N. Massingale, "The Assumptions of White Privilege and What We
Can Do about It," *National Catholic Reporter*, June 1, 2020, https://tinyurl
.com/48p763uw.

38 Sarah Maslin Nir, "The Bird Watcher, That Incident and His Feelings on
the Woman's Fate," *New York Times*, May 27, 2020, https://tinyurl.com/
37823u28.

39 C. S. Lewis, *Mere Christianity*, in *The Complete C. S. Lewis Signature Classics* (New
York: HarperOne, 2002), 33.

40 See Rowan Williams, *Tokens of Trust: An Introduction to Christian Belief* (Louisville, KY: Westminster John Knox, 2007), 145: "And what happens when all
of our defenses against the truth are finally taken away? When we have to
come to terms with God in some unimaginable dimension where our usual
strategies of hiding from ourselves and the rest of reality are not available?

How shall we manage being exposed to God and to our own conscious-nesses as we really are?"

41 As dramatized in C. S. Lewis, *The Great Divorce: A Dream* (New York: Harper-One, 2001).

42 As cited in Reggie L. Williams, *Bonhoeffer's Black Jesus: Harlem Renaissance Theology and an Ethic of Resistance* (Waco, TX: Baylor University Press, 2014), 96.

43 Information about the Four Necessity Valve Turners can be found at www.fournecessity.org.

44 See my further reflections in "What an Unjust World Also Needs: Connecting Vocation and Activism," *Vocation Matters* (blog), July 2, 2020, https://tinyurl.com/17gfz52t; as well as my interview with D., "Hearing the Call to Action," *Vocation Matters* (blog), July 13, 2020, https://tinyurl.com/2tlorjhu. Finally, see the NetVUE webinar, as introduced by Hannah Schell, "Fighting the Good Fight," *Vocation Matters* (blog), July 22, 2020, https://tinyurl.com/5xeovox3.

45 Clydesdale, *Purposeful Graduate*, 88.

46 See especially Luther, "Whether Soldiers, Too, Can Be Saved (1526)," trans. Charles M. Jacobs, in *The Christian in Society III*, ed. Robert C. Schultz, vol. 46, *Luther's Works*, American ed. (Philadelphia: Fortress, 1967), 87–137.

47 Mahan, *Forgetting Ourselves on Purpose*, 27–32, 126–37.

48 Mahan, 126–48.

49 Taylor, *Holy Envy*, 220–23.

50 Scott Clement and Dan Balz, "Big Majorities Support Protests over Floyd Killing and Say Police Need to Change, Poll Finds," *Philadelphia Inquirer*, updated June 9, 2020, https://tinyurl.com/4oc86ogn.

51 Craig Meyer, "'It Is Different:' Tide Is Turning When It Comes to National Anthem Protests," *Pittsburg Post-Gazette*, June 20, 2020, https://tinyurl.com/2bdov92l.

52 "Roger Goodell: NFL 'Wrong' for Not Listening to Protesting Players Earlier," NFL.com, June 5, 2020, https://tinyurl.com/vbqqkj7t.

53 As quoted by Robin DiAngelo in *White Fragility: Why It's So Hard for White People to Talk about Racism* (Boston: Beacon, 2018), 148–49.

54 Howard Thurman, *Jesus and the Disinherited* (Boston: Beacon, 1996), 76. For a theology of "letting go," see Douglas, *Stand Your Ground*, 177–78. Douglas borrows from Rosemary Radford Ruether, "A US Theology of Letting Go," in *The Reemergence of Liberation Theologies*, ed. Thia Cooper (New York: Palgrave Macmillan, 2013), 43–48.

55 Douglas, *Stand Your Ground*, 174–78.

56 Douglas, 193; Luther, "Heidelberg Disputation (1518)," 57 (thesis 20).

57 Douglas, *Stand Your Ground*, 201.

58 Darby Kathleen Ray, "Self, World, and the Space Between: Community Engagement as Vocational Discernment," in Cunningham, *At This Time and in This Place*, 319.

Part 3

1 See "Coronavirus, Climate Change, and the Environment: A Conversation on COVID-19 with Dr. Aaron Bernstein, Director of Harvard Chan C-Change," Center for Climate, Health, and the Global Environment, Harvard T. H. Chan School of Public Health, accessed July 5, 2020, https://tinyurl.com/12fc0dx6.

2 "Davenport's Star Spangled Extravaganza Postponed," *KWQC News*, June 29, 2020, https://tinyurl.com/3v5r5r6m.

3 Eula Biss, *On Immunity: An Inoculation* (Minneapolis: Graywolf, 2014), 19–20. Thanks to Meg Gillett for introducing this book to me.

4 See Patrick J. Deneen, "Wendell Berry and Democratic Self-Governance," in *The Humane Vision of Wendell Berry*, ed. Mark T. Mitchell and Nathan Schlueter (Wilmington, DE: ISI, 2011), 65.

5 Sandel, *What Money Can't Buy*.

6 James Howard Kunstler, *The Long Emergency: Surviving the End of Oil, Climate Change, and Other Converging Catastrophes of the Twenty-First Century* (New York: Grove, 2006).

7 Chris Morris, "As If a Pandemic Weren't Bad Enough, Hurricane Season Could Be a Bad One," *Fortune*, April 3, 2020, https://tinyurl.com/19x4ab5z; Tom Di Liberto, "July 2020 Climate Outlook Has No Good News for the U.S. Southwest," Climate.gov, July 1, 2020, https://tinyurl.com/48jketax.

8 Dan P. McAdams, *The Redemptive Self: Stories Americans Live By* (New York: Oxford University Press, 2005), 3–14; as excerpted in *Leading Lives That Matter: What We Should Do and Who We Should Be*, 2nd ed., ed. Mark R. Schwehn and Dorothy C. Bass (Grand Rapids, MI: Eerdmans, 2020), 549–57.

9 "The suffering that remains" is Shelly Rambo's definition of trauma. See her *Spirit and Trauma*, 15; as well as the discussion in Thompson, *Glimpsing Resurrection*, 5–8.

10 Shelly Rambo, *Resurrecting Wounds: Living in the Afterlife of Trauma* (Waco, TX: Baylor University Press, 2017), 109–43.

11 Thompson, *Glimpsing Resurrection*, 71–117.

12 Michael Corkery, "'Hero' Pay Raises Disappear for Many Essential Workers," *New York Times*, July 14, 2020, https://tinyurl.com/29uyl9ve.

13 A classic articulation is Andolsen, "Agape in Feminist Ethics," 69–83. See also Cynthia D. Moe-Lobeda's discussion of mutuality in *Resisting Structural Evil*, 173–76.

14 See the essay that Mindy Makant wrote later this fall: "Called to Flourish: An Ethic of Care," *Intersections* 52 (Fall 2020): 30–33.

15 Charlie Warzel, "Feeling Powerless about Coronavirus? Join a Mutual-Aid Network," *New York Times*, March 23, 2020, https://tinyurl.com/bkaxc2rm.

16 Tim Wise, *White Like Me: Reflections on Race from a Privileged Son: The Remix*, rev. and updated ed. (Berkeley, CA: Soft Skull, 2011), 179–82.

17 Søren Kierkegaard, *Works of Love*, trans. Howard V. Hong and Edna H. Hong (Princeton, NJ: Princeton University Press, 1995), 18–19, 60.

18 Samuel Wells, "Rethinking Service," *Cresset* 76, no. 4 (Easter 2013): 6–14; as republished in Schwehn and Bass, *Leading Lives That Matter*, 374–87.

19 I am here drawing from Matthew B. Crawford's account of work that requires practical judgments, which can be learned only through bodily practice. See his *Shop Class as Soulcraft: An Inquiry into the Value of Work* (New York: Penguin, 2009), 180–97.

20 My colleague included this quotation and others in Lena Hann, "Finding Purpose in Chaos: Reflection in and beyond the Public Health Classroom," *Intersections* 52 (Fall 2020): 25–27.

21 Wendell Berry, *The Hidden Wound* (Berkeley, CA: Counterpoint, 2010).

22 Joshua P. Hochschild, "Race and Anti-fragility: Wendell Berry's *The Hidden Wound* at Fifty," *Commonweal*, August 5, 2020, https://tinyurl.com/4tupueyb.

23 Hochschild.

24 W. E. B. Du Bois, *Darkwater: Voices from within the Veil* (Mineola, NY: Dover, 1999), 18, as cited by Williams, "What Does He Mean?," 79.

25 Coates, *Between the World and Me*, 107. See also Jennifer Harvey's discussion in "Shall We Awake?," in Evans and Dula, *Between the World*, 51.

26 bell hooks, *Belonging: A Culture of Place* (New York: Routledge, 2009), 38, 118.

27 hooks, 22–24.

28 Jeff Berardelli, "Climate Chaos: Extreme Heat, Wildfires and Record-Setting Storms Suggest a Frightening Future Is Already Here," CBS News, August 24, 2020, https://tinyurl.com/vy9rm5jl.

29 Søren Kierkegaard, *Practice in Christianity*, trans. Howard V. Hong and Edna H. Hong (Princeton, NJ: Princeton University Press, 1991), 120. See also my "Do Christians Love God for Naught? Job and the Possibility of 'Disinterested' Faith," *Word & World* 31, no. 4 (Fall 2011): 389–96, from which I am here drawing.

30 Gutiérrez, *On Job*, 86.

31   Walter Brueggemann, *Virus as a Summons to Faith: Biblical Reflections in a Time of Loss, Grief, and Uncertainty* (Eugene, OR: Cascade, 2020), 51.

32   Bill McKibben, *The Comforting Whirlwind: God, Job, and the Scale of Creation* (Cambridge, MA: Cowley, 2005). Norman Wirzba writes about our calling to care for the natural world beyond utilitarian calculation; see his *The Paradise of God: Renewing Religion in an Ecological Age* (Oxford: Oxford University Press, 2003), 41–47.

33   See Reiner Schürmann, *Meister Eckhart: Mystic and Philosopher: Translations with Commentary* (Bloomington: Indiana University Press, 1978), 63–64.

34   Brueggemann, *Virus as a Summons*, 52.

35   Marge Piercy, "To Be of Use," in *The Art of Blessing the Day: Poems with a Jewish Theme* (New York: Knopf, 1999), lines 12–14, 16–17, 21; the poem is republished in Schwehn and Bass, *Leading Lives That Matter*, 212–13.

36   Berry, *Hidden Wound*, 76.

37   Claire Gecewicz, "Few Americans Say Their House of Worship Is Open, but a Quarter Say Their Faith Has Grown amid Pandemic," Pew Research Center, FACTANK, April 30, 2020, https://tinyurl.com/68cy84bm.

38   Piercy, "To Be of Use," lines 12–13.

39   Oliver Laughland and Adam Gabbatt, "Hurricane Laura: Storm to Bring 'Unsurvivable Surge' of Destruction to US Gulf Coast," *Guardian* (London), August 26, 2020, https://tinyurl.com/1r5xvxfe.

40   Berardelli, "Climate Chaos"; Sukee Bennett, "Inside the Derecho That Pummeled the Midwest," *NOVA*, August 21, 2020, https://tinyurl.com/4j5o8reh; Erin Jordan, "Cedar Rapids Lost More of Its Tree Canopy in Derecho Than Initially Estimated," *Gazette* (Cedar Rapids, IA), August 27, 2020, https://tinyurl.com/22tesy4c.

41   Claire Reilly, "Inside the Luxury Nuclear Bunker Protecting the Mega-rich from the Apocalypse," CNET, July 6, 2020, https://tinyurl.com/2vh1pxek.

42   Wirzba, *Paradise of God*, 20.

43   See "Mars & Beyond: The Road to Making Humanity Multiplanetary," SpaceX, accessed February 15, 2021, http://www.spacex.com/human-spaceflight/mars/.

44   Paul Kingsnorth, "Dark Ecology," in *Confessions of a Recovering Environmentalist and Other Essays* (Minneapolis: Graywolf, 2017), 133.

45   Kingsnorth, 137.

46   Kingsnorth, 141.

47   Dugdale, *Lost Art of Dying*, 79–81.

48   Coates, *Between the World and Me*, 71.

49 Cornel West, "Why Cornel West Is Hopeful (but Not Optimistic)," interview by Sigal Samuel, *Vox*, July 29, 2020, https://tinyurl.com/hhp65rbk.

50 Solnit, *Hope in the Dark*, xiv, 23.

51 Kingsnorth, "Dark Ecology," 143.

52 Kingsnorth, 147.

53 Kingsnorth, 145–47.

54 Søren Kierkegaard, *Fear and Trembling*, trans. Alastair Hannay (London: Penguin, 1985), 68–70.

55 Kierkegaard, 65.

56 Kierkegaard, 56.

57 See especially Delores S. Williams, "Black Women's Surrogacy Experience and the Christian Notion of Redemption," in *Cross Examinations: Readings on the Meaning of the Cross Today*, ed. Marit Trelstad (Minneapolis: Fortress, 2006), 19–32.

58 Bess Levin, "Texas Lt. Governor: Old People Should Volunteer to Die to Save the Economy," *Vanity Fair*, March 24, 2020, https://tinyurl.com/9am6obr2.

59 Levin.

60 "Hurricane Laura Lashes US Gulf Coast with High Winds, Flooding," *New York Times* / ABS-CBN News, August 27, 2020, https://tinyurl.com/3h7ae7dj.

61 Christopher Flavelle, "U.S. Flood Strategy Shifts to 'Unavoidable' Relocation of Entire Neighborhoods," *New York Times*, August, 26, 2020, https://tinyurl.com/ldl6snzp.

62 Eboo Patel, *Acts of Faith: The Story of an American Muslim, the Struggle for the Soul of a Generation* (Boston: Beacon, 2010), xi–xix.

63 Camus, *Plague*, 228.

64 Kierkegaard, *Fear and Trembling*, 65.

65 Coates, *Between the World and Me*, 71; for a discussion of Coates's "unhopelessness," see Joseph Winters, "Between the Tragic and the Unhopeless: Coates, Antiblackness, and the Tireless Work of Negativity," in Evans and Dula, *Between the World*, 99–117.

66 Camus, *Plague*, 232.

67 Weil, "Love of God and Affliction," 70.

68 Mary Oliver, "The Summer Day," in *House of Light* (Boston: Beacon, 1990), lines 18–19.

Epilogue

1 Ed Yong, "Where Year Two of the Pandemic Will Take Us," *Atlantic*, December 29, 2020, https://tinyurl.com/8vwymjbe; Nicki Camberg et al., "A Day

of Deaths 25 Percent Higher Than Spring's Worst," *Atlantic*, December 17, 2020, https://tinyurl.com/9zui7g3e.

2 Adam Serwer, "The New Reconstruction," *Atlantic*, October 2020, https://tinyurl.com/pz732htf.

3 "U.S. Starts Vaccine Rollout as High-Risk Health Care Workers Go First," *New York Times*, December 14, 2020, https://tinyurl.com/57w8v4sn.

4 See Morrison, *Beloved*, 322.

5 From Mary Oliver's poem "The Summer Day," line 14.